FAREWELL ATLANTIS

RECOLLECTIONS

VALENTĪNA FREIMANE

ISBN 9789493418240 (ebook)

ISBN 9789493418226 (paperback)

ISBN 9789493418233 (hardcover)

Translated from the German by Ilze Kļaviņa Mueller

Originally published in 2010 as *Ardievu, Atlantīda!* by Atēna, Riga.

Published in German as *Adieu, Atlantis. Erinnerungen* by Wallstein Verlag, Göttingen, 2015. The German edition contained amendments by the author

Publisher: Amsterdam Publishers, The Netherlands, 2025

info@amsterdampublishers.com

Farewell Atlantis is part of the series Holocaust Survivor Memoirs World War II

Copyright © Wallstein Verlag, Göttingen 2015

Cover image: Valentīna with Dima in a boat on the Lielupe River, summer of 1940

All Rights Reserved. No part of this publication may be reproduced or transmitted in any form or by any means, electronic or mechanical, including photocopy, recording or any other information storage and retrieval system, without prior permission in writing from the publisher.

CONTENTS

PART I
THE FIRST LIFE

Beginnings	3
The Lulows and the Löwensteins	8
Between Riga and Paris	19
Berlin, Meinekestraße 9	25
Just like the movies	43
School begins	56
Riga. Elizabetes iela 23	60
Father and Mother	74
Books. Theater	80
The Luther-Schule	90
Berlin changes – life changes	95
Europe changes	101
Riga, Vidus iela 9	109
First love	122
Like something out of Pushkin	128
Photos	133

PART II
THE SECOND LIFE

Shock without therapy	159
The last act begins	174
Under the yellow star	178
Emīlija	185
Husbands and wives	190
Ghetto	195
People. Destinies	209
The curtain falls in Vidus iela	221
I become a fugitive	226
The Baptists come to my help	234
Perfer et obdura – be patient and tough	239
A milder climate in Pārdaugava	246

Paul Schiemann	254
The solution draws near	269
Afterword	281
Amsterdam Publishers Holocaust Library	283

*This memoir is dedicated to those I love
and who loved me;
those who were human beings
and who saw the human being in me.*

PART I
THE FIRST LIFE

BEGINNINGS

From my earliest childhood, the grown-ups were amused by my unbridled curiosity, by my delight in observing all that was around me. Stored in my memory are scenes whose significance I did not understand until much later, scenes that have never faded.

I realized quite early that I had every reason to be grateful: As in the tale of the good fairies that gathered around a child's cradle, I was showered with gifts when I came into the world, and probably the most important was the unconventional way my parents encouraged all of their daughter's aptitudes and abilities without worrying whether these contributed to practical life. My parents were well-to-do, and some people even considered us to be rich. We did not have large, secure real estate holdings, but there was always money for cultural events, travel, and entertaining. Father was able to secure a carefree existence for us, while Mother was good at cheerfully and easily spending what he had earned. During periods when the sources of our comfort suddenly dried up, my parents were able to do without luxury no less blithely, as long as they still had what was most important – cultural wealth. They considered everything that was happening in the world of the intellect and of art to be extremely important. I was used to the fact that the grownups were constantly reading something, going to exhibitions, operas and plays, exchanging ideas about books and films, getting into heated philosophical discussions and in the process forgetting everything around them. Ever since childhood, immediately talking over what you had read, seen, and heard, sharing the pleasure a book or a concert had given you had seemed to me the only possible way to live.

I was denied nothing. There wasn't a single book on the shelves of my grandparents' comprehensive library that I wasn't allowed to take! There was no such thing as an age limit or other restrictions of the kind. Let the girl read whatever she likes! Whatever she doesn't understand now she'll remember later and then she'll get it. Mother impressed this binding postulate upon every new governess (who would at first try to impose on me the same restraints with which all children are usually tormented). Similar regulations applied to all fields of knowledge. It would have been inappropriate not to answer all my questions as clearly, candidly, and above all as logically as possible.

I am grateful to my parents for regarding me from my birth as an intelligent and discerning being, as a personality. Since I knew no compulsion, no moralizing prescriptions, or intellectual taboos, it was easy for me to accept the fact that you had to take into consideration the feelings and needs of others and the rules of civilized society, referred to as good manners. I thought they were as necessary as traffic regulations: you couldn't race around wildly on the roads either without wreaking havoc. Acquiring impeccable manners was like brushing your teeth at night. My governesses were there to ensure that. From my mother, on the other hand, I learned to converse with others in such a way that they were not bored and sensed my genuine interest.

Many of my parents' Riga acquaintances, regular, solid citizens, believed that I was dreadfully spoiled; the ladies, presumably out of envy, thought my mother was, too. But Father idolized us and could refuse us nothing, though this never involved material demands on my part. I spent my allowance (I could have wheedled a much bigger one out of Father) only for books, movies, and sweets.

I must admit that as a child I was headstrong and unpredictable, subject to tantrums, especially if I imagined people were trying to oppress me or to cramp my style. When I was quite young, I bit my governess' hand when she tried to force me, without explaining why, to do something I didn't want to do. Once, in a fit of rage, I grabbed a couple of eggs and threw them at the kitchen wall. Mama did not lecture me, she did not even scold me, only said: "How ugly and stupid." She looked down at me with scornful astonishment as if I was a changeling that got here who knows how. Her beautiful gray-green eyes lost their clarity and turned as gray and cold as granite. She shrugged her shoulders, screwed up her face, turned around, and left the room. I instantly realized how stupid, ridiculous, and ugly my behavior had been – I didn't want to be that kind of person on any account. That was all it took. From then on I trained myself to achieve more by means of self-control and "eloquent" looks than other children did by yelling and tantrums.

In later years, too, when we had differences of opinion about school-related or other issues, Mama used to say: "*We* don't do that." I loved this "we," I wanted to be part of it and accepted these ground rules for the rest of my life.

Later I understood that this education without commands or straight-out prohibitions saved me from having all kinds of complexes and frustrations that some of my friends had to struggle with all their lives. However, it also promoted certain character traits I regard as weaknesses. For one, for a long time I did not know the meaning of duty, for until I was about eighteen years old, I only did what I liked or what gave special pleasure to someone I loved. It was a different matter that many things other children experienced as an annoying obligation felt like fun to me. In school I was crazy about mathematics: Solving a complicated problem gave me no less pleasure than reading a wise book. I accepted the task of acquiring knowledge because it was fun. But it was left entirely up to me how I was to accomplish this. That is why to this day I find it difficult to perform the kind of unpleasant or boring duties that daily life constantly has in store for us and that we should actually take care of conscientiously.

Another character trait that was later to prove troubling in daily life already became apparent in my childhood. Usually I did not become passionate about doing something unless I was sure I could do it better than others. It was only worth doing if I had more to offer than they did. If it turned out that there were others in my social circle who were better or more capable in a particular field than me, I had no ambition at all; I felt no need to make an effort, to compete with others, but preferred to step aside and enjoy the others' success. Later in my career I was occasionally criticized for this characteristic.

As a child I had to learn to play the piano – an indispensable component of a young girl's education. I deeply loved music; I couldn't have imagined a life without opera and concerts, but that was exactly what proved to be fatal: I didn't like to hear myself play. At the age of ten or eleven, I declared to my parents that I no longer wanted to take piano lessons. I'd rather put on a Horowitz record, I said. My parents allowed themselves to be convinced. Five or six years later I also gave up drawing, which had been my passion for a while.

Much later, in another life, I was tormented by the fact that my writing seldom met my own standards. My thoughts run ahead of my writing hand, and that makes it hard to fix the thought, so that I am almost never satisfied with what I have written. This causes me torment that I wish I could avoid, although my head is full of unwritten texts.

Paper, pen, and typewriter, not to mention the computer, are not my allies. Yet even as a child I liked to tell stories. I need direct communication, living contact, I have to see the expression on my interlocutor's face, see their reaction. Recently, at a party in Riga, I met a lady my own age who recognized me, whereas I could not remember her. "We used to live in the same house as your grandmother," the lady prompted me. "We met in the yard. You had come to visit from Berlin. The governess didn't want to let you play with other children, but you gave her the slip and told us about movies you had seen and books. Also you had pictures of actors with actual autographs. We were a bit jealous, but we really liked the stories." The people who were present laughed heartily and said I had obviously not changed at all.

When the Soviet tanks rolled into Riga and my first life ended, I was eighteen. I had often heard my usually taciturn father express the idea that one could take everything away from a person – except for what was alive in their head and heart. This, said Father, is our only true, inviolable capital. Thus I was a wealthy person who needed to fear nothing and obey no one. This certainty gave me a peculiar sense of security and freedom. I came to the conclusion that freedom does not depend only on social and political conditions, which often cannot be influenced by the will of an individual. No, freedom is also a personal quality. People are free because they are grounded in something that empowers them to be free.

This capital has nourished me all my life. It's another reason why I feel compelled to write about my family, to describe the people under whose protection I grew up. It is my duty to the dead, a task I've dreaded to tackle for many years. One of my friends in recent years was the Hungarian writer István Eörsi. After the 1956 uprising he spent years in a communist prison and wrote a book about his experiences: *Remembering the Good Old Days*. "The dead, whom I feared to visit," he says, "are signaling to me that they are gradually running out of patience." I too must make haste.

I have often reproached myself for asking my parents so few questions. Like all children I believed they'd be there forever. Likewise, it would never have occurred to them, the grown-ups, that soon there would no longer be anyone from whom one could find out specific details about our family history. That out of our large circle of relatives I would be the only one to survive.

In the early days of my life history there are large gaps I'll never be able to fill anymore. More than once, especially when it came to filling out the insidious forms during the Soviet period, I've been incapable of answering a number of basic questions precisely. The powers that be at the time always found me suspect, and the blind spots in my biography increased their mistrust even more.

THE LULOWS AND THE LÖWENSTEINS

The forebears of my father, Leopolds Lēvenšteins, settled in the Duchy of Courland in the late 17th or early 18th century. The immigrants to Courland, both Germans and Jews, were for the most part craftsmen and traders, and were welcomed by the local people. The name of the Loewensteins (the original spelling was Löwenstein or Loewenstein) goes back to a little old town in the district of Heilbronn in Baden-Württemberg. When in the course of history Courland fell to the Russian Empire, the umlaut "oe" was replaced by "e," since the Russian and later the Latvian form of the name had to be entered in documents next to the German form.[1] In Courland Father's ancestors became related to the Rozentāls clan; a branch of the latter was baptized soon thereafter and married into Latvian families. The Löwensteins and some of the Rozentāls kept the faith of their fathers and settled in Riga at some time in the beginning or

---

1. Incidentally, to this day there has also been a princely house of von Loewenstein. It was interesting for me to discover that when Hitler came to power Prince von Loewenstein turned his back to his native land in deep disgust and lived in the U.S. until the end of the war. There he was well known for the generous help he provided for political refugees – including those on the left, whose views he definitely did not share.

middle of the 19th century. That's all I remember of the stories of Oma Rebekka, my paternal grandmother.

Father's forebears continued the German tradition. They were a peaceful middle-class family who lived modestly, without pressing financial worries. It was only rarely that a member of the hard-working though not very shrewd family achieved a high degree of prosperity. My paternal grandfather died when I was still quite young; I have only vague memories of the gaunt man with the white goatee. He worked as the head clerk or chief accountant in a German company – a respected, fairly well-paid position, though it wasn't easy for him to finance a suitable education for all six of his children. He sent his third-oldest offspring, my father, whom he considered to be especially talented, to the renowned Deutsches Klassisches Gymnasium in Riga. The rest of the children attended less prestigious commercial schools. Since he felt responsible for the education of his younger sisters, Father began earning money by giving private Latin lessons while he was still in secondary school. (Now and then, during the Soviet years, I used to meet gray-haired gentlemen who had been his pupils.) For my father, responsibility for the welfare of his family members ran in the blood – it was a matter of course.

The students of the Riga Deutsches Klassisches Gymnasium were primarily the sons of the German nobility and the city's patricians. Several of them remained on friendly terms with Father in later years as well. One lifelong friend was a certain Baron Korff, an amiable, frequently ailing man whose visits to our home I remember well. I also met two of Father's teachers, the brothers Kurt and Roderich Walter, who had taught his favorite subjects, German, Latin, and history. The Walters, who became my teachers, too, twenty years later, told me that Father had been a very popular student because of his talent, his even-tempered, self-possessed character, and his athletic successes. It was hard for me to imagine my father as a successful short-distance sprinter and as a member of the Kaiserwald cycling association. However, a thick, richly illustrated album about the 1912 Stockholm Olympic Games had been preserved at our house.

In it, I could admire Father – a slender young fellow with a small mustache, a member of the Olympic team of the Russian Empire.

At the Classical Gymnasium Father enjoyed a thorough humanistic general education. He was particularly fascinated by the world of classical antiquity. As a result, as a child, I got to hear many exciting stories about the ancient Greeks and Romans before I began reading about them myself. Father's dream had been to study classical philology, and after graduating from high school he did so for a year somewhere in Germany – until he realized that with this profession he could not earn enough to support his family. That is why he went to St. Petersburg and enrolled in law school, inspired perhaps by his deep respect for Roman law, the Lex Romana, which he later instilled in me as well.

Father's older sister Lonni had had a serious infectious disease as an infant. She was hunchbacked; also, learning and abstract thinking in general did not come easy for her. She remained single and lived with her parents. Day in and day out she was busy doing housework and was an excellent cook. Her sweet, friendly nature had already impressed me as a child, for I saw how much warmth and affection she could give even though nature had not been kind to her.

My father was born in Riga in 1894. His only brother Max had been born a year earlier, and the two looked so much alike that everyone thought they were twins. When I hadn't seen Father for a while due to his travels, there were times I mistook one for the other and greeted Max with the joyful exclamation "Papa is back again!" Afterwards I was terribly embarrassed. I listened entranced to Father's stories about the tricks the two brothers had played on people as they took advantage of this uncanny resemblance.

Max was a student at a commercial high school where nobody knew Leopold, and sometimes, when he was not prepared for a test or even an exam, Father went and took it in his stead. To my great delight they never got caught.

Father's sister Anna and her husband, Michail Kalabus, were to play an important role in his life. During World War I the Jews were forcibly evacuated from Riga and Courland into the Russian interior because they were suspected a priori of being friendly to the

Germans. Those who were lucky could find accommodation somewhere with relatives, and Anna reached her brother in Petrograd by a circuitous route. At that time Father was still at the university; he had not been drafted into the army because he was nearsighted. For a while he served with the railroad.

Anna took courses, and she and her fiancé worked in the office of a certain Nobel. This was not the famous Nobel, but Emanuel, his nephew, the son of Alfred's late brother Ludwig. The Nobels had extensive estates all over Russia. After the October Revolution these were nationalized. Taking advantage of the initial confusion, by means of all sorts of maneuvering, two law students – my father and one of his fellow students, the Polish Count Lubienski – managed to help Nobel to rescue part of his fortune and get it out of the country. Nobel never forgot that they had rendered him this service. It was thanks to him and his influential references that Father, upon his return to his native Riga, was able to establish himself professionally so rapidly and successfully in the international financial scene.

While still in Petrograd, as a sign of his gratitude, Nobel gave my mother a fabulous ring from India upon her engagement. It seemed like something out of The Arabian Nights, and later became my mother's distinguishing mark, as it were. The rare gem – a large emerald cut *en cabochon* – was magically beautiful. Sparkling green, it rose above the setting, which was emblazoned with diamonds. No matter what other jewelry appeared in Mama's possession in the course of her life, she never parted from this ring. She regarded it as her talisman and claimed, smiling at her own superstition, that it really did protect her and brought her good luck.

During the years of war and revolution only my father, his sister Anna, and her fiancé Michail lived in Petrograd. His sister Edith had wound up in Saratov. Max was serving in the army, while Father's parents had remained in Riga with the oldest and youngest daughter. On the other hand, Mother's family, who lived in Liepāja, was forcibly evacuated when the war broke out and also ended up in Petrograd, where some of their relatives were living. That's where my parents first met.

My mother's family, to whom in childhood I was much closer

than to the relatives on my father's side, always seemed mysterious to me. In Ancient Hebrew the archaic last name "Lulav" which Russian officials had changed to "Lulov" referred to the palm branch that in ancient times, when the sanctuary of Jerusalem, the Great Temple, had not yet been destroyed, was carried in solemn procession through the city in front of the Ark of the Covenant. Such palm branches were carried by members of a special family chosen for this purpose, who were therefore also given this family name.

While nothing is known about the paths that through the centuries finally led our forebears to Russia, the Lulaf family, from generation to generation, had preserved a legend that goes back to the 2nd century C.E. Mama told it to me when I was little, and it made a great impression on me: Our ancestors are supposed to have lived in Alexandria. They ended up there when the Romans subjugated the ancient Judean kingdoms of Israel and Judea. After the destruction of the Second Temple in Jerusalem, after the uprising and the suppression of the stubborn resistance began the great diaspora of the Jews. Early on, a sizeable Jewish community had formed in Alexandria, which included many learned men. In the famous library, the Lulafs joined a philosophy discussion group of the local Greek Neoplatonists. They engaged in debates, made friends – and even began intermarrying across the boundary lines between religions. This story filled me with enthusiasm and stimulated my imagination, although Mama warned me not to take everything at face value; perhaps in reality it had not been quite like this; a legend, she said, was just a legend. But, said Mama, it wouldn't hurt to live as though it was the truth so you wouldn't have to be ashamed in front of your wise forefathers.

Mama's forebears had been forced (I don't know under what circumstances and exactly when) to settle within the so-called *Cherta Osedlosti* (Pale of Settlement) in Russia – a zone where Jews were allowed to live and that comprised a part of the western governorate of the Russian Empire: parts of the Ukraine, Belorussia, the Polish-Lithuanian territory, and Latgale, which belonged to the governorate of Vitebsk. In the remaining parts of Latvia, the governorate of Livonia and Courland that was de facto administered by the German

Baltic aristocracy, there were other administrative regulations that were to some extent favorable to the Jews. I know our family history really well only from the point when, in the second half of the 19th century, the Lulows received permission to move from a small shtetl somewhere on the Belorussian-Ukrainian border to St. Petersburg. There they set up an export company for lumber and fish; a subsidiary was founded on the eve of World War I in the Courland port city of Liepāja, called Libava in Russian, where the Lulows had been rooted for some time.

In his youth, while still in Russia, Grandfather had learned and worked at the trade of lumber *sorter*.[2] Initially he worked in the woods where the lumber was felled, but later he went into the lumber trade and founded his own business. He owned forests in the vicinity of Valka near the border to the Estonian language area. Grandfather's companions were the first Latvians I remember. When in the mid-1920s I visited my Lulow grandparents in Riga, Grandfather had already retired, and only occasionally he got carried away telling me about his beloved woods, and also about how the woods had first appeared in the lives of his ancestors: In the middle of the 19th century one of his forebears served in the Imperial Russian Army as a so-called Nikolai soldier. These soldiers were drafted into the army for twenty-five years, but afterwards, if they survived, were pensioned off with a piece of land. Our forebear got a piece of forest. It was for this reason that one of the sons of the family usually chose a profession that had to do with the forest in one way or another. This forest of my grandfather's family has remained in my memory as a romantic image – and not as Grandfather's property or line of work.

Grandmother Esther's maiden name was Michaelis (or Michoels, an alternative pronunciation of the Hebrew spelling). Grandmother told us that she grew up in a family of teachers and scribes. One of her relatives, whose last name was Wowsi, had adopted the stage name Michoels – that was Solomon Michoels, a world-famous actor and stage director and, from 1928 until his death in 1948, director of the Moscow State Jewish Theater. He was originally from Daugavpils

---

2. Sorter: assessor, quality inspector

(Dünaburg, Dvinsk) and had graduated from secondary school in Riga. While they were university students in Petrograd my parents and he were friends. Shortly after the war I had the good fortune of seeing him in a comedy onstage, and also in a film fragment as King Lear, a role played by this great actor that had often been described in theater studies literature. I didn't get to know him personally. In January 1948, in the course of the persecution of the Jews during Stalin's last years, Michoels was murdered by the Soviet secret service while staying in Minsk as a member of the jury nominating theater awards. The official version was that he had been killed in an auto accident. His theater was closed, and the leading artists were imprisoned or sent to labor camps.

By some miracle I had been able to save a large-format anniversary edition, illustrated by outstanding artists, of Gogol's *Dead Souls* that Michoels had given my parents as a wedding present, with a dedication. Because of this dedication, the luxury volume was confiscated by the KGB in 1950 during a search of my Riga apartment, and I was in serious trouble, because Michoels' name was no longer allowed to be mentioned at the time. Certain scenes in which he could be seen were even cut from the Soviet feature film *Tsirk* (Circus, 1936). During the so-called thaw, he was rehabilitated and paid tribute to as an artist; admittedly, the false version of his accidental death was maintained for a long time to come.

My mother, Eva, was born in Liepāja in 1899. In contrast to Father's German-speaking family, the daily life of the Lulows was defined by the Russian language and culture. Much later, I accidentally discovered that the Latvian writer Zenta Mauriņa had attended the same Liepāja Russian Girls' Gymnasium at roughly the same time as Mama. After the outbreak of World War I, when the entire family was forcibly evacuated to Russia, my mother decided to go to relatives in Petrograd in order to study law in the higher women's courses. At that time, female students were admitted to the university's law school only in exceptional cases.

Grandfather used to say, half jokingly, half seriously, that from time immemorial a remarkable phenomenon could be observed in the Lulow-Lulaf family: The first child frequently had blond or red hair and gray or blue eyes, the second was dark blond with brown eyes, the third and all additional children, on the other hand, had dark hair and eyes. In those days large families were the rule; one that had only three children – as in Mama's case – was considered to be modest-sized. As a child I took Grandfather's joke at face value, for Mama and her younger siblings provided clear evidence for his assertion. My mother was unquestionably attractive: slim, with an ideal figure, her luxuriant, glossy, golden hair slightly wavy, gray-green eyes, and a radiant smile. But the source of her attraction was not her external appearance alone. In the circles in which Mama moved as an adult, there was no lack of beautiful women – neither in Riga nor in the film and theater circles of Berlin, not to mention Paris. And yet she immediately became the center of any social gathering. Even as a little girl I got a kick out of observing how every man who saw her for the first time was immediately blown away. Even years later many people remembered my mother's almost mystical charisma. She was an astute conversationalist, full of wit and irony, and passionately loved the arts. It was only when I was older that I really understood how vital and full of joie de vivre she was.

Her brother Georg, nicknamed Žoržik, two years her junior, resembled her both in appearance and in terms of his cheerful, carefree nature. He had the same sense of humor, astuteness, and charm, which made him so dangerous to women. Even before his return to Riga in 1922 he had obtained a diploma as a railroad engineer in Russia, but did not find a steady job in his field in Latvia. Žoržik was hopelessly impractical. While he was able to work conscientiously when directed by others, he had no head for business at all.

Completely different from her two older siblings was the baby of the family, Cäcilia or Cilia as everyone called her. She had serious, almost classical, and somewhat melancholy features, straight black hair, and big dark eyes. Reticent and quiet, Cilia was conspicuously musical; it looked as though, too shy to communicate with words, she could reveal herself unreservedly at the piano. She played wonderfully well, but she and the whole family regarded her shyness, which made any appearance before strangers a torture, as an insurmountable obstacle to a career as a concert pianist. Cilia was the only one in the family who lacked the vitality and joie de vivre that allowed the Lulows to accept with ease material and other worries that are, needless to say, always part of life. In love, too, Cilia was constant: Once she fell in love and then got happily married, she no longer wished for adventures and new experiences.

Mama's whole family was very close to me. When I was with them, I felt safe and secure; they gave me not only love and confidence in my abilities, but also many stimulating ideas in all spheres of life. What is more, when I was with the Lulows, I could always expect exciting surprises. I called them all by their first names or nicknames – in contrast to Father's relatives, whom I addressed as Aunt or Uncle.

I liked the paternal side of my family in a different way. I respected them, but I did not admire them. In my eyes they were preoccupied with nothing but mundane trivia, and hopelessly prosaic. Only Father's youngest sister Eugenie – Aunt Jenny – was different: She had a very lovely voice and lived in music. After she finished secondary school, she went to Germany, supported by Father, in order to complete her vocal training. There she got married and from then on lived in Königsberg. Although Mama got along with her better than with Father's other sisters, we only rarely met her in Riga or in Berlin.

I spent the Riga periods of my childhood mainly with Mother's family; for me it is my Lulow grandparents' apartment in Elizabetes iela 23 that is associated with the aura of "home." Nowhere else and never since have I experienced a place where I lived as a "haven of peace" again. The name of "Riga" was for me identical with the lovely Art Nouveau building in Elizabetes iela. This emotion extended to the house next door as well; a huge stuffed brown bear, erect and menacing, stood in its large foyer; I had tender feelings for it, perhaps since because of our many journeys and relocations I had to do without a pet of my own.

With the great wave of war refugees and forcibly evacuated people who gradually returned to the newly founded republic of Latvia in 1921, the two Jewish families of the newlywed couple also came to Riga. Mother's relatives did not go back to Liepāja, but remained in Riga, where, in Elizabetes iela 23, they dropped anchor for the coming years. It was in this apartment that I was born on February 18th, 1922.

In those days, after the return from Russia, Emanuel Nobel, as I already mentioned, played an important part in Father's life. The fact that Father and Count Lubienski had been able to rescue him from a precarious situation testified to their competence and ability to react to any given circumstances quickly and appropriately. Nobel saw to it that Father had access to the international world of finance, while Lubienski took part in the finale of the Polish fight for independence and then entered the diplomatic service. I don't know whether Nobel's grateful friendship was useful for his career as well. In the 1920s, Lubienski regularly came to Riga as a Polish diplomat and was a frequent guest in Elizabetes iela – and a loyal admirer of my mother.

It was only many years later that I became fully aware that Father had renounced his true calling – history and classical philology – in favor of a more lucrative profession so that his sisters and later Mama and I would lack for nothing. He did not feel by any means that this was a sacrifice, but rather an honor bestowed on him by fate. He never doubted for a single moment that he had the loveliest and most charming wife and the smartest, most wonderful daughter in the world. In order to make it possible for us to have a decent life and to be able to fulfill all our wishes, he had to make a lot of money. I imagine that Father, being talented and determined, would have gone far in the humanities, but stoically, day in, day out, he continued to attend to his business. I can still visualize the little edition of Marcus Aurelius bound in Morocco leather that always lay on his nightstand as others have a Bible. He would sometimes read to me passages from it in Latin. He was indeed a stoic.

Although my parents after returning from Petrograd had spent barely two years in Latvia, Latvian citizenship was held in very high esteem in our family. I remember conversations about how significant it was that, as was customary in the Western democracies, ethnicity was not recorded in the Latvian passport. (This was different in the Russian and later in the Soviet passport.) The only thing that was noted in the passport was religious affiliation, unless the passport holder expressly objected. The passport documented one's citizenship in a young, democratic republic with an exemplary constitution. Psychologically, Father considered this to be an important factor in strengthening the citizens' loyalty to their state. Even when my parents were later living in Berlin, the capital of the Weimar Republic, it never occurred to them to change their citizenship for the sake of convenience. Riga, now the ancestral seat of their large family, was home, a haven of rest in which you recharged your strength and energy before setting out for new enterprises far away.

Around the time of my birth, my father had established contacts from Riga to several large banks in Western Europe, especially to those of the Lazard Brothers in London, which were part of the Rothschild Group. As those who were in the know later told me, Father acted as an unofficial intermediary between the young Latvian government and the Lazard banks, which were willing to grant credit to Latvia. In my first semester of business administration at the university in 1940/41, the highly esteemed Professor Dunsdorfs told me that the British banks had granted quite advantageous credits. The substantial loan had been of crucial importance for Latvia's economy, which had been devastated by the war, and where both the agrarian reform and the development of industry demanded comprehensive investments. Knowing about my father's role in the reconstruction of Latvia (even if it was a myth) made me secretly proud and was the reason I was attached to my Latvian passport, which I received at the early age of ten.

Already while he was in law school, Father had realized that the actual work at a court of law held little interest for him. He wanted to be neither a judge, nor a prosecutor or solicitor. Appearing in public, holding a public office, being in the public limelight did not appeal to him in the least. Father specialized in international financial law. Thus the fateful incident in Petrograd had had a decisive impact on his career.

BETWEEN RIGA AND PARIS

Our life outside of Latvia was not to come to an end until 1936, after ten years in Berlin; after my parents were forced to accept the fact that nothing would change for good in Hitler's Germany from then on, they returned to Riga to stay. All these years we had been going to Riga in the long vacations and for the holidays for renewal in body and soul within the family circle. I spent the summer months with Mama's family in a big villa in Jūrmala, together with the families of Žoržik and Cilia. We usually arrived a week before Midsummer and stayed till the beginning of September.

My earliest memories are of Paris. Since I was one and a half years old when we came to France, it is hard to say whether these are really my own memories or whether I was told them so graphically that I finally thought I could remember them myself.

The first of many governesses who looked after me in the coming years was a Russian *nyanya,* who was called "Madame Charloff" in the French manner. She had come with us to Paris from Riga – Russian nannies in those days were regarded as the best. When I could already talk, my governess was Nurse Olga, a German Balt who always wore a nurse's uniform in the house – a light blue dress with a starched white apron, white collar and white cuffs. On the street she wore a dark blue cape and a dark blue cap with a starched white edge. She had been trained in educating preschool-age children according to the Pestalozzi method in Switzerland, and now she drilled me until brushing my teeth and bathing felt like second nature to me. In Berlin I got a French governess; at that point I had already started reading books. Mademoiselle Speer, who had studied French literature, was Swiss and came from Geneva. She was always keeping on at me how well-behaved the children had been in her last situation with the family of a French general. Mademoiselle was a Calvinist and forever influenced my bleak view of that religious orientation.

Our life circumstances were the reason that at an early age, almost simultaneously, I began speaking three languages: German, Russian, and French. Evidently the calculation of hiring a governess who came from a different language background worked.

Mama said that materially speaking the time in Paris had been the most carefree in our family's life. It coincided with the so-called Golden Twenties, Roaring Twenties or Années folles when the economic upswing both in the U.S. and in Europe seemed to be limitless, and even defeated Germany had already survived the crazy inflation. In Paris Father initially worked as an expert on international finance, but soon founded his own bank together with his friend Michel Olian. However, he sold his shares a few years later to his partner, with whom he continued to work closely. He preferred life as a freelancer, which was perhaps more risky but offered him more interesting and more versatile work.

I can't remember our Paris address – all that is left is the impression that the apartment was enormous. I can still see the big entrance hall – on one side of it were my parents' rooms, Father's study, the dining room, and the big salon, while on the other were my room, that of the governess, and a large kitchen. I particularly recall the salon. Low divans upholstered with exotic fabrics, strange art objects, allegedly from Africa... furnished completely differently than the Elizabetes iela apartment. Art Deco, as Mama later explained to me.

I rarely came into contact with the social gatherings in the other part of the apartment, since I had to go to bed before the real life began. But as soon as I was older, I had to "present myself": I had to learn to approach strangers without the governess' support and to get acquainted with them. Naturally I was supposed to show myself at my best. But Mama transformed what is usually forced on children as a logically unfounded code of conduct into a game. She would describe a specific scenario, for instance: This afternoon, several ladies are coming to have coffee with me; let's show them what a model child, what a *petite fille modèle* we have – they'll be astounded that you know how to behave as if you were at the British court. Thus I modeled myself on the illustrations of French children's books, and afterward Mama and I discussed what impression I had made. We enjoyed an affluence that was no longer imaginable in the later crisis and post-crisis periods. In Riga, beside a maidservant, Mama had recently hired a parlormaid as well. In Paris the servants did not live in the same apartment as their employers, as was customary in Eastern Europe, but on the top floor, usually the attic, in their own rooms, which usually also had sanitary facilities. This made it possible for servants to keep to regular working hours and not to have to spend their time off under the eyes of their employers. If it was ever necessary to call on the help of the staff late at night or on Sundays, these times were considered to be overtime, which were naturally paid extra. In Riga it was different: In the large apartments there were "maid's rooms," and the maidservant had to resign herself to unregulated working hours. My parents said this was customary all over Eastern Europe, a relic of a former way of life in Russia, where vestiges of serfdom had survived for such a long time. In Paris we had a car with a chauffeur, but later in Berlin and in Riga there was no question of that.

Occasionally I would hear from the cook or the governess that there were poor people in the world and even in Latvia. I also knew that Grandmother's washerwoman in Riga had a hard life. My grandparents tried to help her every way they could. As is customary in Jewish communities, not only in Riga, Grandfather and Father actively supported the poorer members of the community. I remember they helped a very nice and cheerful shoemaker to set up a workshop and adjoining apartment for his large family. Now and then we would bring him shoes to repair, and I felt how pleasant it is to do good and to receive genuine sympathy in return.

My ideas of poverty were pretty naïve. Somebody had told me that there were people in Latvia who lived on black bread and herring. In books I often read about poor children, but I didn't know a single one. Poverty had something to do with hard work, but being unemployed, I had been told, was even worse. Basically you could rest, but there was nothing to live on. I agreed with my parents, who sometimes said there was a lot of injustice in life. It was clear to me that every child has a right to live well. But I cannot claim that I really gave the matter much thought.

Once, on a walk with my governess in Paris, I discovered a group of workmen who were busy repairing the pavement. They had sat down at the roadside to have their lunch. I was amazed – a workman is not well-to-do, I knew that, but these men were breaking off great big chunks from a long, long loaf of white bread, taking huge bites of chocolate and washing them down with red wine from a bottle. In Riga white bread was considered to be a far greater delicacy than "coarse bread," as rye bread was called in Latvia, wine was not served every day, and such enormous slabs of chocolate were few and far between. How was I to know that rye bread did not exist in France, that local wine was cheaper than milk, and that chocolate in the days when France was still a major colonial power did not cost much. For laborers, chocolate was no doubt a more appropriate food than other, less exotic things. Although I was not even five years old then, I can still visualize this scene. At home I announced: "Poor people can be happy too!"

I still have fragments of memory from a trip to Nice we took together with the Olians, the family of my father's friend and partner. We traveled in two cars, rather impractical cabriolets that had retractable roofs; one was driven by our chauffeur, the other by Monsieur Olian, Misha, as we called him. Sitting in Misha's car were Father, Mother, and Misha's wife, Lilly, Mama's friend, while in our car were Tatiana, the Olians' little newborn daughter, the two nannies, Mama's maid, and I. I don't remember the long drive to the Mediterranean, or any of the stops along the way, although this was not an everyday event. Only one single static scene has remained in my memory: I see the two cars with their passengers and Monsieur Olian's unusual motorist's outfit, which was fashionable at the time – a leather jacket, leather peaked cap, and dark glasses. My mother told me all the rest. At any rate, we spent spring on the Riviera and then, after the end of June, spent the long vacation in Jūrmala, on the Bay of Riga.

In Paris Mama quickly acquired a large circle of friends and acquaintances, consisting mainly of Russian intelligentsia and French artists and film people. The chansonnier Maurice Chevalier, who was very popular at the time, came once. His hit and trademark chanson was "Valentine," which appeared in 1922 – a piquant, slightly risqué song about a charming girl with a tiny behind and cute little breasts, who in the next verse, a few years later, has turned into a rather portly lady, recognizable only by her frizzy hair, pitifully repeating, "But I am Valentine, Valentine, Valentine." We had a record on which Chevalier sang this naughty song, and I listened to it many times. Mama wouldn't have been Mama if she hadn't encouraged me to memorize the song forthwith. I had no doubt that Maurice Chevalier had dedicated it to none other than me, and I sang it with great enthusiasm. I no longer recall whether I was brought to the guests or whether the guests came to me into the nursery; in any event I found myself face to face with Chevalier and in all seriousness launched into "Valentine" – the audience split their sides laughing. This was the only artistic triumph of my life.

One of my other vague memories is the following episode: One spring, when the family was again going to the Côte d'Azur, we made the empty apartment available to Sergey Prokofiev, who had just arrived in Paris. When we got back, we discovered that our piano was totally ruined. It was like a horse worked to death and abandoned on the battlefield.

I also recall a few Russian writers from the ranks of the so-called white émigrés. One of them, Yuri Felsen, was devoted to Mama to the point of self-sacrifice. He dedicated poems to her and made her the heroine of a novel about a femme fatale.

Perhaps Mama had already discovered her love of French culture and way of life earlier on. In any case, from her first moment in Paris she felt like a fish in water, and when we lived in Berlin and later in Riga, she went to Paris as often as possible and sometimes stayed there for longer periods. Both in Berlin and in Riga, she would order the latest French books, which were sent to our address in great big parcels. Since nobody stopped me from reading these novels, I was equipped, even as a teenager, with thorough knowledge about male-female relationships – including unconventional variants of love.

As for German books, Mama read them only with careful discrimination, while Father devoured them in huge numbers. From the time I was little, he would not only give me the books that meant a lot to him, but also loved to arrive home loaded down with editions of collected works.

At the time we left Paris, in 1926/27, I had started reading passionately on my own initiative. This step is far more significant in a person's life than we generally assume. Up to that point children observe what is going on in their immediate vicinity, take note of it and become socialized. When they read a book or watch a theatrical performance, they become observers, where there is a certain distance. That is how their imagination, emotions, and analytical thinking begin to mature.

BERLIN, MEINEKESTRASSE 9

From early on, at two or three years of age, it was obvious to me that the world is huge and that every place is different – and that you don't have to be afraid of that. Speaking several languages in order to communicate with people seemed totally natural to me. Greeting people in their home in their mother language means showing them respect. Even as a child I made the pragmatic observation that strangers become friendly and are happy to talk to you if you address them in their mother tongue.

I began to speak and soon to read German, Russian, and French without actually having studied these languages, and regarded none of them as a foreign language. Since I regularly spent longer periods in Riga and Jūrmala visiting my grandparents, I also acquired Latvian, though my vocabulary remained limited to practical topics and children's games. It was not until later that I discovered Latvian literary language and culture along with it.

Sometimes people have asked me whether as a child I did not confuse the many languages. Obviously the mistaken belief that speaking several languages might cause a jumble in a child's mind persists to this day. However, in recent years, studies have shown that the early playful and natural learning of several languages activates certain areas in the brain. This not only makes it easier to learn additional languages, but also to memorize various theoretical formulations and terminology in later years.

I found it really easy to learn further languages – beginning with Latin and English – in the conventional way. With true enjoyment, on my own, without a teacher or textbook, I later acquired a few more languages (at least to the point where I could read them). The diversity of impressions taught me early in life to observe, to compare, and to analyze. Above all, my profound conviction that every human being has a right to be different became stronger and stronger.

We arrived in Berlin in the winter of 1926/27 – at first Father and, once he was firmly established, Mama and I. Among other things, Father represented two Latvian export firms in international matters. He also worked at the stock exchange. I had no concrete idea of what he did, one reason being that Mama avoided discussing anything as banal as making money. What was crucial was Father's own attitude. As a man of classical culture, though keen on his professional work, he regarded it as too coarse and in a sense "immoral," inappropriate for his queen and his princess. He liked his women to bloom like flowers in a hothouse, delighting the world with their fragrance. Moreover, like a physician, as a lawyer he had to maintain professional secrecy in the interest of his clients. That is why I know only two large companies Father worked for at the time: the chemical company I.G. Farben and UFA, Germany's largest film production and distribution company.

Unlike in Paris and Riga, we did not have our own apartment in Berlin. In keeping with their lifestyle and circumstances, my parents preferred to live in a so-called residential hotel or comfortable guesthouse that provided all domestic services and where the guests found accommodations for an extended period and sometimes even for years. Mrs. Bergfeld, the proprietor of our hotel guesthouse, who was Latvian, was one of the most extravagant figures of my childhood. Even before World War I, she had come to Berlin upon her marriage, and the apartment building in Charlottenburg had been left to her by her late husband. It was located in Meinekestraße, a peaceful side street of the rather busy Kurfürstendamm with its theaters, movie houses, restaurants, and exclusive stores. World War II spared this part of Berlin, so that the street of my childhood between Ku'damm and Lietzenburger Straße still looks almost exactly the way it did then. Today, however, Meinekestraße 9 houses the Hotel Residenz Berlin.

Our financial options in Berlin were no longer as ample as they had been in Paris. Soon after we settled in Meinekestraße, we were hit by the world economic crisis. We could no longer afford to keep servants – except for my governess, for Father spared no expense when it came to my education. Possibly my parents were also not sure whether they would stay on in Berlin or return to Paris.

The Pension Bergfeld, something between a hotel and an apartment building, proved to be ideal for the needs of our family. In the two-room apartments with built-in kitchenettes, or single rooms with corresponding facilities, the guests lived with every comfort.

On our floor there were few apartments, though there were two drawing rooms that were available to all the guests. The smaller of the two was the music salon, where there was a grand piano. People who wanted to have a party or celebration could book one of the drawing rooms. Guests were free to order breakfast in their apartment; lunch was served in a large dining room, which was also located on our floor. Mrs. Bergfeld's cuisine had an excellent reputation, so that not only the guests of the hotel came to lunch, but their friends and acquaintances as well. Moreover, in the breaks between the morning rehearsal and the evening performance, actors and directors from neighborhood theaters also used to show up. Supper, like breakfast, did not necessarily take place in the dining room; while it was possible to have it served there, people usually had it brought into their "own" four walls.

The fame of Mrs. Bergfeld's cuisine was based on the much-vaunted foods from Latvia. In this Ku'damm neighborhood, everybody knew that Mrs. Bergfeld received direct shipments from Riga several times a week. Latvian butter and other products were available in Berlin shops as well, but they were considered to be delicacies and were therefore correspondingly expensive. From the conversations of the grown-ups, I knew that German groceries were of lesser quality. It was we, the proud Latvian citizens in particular (and there were occasionally a number of them living in Pension Bergfeld), who made fun of the fact that the Germans had two kinds of margarine: One was called margarine and the other butter. Even I found German milk and butter inedible.

Mrs. Bergfeld's supply system functioned flawlessly. She had the food sent to her regularly by her relatives from Latvia by the Riga-Berlin express train. All she had to do was come to terms with the conductors – they would receive the packages in Riga and hand them over to Mrs. Bergfeld's maidservant Agnes in Berlin, who would be waiting on the platform together with her fiancé, a fireman. Instead of the modern refrigerators, iceboxes with natural ice were used at the time, and since the train was not en route too long, the food stayed fresh. (At the time the railroad tracks in Latvia had the same gauge as in the rest of Europe, so that the distance between the two capitals could be traveled in 24 hours.) Thus Mrs. Bergfeld could serve genuine Latvian delicacies to her guests: the prized yellow butter with its fragrance of hazelnuts, thick, velvety sour cream, and salt- and freshwater fish, some of which – such as lampreys, smoked Baltic herrings, or lightly salted salmon – were not available in Germany.

It was in Berlin that the cinema entered my life: I spent an entire decade of my childhood among film people. I encountered them not only on the screen but also in Mrs. Bergfeld's guesthouse, especially at her lunch table.

As I mentioned earlier, Father worked for UFA. With its big studio in Babelsberg, it was the second most important center of the film industry after Hollywood. The '20s and the early '30s up to Hitler's ascension to power were the heyday of silent film and early sound film; the movies produced in Germany captured audiences at home and abroad. In Latvia they were among the most popular films.

UFA not only sold movies abroad, but in turn also acquired the rights for foreign films for distribution in Germany. It was part of my father's job to draw up the relevant contracts, which is why my parents were irresistibly drawn into the circles of the German film scene. I'm sure that if my serious and matter-of-fact father had not had such a charming wife, all the actors and other film people would hardly have visited our home. Father was primarily in contact with the various producers who worked for UFA. One of them, Erich Pommer, has gone down in film history as a prime example of his profession. He was in charge of one of the independent production units under the umbrella of the great film company and stubbornly and successfully pursued a clear objective: to produce films that were not only artistically significant but also made money. Between 1918 and 1932, Pommer's era in German cinema, he was responsible for works ranging from *The Cabinet of Dr. Caligari*, *Metropolis*, *The Blue Angel*, to famous musical comedy films like *Der Kongreß tanzt*. My parents met Pommer during the last years of this period. In their conversations I heard names such as Murnau and Fritz Lang, Sternberg and Marlene Dietrich, whose films I got to see even as a child. I particularly remembered the names Heymann and Holländer because their famous hits – with Latvian lyrics – were also popular in Riga.

As for Pommer himself, I only occasionally saw him at our place. Naturally my parents followed his later fortunes and spoke about them at home. As a World War I veteran he had been awarded the Iron Cross and other medals. We were still in Berlin when Pommer was driven out of the film world he himself had created. Forced to emigrate because he was a Jew, he worked in England for a while and later went to Hollywood, but never felt really at home in the unfamiliar cultural milieu. After the war he briefly returned to Germany. He was unable to resume a career on the basis of his earlier successes either here, in his ungrateful native land, or back in the U.S. – and he was no exception.

Naturally, of the visitors at Pension Bergfeld, I was chiefly interested in the actors I admired on the screen. The rest of the film people – directors, cameramen, set designers, and scriptwriters – were to a certain extent overshadowed by the actors, whose faces were ubiquitous, not only on the screen but also on posters, portrait postcards, and cigarette cards, which were very popular at the time. It was almost impossible to avoid seeing them – just like the Sarotti chocolate ad, a little Moor in colorful garb that greeted me on every street corner from the advertising pillars.

As soon as I became at all interested in movies, I was told by my parents I could watch whatever I wanted to: "You won't understand whatever you're not supposed to in any case!" In those years, for me, life and film must have been totally blended. I constantly kept discovering situations and relationships that were exactly like the movies. On Ku'damm, directly across from Meinekestraße, there was a little movie house I was allowed to go to even without my governess. The staff closed their eyes in regard to age limit, happy about every ticket they could sell – especially for matinees, when the hall was half empty. There I watched everything without exception, but above all I tried not to miss a single movie that featured two actresses who strongly reminded me of Mama: Jeanette MacDonald, an American who became famous playing in musical comedy films and thanks to her pleasant, clear soprano voice was also very popular in Latvia, was the spitting image of my mother. The features of the second actress were somewhat sterner, but she too resembled Mama – the German film star Brigitte Helm. Since her debut in Fritz Lang's *Metropolis*, her career was meteoric, only to crash-dive when the Nazis came to power. She was a true blonde German beauty, but she fell out with the leading directors of the Nazi film industry – and was given practically no more roles.

Both Mama's and my favorite among the film people who regularly rented accommodations at the Pension Bergfeld was Anny Ondra, a Czech from Galicia. Her real name was Anna Sophie Ondráková. Her partner at the time, with whom she shared her apartment, was the stage director and actor Karel Lamač. Both of them came from Prague, where Anny had first become known as a dancer, and he as an actor in Czech movies. Back during the silent film era they got assignments in Germany, where they quickly advanced to star status. From time to time, they would go home to the Czechoslovakian capital, where a film industry was developing. The competitive Barrandov Film Studios, which were then being developed, belonged to the Havel family. Anny and Lamač must have come to Berlin at roughly the same time as we. Anny celebrated her first big success in 1928 with the silent film *Saxophone Suzy*. Lamač made a large number of films in Berlin and Vienna, mainly with Anny, but also musical comedies, for instance with the Hungarian star Marta Eggert. All these films were shown in Riga as well, and the audience loved them. When I went to visit my Riga grandparents, I could brag that I knew these stars.

Anny was unbelievably nice. "I'm just a simple girl," she liked to say. To a certain extent that was true. Anny was very attached to my mama and admired her. "You're lucky to have such a mama," she would often tell me. "I too have been learning a lot from her – for instance, how to dress and make conversation." Before Anny went to an official reception or a ball, she would often come to our house to get advice as to what her outfit or her appearance still lacked. Mama was amused and usually recommended that she take something off: "Less is more!" This sentence has stuck in my memory. We loved Anny for her sincerity and her naturalness, and she too became fond of me and spent a lot of time with me. She was troubled by her own childless life. Speaking to me as to an adult, she once explained to me that she had to renounce this pleasure solely because of her career. Perhaps I filled this gap. At any rate, Anny wanted me to accompany her everywhere – and saved me from the governess.

I liked it that Anny spoke to me as though I were her confidante. She took me with her to the film studio, to the café, ordered oodles of cake and ice cream, and watched sadly as I stuffed my face. She was forbidden to have any, she said – according to her contract with the film studio she mustn't gain an ounce. Time was her enemy, the audience would immediately forget its darlings if they were not constantly present; and anyway, time was very cruel to women (especially film stars!). I polished off my cake, listened with curiosity, and felt very sorry for Anny.

The public at the guesthouse was so diverse, every personality so distinctive, that the lifestyle and the relationships among the guests were also unconventional and permissive. Much that was unthinkable or frowned upon in the middle-class society of the time was taken for granted here. In one top-floor apartment lived two nice, polite gentlemen whom I often encountered at lunch. People said they were practically married. Nobody seemed to think it was anything special.

I was the only child among all the adults. Unlike Mademoiselle Speer, who was constantly getting upset and taking offence, I followed the example of my parents and accepted the fact that life was multifaceted as something totally natural. For a while Anny and Karel had a third partner and roommate – the cameraman Otto Heller, also from Prague. The three lived as a family on our floor in a large two-room apartment. Their life as a threesome did give rise to a lot of furious gossip. Otto Heller, whom for some reason I called Fritz, was a cheerful young man who was always ready for new pranks. When political conditions changed and the Nazis came to power, the trio broke up, and Otto Heller, who, as it turned out, was Jewish, left the country – first he went to Vienna, then to London. For a while my parents managed to keep in touch with him, but at some point their contact broke off. A good quarter of a century later I discovered that Otto had become a classic as a cameraman. He had shot several famous movies, including *The Ladykillers*, my favorite British comedy.

My parents were still in Berlin when Anny left Karel Lamač and moved out of the guesthouse. She had fallen in love with someone else – the boxer Max Schmeling, whom she married soon thereafter. In 1936, after he defeated the American champion Joe Louis, the legendary "Brown Bomber," Schmeling had become the world heavyweight champion and a national hero. Despite all the homage and privileges, he continued to be a decent human being, who during the Nazi period did not tarnish his honor either by betraying, or by indifference toward, his persecuted colleagues. Anny and Schmeling spent a long life together. For all the years I was separated from the rest of the world by the Iron Curtain, I received only indirect news from Anny. I was determined to locate her if I ever reached the West. In 1989 I managed to do so, but Anny had died two years earlier. I was very, very sorry. Max Schmeling survived her by many years and died, almost a hundred years old and still as popular as ever, in 2005.

Since not only in Riga but also in Paris and Berlin Mama socialized with Russian émigrés, I met film people from these circles as well. A group of young film directors had formed in Berlin, and some of them later became well known. Some had studied in Russian theater schools and had even had the opportunity to study with Stanislavski. One of them, who visited us quite often and therefore could practically be considered an uncle, was Anatole Litvak. Since he was an exciting storyteller, I usually tried to sit as quiet as a mouse and to remember the many names he dropped, which were associated with all kinds of events.

Born in Kiev, he had graduated from secondary school very early and by age 23, when he left the Soviet Union, had already studied philosophy in Petrograd, graduated from acting courses with Vakhtangov and Meyerhold in Moscow, and had also acted in a couple of silent movies.[1] He'd been lured to Berlin by a friend, another Russian émigré – the somewhat older film director Nikolay Volkov, who was working quite successfully on German silent film productions.

"I can't judge whether he has talent," said Father, who appreciated Anatole for his eagerness to learn, "but thanks to his curiosity and intelligence his productions will no doubt never sink to substandard levels." For a start, Anatole learned the art of montage, and Georg Wilhelm Pabst chose him for his team as a cutter. After he had cut several Pabst films, including *Joyless Street*, and had worked with Volkov as his assistant, Litvak made his own first film in 1930: *Dolly macht Karriere* (*Dolly Gets Ahead*). I didn't get to see it, but I did see his next two films in Riga, which were a huge commercial success: the musical comedy *Nie wieder Liebe* (1931) with Lilian Harvey, who was popular all over Europe, including Latvia, and *Das Lied einer Nacht* (The Song of Night, 1932) with the famous Polish tenor Jan Kiepura. Even after Anatole moved to Paris, my parents stayed in touch with him, which is why I was able to follow his further career. One of the five films he made in France became an international hit, including in the U.S.: *Meyerling* (1936), the first sound film about the tragic suicide of the Austrian heir to the throne, Rudolf, and his mistress, with Charles Boyer and a young Danielle Darrieux in the main roles. (I can testify to the fact that it provoked floods of tears in

---

1. The 1922 silent movie has not been preserved; only a few stills are in existence.

Riga as well.) Now Litvak had arrived, and an invitation to Hollywood followed. The same winter that my parents returned to Riga from Berlin, Anatole said goodbye to the Old World.

His last letter reached us in 1938, in the year of the fateful Munich Agreement: Anatole, who had switched from RKO Pictures to the famous Warner Brothers, had given up his bachelor's life and married Miriam Hopkins, the star of his first American film. While already living under Soviet conditions, at the start of a new difficult phase of survival, I suddenly heard his voice in a French radio broadcast. My heart gave a sudden lurch. In his perfect French, he was thanking General de Gaulle for the Cross of Honor he had been awarded (later he also became a Knight of the Legion of Honor). As it turned out, Anatole had served in the U.S. Army and been in charge of a documentary film team together with Frank Capra. They filmed the Normandy invasion of the American and Canadian troops and the military operations in France.

I never saw Anatole Litvak again, for during the Soviet era I was not allowed to travel to the West, not even as a tourist. He died in Paris in 1974.

It was mainly Anatole who was dying to have Mama play in the movies and kept offering her parts. But Mama was not in the least tempted by something millions of women dreamed of. She didn't need this dream – real life offered her plenty of plots. Mama loved to party at night and to dance a lot, which is why she was in the habit of sleeping till noon and having breakfast in bed. I remember she laughed and said to Litvak: "You want me to get up at the crack of dawn, spend hours putting on makeup, and stand in front of the camera at 8 a.m.? No way!" Moreover, as a smart and sufficiently self-critical woman, she was well aware of her strengths and weaknesses. She was not photogenic, the camera was not her friend. Never, in not one photograph did she really look like herself. Obviously her true power lay not in her features, which can be captured by optics, but in her charisma, in the vitality that emanated from her whole personality. She was quite aware of it, and that was why the cinema, while it was a pastime, held absolutely no interest for her.

I still have pleasant memories of another young acquaintance of my parents who had something to do with the cinema – Hermann Kosterlitz. Originally from Berlin, he was a friend and colleague of Lamač and Anny. Karel jokingly called him "our child prodigy" because he was not even 22 years old when he sold Lamač his first script. He wrote only comedies, which in retrospect does not surprise me when I think of his fun-loving nature and the amusing drawings and caricatures with which he made not only me but the adults laugh as well. While we were still in Berlin, his Czech partners were joined by Hungarian ones. Kosterlitz made movies not only in Berlin and Vienna but also in Prague and Budapest. There he discovered a new film star: the Hungarian Franziska Gaal, who like Anny was ideal for comedies that had a somewhat clownish, endearingly comical, temperamental diva as their center. I saw his films that starred Franziska Gaal – for instance, *Peter* and *Kleine Mutti*, both made in 1934 – in Riga, where they were a big box office success. He soon vanished from my horizon.

My parents had barely had time to settle down properly in Riga when Kosterlitz, who was discovered to have fateful Jewish forebears, left Berlin and landed in Hollywood, where he adopted the name Henry Koster. For a start, he was given a risky job no other director wanted to take on – making an unknown and inexperienced singing fifteen-year-old by the name of Deanna Durbin into a star. Like all teenagers in Riga, I too was crazy about the series of five musical films with this likeable young star, whose unexpected worldwide success saved Universal Studios from bankruptcy. The second of these films in particular, *One Hundred Men and a Girl* (1937), which also featured the famous conductor Leopold Stokowski, can still occasionally be seen at art house cinemas. I took one of his later films, which I did not get to see until many years until it first appeared, into my heart: *My Friend Harvey* (1950), with a six-foot, three-and-a-half-inch tall invisible white rabbit, who turns out to be the guardian angel of the protagonist played by James Stewart.

In those days, two types of feminine beauty dominated in life and on the silver screen: the modern, androgynous *garçonne* – boyish, slim, with small breasts and short hair, emancipated and independent, what the Americans called a flapper. And the so-called ladylike type, which, as far as I can tell, is completely extinct today. In German cinema it is aesthetically most perfectly embodied by Lil Dagover. Agnes Esterházy, a friend of Mama's I didn't like, completely fit the type; she had also enjoyed an education that was commensurate with elegant salons. With her black, slicked down hair that was usually wound into a bun, her lovely black eyes, and erect, full figure, she stood for a chic, luxurious lifestyle. In the '30s both these ideals of beauty seemed to vanish; in actual fact they merged into one when slim yet feminine figures became fashionable.

Recently I saw Agnes Esterházy in Pabst's silent film classic *The Joyless Street* and ascertained that, seen through modern eyes, she looks even less interesting.

The family background of Agnes Petersen, Mama's other friend, a German, was less genteel. She was not as well-known as Agnes Esterházy, but undoubtedly superior when it came to beauty. I remember Mama's words; Agnes, she said, was a very kind person, sensitive and vulnerable. She had a romance with Oscar Dancigers, a friend of our family from when we lived in Riga, who during this phase of his life was preceded by the reputation of an irresistible womanizer. I did not doubt it, for I and Mama also liked him a lot. Agnes was a lover for Oscar, while my mother was a kind of icon he worshipped devotedly. Even then such nuances in male-female relationships were clear to me.

The name Dancigers (German Danziger) was very familiar to people then living in Riga. As the historian Marģers Vestermanis informed me, the Dancigers, a Jewish family who had converted to Christianity two generations ago, were the most important sponsors of the Riga Herder Institute founded in 1921. They were wealthy people and owned large dry-cleaning businesses in the city. Right after World War I, Oscar's brother Georg (later Georges) had gone from his native Tukums to Riga and then to Paris, where he worked in film distribution. In 1945 he and his friend, the Russian émigré Alexandre Mnouchkine, founded the film production company Les Films Ariane. Both were highly educated men, something that cannot be said of all the heads of the film industry. As the years went by, along with somewhat more modest entertainment production, they created quite a few outstanding cinematic masterpieces that today have a firm place in the history of film. The two gave their production company the name of Mnouchkine's daughter Ariane, born in 1939, who later founded the world-famous Théâtre du Soleil.

Oscar, on the other hand, the younger (and might I add, the more handsome) of the Dancigers brothers, enjoyed the wealth acquired by his parents; he earned no money, but merely spent it as he traveled through Europe, drawing attention to himself even in the circle of good-looking film stars. Women fell for him by the dozens, and he loved them too, without being particularly choosy. Probably that was why he constantly had to commute between Berlin, Riga, and Paris, since he was eagerly awaited everywhere. In summer he mainly stayed at the Riga seaside in Jūrmala, and I have several photos where he can be seen on the beach in the company of my parents, uncles, and aunts.

Together with Agnes Petersen, Oscar Dancigers would also appear at the Pension Bergfeld, and I recall a particularly spectacular episode involving them both. At the time I was about seven, and my friend Paulchen Salzmann, who also lived on Menekestraße, was about ten. We loved to observe the grown-ups, to eavesdrop on their conversations, and discuss our impressions later. Once, as we often had before, we had made ourselves comfortable behind the grand piano, where heavy draperies concealed our hiding place. Oscar and Agnes came into the salon, naturally without seeing us, and we witnessed a highly dramatic scene. Here's what we understood from the situation and a few words: Oscar had just told Agnes that it was over, and Agnes looked devastated. Evidently they had retreated into the salon in order to conclude the difficult conversation. Her voice choked with tears, Agnes begged: "Play our song for me one more time..." Oscar sat down stony-faced at the piano behind which Paulchen and I crouched with bated breath, and began to play. When he was finished, he slammed the piano lid shut, said, "Goodbye and thanks for everything," and left. Agnes remained sitting in the corner of the sofa for a while, the picture of misery; then she, too, left the salon. Paulchen and I were speechless: How lovely it had looked! Just like the movies: two beautiful young people, a grand piano, a farewell melody, tears... We agreed that it was even better than the movies, because we had been part of it ourselves. Many years later I had to smile about these memories; in my hiding place I had witnessed a scene that could have come from *Casablanca*.

Later, after countless stormy romances, Oscar became more dependable and joined his brother, who introduced him to the film business. Oscar secured his place in the history of film as a producer in Mexico. After a ten-year hiatus, he was the first to take the risk of financing films by the director Luis Buñuel, dubbed "accursed" at the time – including *Los olvidados* (*The Forgotten* and *The Young and the Damned*, 1950). Much, much later I read Oscar Dancigers' name as the producer in the credits of Louis Malle's feature film *Viva Maria!*, which was made in Mexico and starred Brigitte Bardot and Jeanne Moreau.

As a child I got used to looking on life as a movie; involuntarily I began to see theatrical scenes all around me that were often far superior to what happened on the screen. Take Mrs. Bergfeld. She could have been put in a comedy straight out of our guesthouse and nobody would have believed she was not a fictional character. Whenever I was able to escape from my blasted governess, I would run into the kitchen, where another, no less interesting life was going on. The governess was shocked by my "plebeian tendencies," but Mama allowed me to make friends with whomever I wished – there was nothing that could be done about it.

In those days, of course, I was unable to properly appreciate Mrs. Bergfeld's fantastic capacity for work. She had only one full-time helper – a maidservant by the name of Agnes – and the two of them slaved away from early morning until late at night. They went shopping, cooked, and baked. Only for heavy jobs, a cleaning woman and a strong handyman would come at specific times. Basically the whole big house with its many inhabitants rested on Mrs. Bergfeld's shoulders. Being a wealthy woman, she could no doubt have hired more help. I don't think she was reluctant to do so in order to economize. I heard my parents say that she, who wanted everything to be perfect, quite simply did not trust anybody. She could only guarantee impeccable order and quality meals if she had a hand in the work herself. I can't remember ever having seen her tired, unfriendly, or grumpy.

Mrs. Bergfeld had devised an ingenious system to avoid wasting even a second in the course of the day. In accordance with her roles, from making soup to being a hostess, she also had to change the clothes she wore. In the early morning she put on all the outfits she needed one on top of the other and took them off layer by layer like the skins of an onion as the day went on. It seemed like a game to me, and as often as I could, I would dart into the kitchen to watch Mrs. Bergfeld's wondrous transformations. Next to her body she wore the dress for the evening; over that was a suit in which she appeared in the dining room at lunch. On top of that in turn were the overalls and apron she needed for kitchen chores, and when the weather was cold, when she went shopping in the early morning, a coat had to fit over all the rest of the clothes. It didn't bother Mrs. Bergfeld that, decked out like this, she was as broad as she was tall. After transforming herself into a kind of cabbage, she rolled through the kitchen and dining room at great speed like a little ball. I always tried to guess which dress would appear when Mrs. Bergfeld peeled herself out of the next layer.

No less than Mrs. Bergfeld with her dramatic transformations I was drawn to the guesthouse kitchen by the maidservant, Agnes. She was infinitely sweet and good-natured, and very fond of me. Agnes wore the same neat work clothes all day long. She was very clean and was constantly scrubbing her big red hands with kitchen soap and a scrubbing brush. Her face was just as red – though I never got to see how and with what she scrubbed it.

No longer young, Agnes must have been at least thirty-five, but was still unmarried. It's true that she had a fiancé, the above-mentioned fireman. They'd been thinking of getting married for years, but still hadn't saved up enough money. He had formerly been a taxi driver and was now saving for a cab and a house of his own. On their few days off, they would go off somewhere to have a good time. Sometimes Mama gave me permission to accompany them. It is thanks to the two of them that I got to know a different Berlin, a city that was radically different from the one I would see on walks with

Mama or Mademoiselle Speer. This was the world of the workers, the simple people, where everyone drank beer from big steins as they chowed down on big or smaller sausages – and where for the first time I came in contact with men who were drunk. They were all incredibly nice to me and regarded it as their sacred duty to teach me how to speak a proper Berlin dialect.

My experience of life was considerably expanded when I became better acquainted with the women from the fashion salon of Mama's friend Maria. "Marmikha," as we lovingly called her, had come to Berlin during the first wave of white emigration and had married a German, Mr. Salzmann, here. Her son, my friend Paulchen, whom I've already mentioned, was three years older than me, a bookworm like me, and in spite of the difference in our ages did not mind being friends with me. We met almost daily to talk about books and movies and about life in general. The Salzmanns had a big apartment kitty-corner from the Pension Bergfeld. I don't know what Mr. Salzmann did for a living, but evidently it was necessary for Marmikha to help her husband so that they could maintain their standard of living. She, an educated lady whose attitude toward the material side of life was careless, typical of the Russian intelligentsia, had actually managed to open a fashion salon in Meinekestraße and to make a success of it. Four qualified seamstresses worked for Maria Mikhailovna, who designed her dresses herself with excellent taste and artistic intuition. While I was there, the salon was already famous all over Berlin.

The Salzmanns were a mystery to me. Mr. Salzmann was the absolute opposite of his wife. They never came to visit us together, but always separately – Mr. Salzmann to see my father and his wife to see my mother. I simply couldn't understand how two people who were so totally different could become a couple and get married. Mr. Salzmann, whose first name I never heard, remains indelibly engraved in my memory because he embodied all the clichés of a typical Prussian. As a young man he had served in the imperial army and then fought in the front lines during World War I. The Prussian military style was ingrained in his very bones. The one who suffered from this the most was my friend Paulchen, the victim of his father's Spartan educational methods. His room, with its bare, white walls, without decoration of any kind, without a single picture, was furnished only with the most basic necessities. He slept on a narrow iron bed frame, under a thin, gray woolen blanket without a top sheet; the pillow was hard and flat. At the time I didn't know that soldiers in the barracks slept in such beds. But to my mind the most terrible thing was the fact that Mr. Salzmann, who got up at 6 a.m. because his work began very early, roused Paulchen as well and made him take an ice-cold shower and do gymnastics in his underwear in front of the open window. Our dear Marmikha secretly tried to save Paulchen from the daily iron schedule and discipline, and invented all kinds of excuses for him.

Paulchen found refuge from his despotic father among the seamstresses, who worked in a large room behind the reception and demonstration rooms of the fashion salon. There, we spent many lovely hours. A seamstress by the name of Hanna was particularly fond of me. Like Agnes, she had a steady boyfriend – also a driver, who already had his own taxicab. They too were saving money in order to be able to marry. Hanna often invited us to go for a ride in her boyfriend's taxi, and so we crisscrossed Berlin and got to know the city within a larger radius than with Agnes. That is why today I can remember a Berlin that vanished forever in World War II.

I admit that in spite of its size and vastness Berlin made no particular impression on me. To me it seemed more impoverished than Riga; perhaps because no one had showed me the outskirts of Riga, so that I knew only the splendid center and the carefree people who frequented it. Our taxi driver's friends kept cracking jokes, and he himself always had an anecdote ready about the sights of the city he showed me and Paulchen. Thus I got the impression that every architectural monument in Berlin had a nickname, sometimes quite a racy one. The four of us sat in the beer gardens of Berlin and watched the men and women, their faces flushed (for some reason they all seemed fat to me), drinking beer, singing at the top of their voices, and dancing. When the weather was bad, we'd go into one of the countless Berlin corner pubs. I talked Berlin dialect for all I was worth, and we never stopped laughing for a minute. Mademoiselle Speer threw in the towel, embittered and deeply offended because Mama had given all this her blessing.

In those days I had another friendship that shocked my governess just as much. In an apartment on the courtyard side lived a girl called Steffi. Her mother was divorced and worked right around the corner on Ku'damm as a salesclerk at Wertheim's, one of the biggest and most modern department stores in prewar Berlin. It's true that Mademoiselle Speer had intimated to Mama that Steffi's mom was a "fun-loving lady" who was known to change her male friends frequently, but got no encouragement from Mama. Steffi was one or two years older than me. When she came home from school, she would first go to her mother, and whenever I could, I would join her. In the department store, I again discovered a new, hitherto unfamiliar world. We wandered through the floors and departments, looked at the beautiful merchandise, imagined what we would love to buy and what we would do when we had bought it, and chatted with Steffi's mother's fellow salesgirls. They were very friendly, and I had the impression that they all felt they were one big family. Such a milieu was totally new to me, and again I said to myself: It's just like the movies...

JUST LIKE THE MOVIES

Mrs. Salzmann's clientele came from the ranks of the so-called better society, and since Mama often took me with her, I had plenty of opportunity to study the various types of lovely ladies and their no less elegant wardrobes at the salon. Marmikha was not only Mama's friend but also knew how to make business use of this friendship. During the international financial crisis, she literally made Mama into her poster child: Though my parents' social life in Berlin went on as usual, money had become tighter; Mama could not change her wardrobe as often as before. Marmikha made her friend an offer that she should wear the demonstration models of her salon at soirees, premieres, and other public events. She was to wear them once and then return them to the salon. Since Mama as a rule got compliments for her wardrobe – "Oh, what a chic new dress!" – all she had to say was: "Thank you! I had it made for me at the Salzmann fashion salon in Meinekestraße" and add a few words of praise about the outstanding quality of the workmanship.

I remember an episode that was almost like the plot of a movie: Mama had a childhood friend by the name of Lydia. The daughter of a Jewish pharmacist from Kuldīga, she had escaped provincial life in Courland and gone to Paris to study music there. I liked her a lot, especially because of her sharp wit and her tongue, which was no less sharp. After World War I, students from the Baltic states or from Poland, including Jewish girls from very modest circumstances, could often be encountered in Western Europe. Often they had graduated from a German or Russian secondary school, spoke several languages fluently, and had a broader horizon than their fellow students in France or Germany. It took character and determination to break out of the narrow circle of the Jewish petty bourgeoisie. If the girls were beautiful to boot, the attention of their new community was immediately focused on them. The meager resources of the Kuldīga pharmacist did not permit him to finance his daughter's stay and education in Paris lavishly, so that from the start Lydia had to consider how she could earn a little extra money. She soon got offers to be a model for painters and photographers, work that would not keep her from continuing her studies. Her Polish friend Bronia followed a similar path – she too stood out due to her appearance, education, and intelligence.

Lydia's spectacular looks attracted the attention of Paul Cartier, one of the best-known jewelers of Paris. He hired her to advertise his jewelry. The Cartier company, among other things, had rented a box at the opera. This is where Lydia sat on certain evenings, elegantly dressed and flashing her jewels. Usually she was accompanied by a gentleman in tails or a tuxedo who was actually guarding the jewelry. There she sat, allowing the audience to admire her. Nothing else was expected of her, and she was paid to be there. Lydia, who adored opera, felt this work was a gift from heaven. Because of their mutual love for music, Cartier's nephew became interested in her, and she became Madame Cartier. Now she herself had to keep an eye on her jewelry.

I can still see the portrait of beautiful Madame Cartier on the cover of *Vogue*. The name of the Kuldīga pharmacist, on the other hand, was not mentioned anywhere. Lydia's friend Bronia, who became well known in Parisian artist circles because she was working as a photo model for Man Ray, finally married the film director René Clair, with whom she had a long and happy marriage.

In Mrs. Salzmann's salon, dresses for the wives of various foreign diplomats were also made. Thus, by a paradoxical coincidence,

Natalia Rosenel, a Moscow actress, was having her clothes made in the salon of a white émigrée. Madame Rosenel, as she was called, was married to Anatoly Lunacharsky, then people's commissar for education and temporary ambassador of the USSR. Since he liked to accompany his wife, Mama met them both at the Salon Salzmann. Lunacharsky, who unlike other people's commissars was highly educated and was even a writer, began visiting the Pension Bergfeld – naturally without his wife. Lunacharsky's weakness for beautiful ladies was generally known – a weakness that could easily put such a high-ranking Bolshevik official into a dangerous situation. Of course, he fell head over heels in love with my mother. But that was not the only reason that my father treated the new acquaintance rather coolly and left the house, if possible, whenever Lunacharsky appeared. In spite of his wit and entertainment value he was perceived as a menacing presence.

For reasons unknown to me, Lunacharsky insisted on speaking only French to me. Perhaps, it later seemed to me when I thought about this whim of his, he really wanted at least occasionally to forget his historical role, with which by this time he was quite disillusioned, and to feel like a totally normal person in whose presence people did not have to feel mistrust and be vigilant. I remember Lunacharsky and Madame Rosenel very well – not so Ilya Ehrenburg, however, who had also lived at the Pension Bergfeld a few years earlier. From Mama's stories I only know that he had fallen violently in love with one of Mama's friends from Riga, Aunt Katya. She was a Russian emigrant, and had married a man who lived in Riga. Whenever she got bored in Riga, Aunt Katya escaped to Berlin to have a bit of fun. There she met Ehrenburg, who at the time was also considered to be an emigrant from the Soviet Union, and so began, as Katya put it, a *burniy roman*, a stormy romance. I put away this story as well in the treasure chest of my memory, where over time I accumulated a considerable amount of knowledge about the two obviously most important spheres of life: love and art. It would all be of use to me one day.

When Lunacharsky frequented the guesthouse, I was already making my observations and drawing my conclusions from them. I had seen his wife only at the fashion salon, and had a faint memory of her as a person who was covered from head to foot with pearls and diamonds. For Mama she was a prime example of *mauvais goût*, extreme tastelessness; she was also horrified by her brazenness: Everyone knew that this jewelry came from the confiscated personal treasures of the Romanov imperial family, which as masterpieces of the jeweler's art had been handed over to various Soviet museums – and now adorned so-called *nomenklatura* wives.

At the time, Lunacharsky had come to Germany with commissions in the sphere of culture, and particularly of the cinema. In 1928/29, the Soviet film company Mezhrabpom[1]*, founded in 1923, was making two German-Soviet co-productions with Prometheus Film in Berlin. That was why Russian film directors and actors were staying in Berlin, some of whom refused to go back to the Soviet Union. In 1929, the company made Tolstoy's *Living Corpse* with Vsevolod Pudovkin in the leading role. It was directed by Fedor (also Fyodor) Ozep, who had brought with him his star Anna Sten – the daughter of a Russian variety dancer and a Swedish ballerina who had started her screen career in 1926 in the Soviet silent movies. In the fall of 1930, in Berlin, they made their successful film *The Murderer Dimitri Karamazov*, in which Anna Sten played Grushenka by the side of Fritz Kortner. When Ozep first entered our circle of acquaintances, I couldn't even imagine that I would marry a relative of his ten years later in Riga. Both Ozep and Anna Sten remained in Berlin and became so-called *nyevovrashchentsi*, "those who did not return home." Soon they would both go their separate ways: Ozep made movies in Berlin and Paris, while Anna went to Hollywood and later married and went to England.

At the time I did not completely understand what kind of a man Lunacharsky was and why people exercised caution where he was concerned. I was only struck by the fact that in Lunacharsky's presence our guests hardly ever spoke about politics, but rather about literature and art – areas about which he was extremely well

---

1. Acronym of Mezhdunarodnaya Rabochaya Pomoshch: International Workers' Assistance.

informed. Some tried to keep a discreet distance from him. In his native country, Lunacharsky would soon fall from grace. He was fortunate to die in time – before Stalin, whose mighty shadow already loomed menacingly behind him, was able to destroy him.

It was not for nothing that Father avoided Lunacharsky. He knew that the tentacles of Soviet power had penetrated far into Western Europe. "Any contact with representatives of this state, even a business one, is risky, no matter how neutral and innocent it may appear," he said once. How right he was!

In the early 1930s, when I was already going to school in Riga and living with my grandparents in Elizabetes iela but spending holidays with my parents in Berlin, a certain Schönmann family had moved into the Pension Bergfeld. The couple seemed very unusual to me because they were an extremely poor match. Stanislaw Schönmann was half Polish, half Jewish, while his wife was Finnish. They spoke Russian to each other, and he called his wife by her patronymic, in the Russian fashion: Ekka Jonovna. To my eyes the red-haired Ekka was thoroughly exotic, for Finland was considered to be an unknown country somewhere at the other end of the world, far north, where the polar bears live. In those days it hardly played a role in European cultural life. Ekka Jonovna was friendly but silent and reserved. Mama said she was surely a very lonely woman. Her husband Stanislaw or Stasik, as everyone called him, was the absolute opposite: extroverted, witty, and charming, the soul of any party, as people used to say, and even I could feel his charisma. Besides, he was surrounded by mystery: At the guesthouse, he appeared only sporadically, kept disappearing for longer periods, and often left his wife and son in a rather precarious financial situation. News would then arrive from various European metropolises like Paris, Brussels, or Geneva, something that Paulchen's stamp collection profited from. Jean, the son, must have been seven or eight years older than me, perhaps he was already at the university, and he looked at least as handsome as his father. Stasik courted my mother, which was nothing unusual, but to my surprise this time Mama apparently did not remain indifferent. Father could not possibly help being aware of this; however, his only reaction was that he teased her about this a little now and again.

I had heard with half an ear that Stasik was engaged in some kind of business of which Father said that it was not exactly sound, but even dangerous. There were people who called Stasik simply an adventurer. Once Father hinted that Stasik had gotten involved in a particularly risky game. But I was interested in a new rumor that gradually spread through the guesthouse and that my mother did not like at all – namely, that Stasik supposedly had a second family in Belgium: a wife named Yvonne and a little child. It was said that he regarded both wives as equally legitimate and commuted back and forth between them. Just at that time the drawing-room comedy *Eva or Yvonne,* with Henny Porten in the lead, was playing at a theater on Kurfürstendamm, and since Stasik did not conceal his passion for my mother, everybody joked that the play was evidently about him.

In my German school in Riga we had holidays again, which I was even allowed to extend so that I was able to stay with my parents in Berlin. Toward noon one day I was sitting with Mama, who was still having breakfast in bed. The phone rang. I picked up, it was Father: "I'm glad you're there. Where's Mama?" – "In the bathroom." – "All right, listen: I'm going to talk to her now, but please don't go away. I've got some bad news: Stasik's been killed, it will be a great shock for Mama. Maybe she'll feel faint. Please stay with her and see if you can help her. I'll be with you as soon as I can."

Mama comes from the bathroom, picks up the receiver: I know what Father is telling her, and I'm sure he goes into more detail. Mama turns pale, doesn't breathe a word, but nothing else happens, she knows how to control herself.

A moment later she realizes she needs to console poor Ekka Jonovna, who is now all alone in the world, without friends, without a home, without a country, and god knows whether Stasik has left her anything to live on.

Father had expressly warned people against Stasik, had called him reckless and foolhardy. My father was well-informed about international affairs; it was part of his job as a lawyer to steer his clients through the labyrinth of the laws of various countries and whenever possible to apply them in their favor. He also knew the contradictions and weaknesses of the laws, which he circumvented if possible, though without ever openly violating them: This would have gone against his sense of justice, as he always pointed out to me. Stasik couldn't have cared less about such considerations, he often acted recklessly, even reprehensibly, and got involved in complicated business affairs without having the required knowledge and experience. That was what had happened this time as well.

As it turned out, he had wanted to dabble in the most dangerous business of all – arms trafficking. Stasik had many acquaintances among the Russian émigrés in Western Europe. At the time, the idea of a conspiracy against the Soviet power, led by General Kutyopov, was brewing among them. Among other things, their intention was to infiltrate former army officers into Russia and incite the populace against the government. Stasik was planning to supply them with weapons. Naturally the czarist officers living in exile could not be expected to come up with significant sums of money. That is why, in parallel with these secret connections, he was officially collaborating with the Soviet embassy in Paris. As a middleman, he brought together producers and buyers. In his exaggerated opinion of himself, Stasik had imagined that he would play this double role brilliantly and fool everyone. At the time he rarely showed up in Berlin; he traveled all over Europe, but mainly stayed in Paris.

The official version of events was as follows: The Soviet embassy had hosted a grand reception on a yacht anchored in the Seine – a party with the usual pompous posturing, streams of vodka, and mountains of caviar. Allegedly Stasik, blind drunk, fell into the Seine and drowned. In other words, an accident. But everybody knew that Stasik didn't drink, no one had ever seen him totally drunk, let alone so drunk that he would have fallen overboard. Everybody realized that Stasik had been murdered; perhaps he had been stunned and thrown into the river, but it was also clear that it would make no sense at all to demand a police investigation. People were simply furious that Stasik, who was secretly collaborating with the white émigrés and hoodwinking the embassy, had been so foolish as to accept its invitation.

And so he vanished from our lives. Later we learned that Ekka had located some relatives and returned to Finland. Her son Jean moved to Paris and began working for the film industry; a stormy affair with the French star Viviane Romance created quite a stir in the film world. After that he lived in Egypt for a while making movies. At some point we lost sight of him.

And yet Jean left me the memory of a beautiful episode. I can't have been more than twelve years old, and so Jean was around twenty. He was quite aware that I had a crush on him, and one day he invited me to an evening performance. There were two big variety theaters in Berlin – the Wintergarten and the Scala. Even Beniamino Gigli had sung at the Scala – I had gone to the concert with my parents, With Jean, however, I spent an unforgettable evening at the Wintergarten, where a circus legend, the famous musical clown Grock, was appearing. Naturally I remember how masterfully he played several instruments at a time, but that wasn't why the evening was so special for me. What was unforgettable was the feeling that I was going out in the company of a young man for the first time in my life, exactly like a grown-up young lady. I was tremendously proud.

When silent films were replaced by talkies in Germany once and for all, new residents appeared at the Pension Bergfeld, new guests had their lunch there, and conversations revolved around their work. Sound equipment had been patented in America in late 1927, and already in the following year the production of sound films was running at full tilt. Germany, which was the first to acquire the patents, was hot on the heels of the U.S. In France, however, in the big film studios of Joinville near Paris, they had no sound equipment for some time to come; that's why the soundtracks of the first French sound films were recorded in Babelsberg. Thus René Clair's *Under the Roofs of Paris* was given its soundtrack in Babelsberg. Of course, all this was discussed in Meinekestraße eagerly and at length.

During the transition period from silent films to talkies, synchronization, i.e., adding a soundtrack in another language to a finished movie, was not possible yet. Therefore at UFA potential box office hits were made simultaneously in different language versions – in German, French, and English, for the British too were slow in acquiring sound equipment.

Here is how it worked: Once a scene, in German, was in the can, it was shot again following the same script (translated into the respective language, of course) with the same sets and the same music. This method could be used only by UFA, for the whole thing was a laborious and expensive affair. This is how in Babelsberg, for several years, a whole series of German films were made in three versions. There were several German actors who were fluent in English or French, or both in rare cases. Lilian Harvey, for example, played in all three versions, though each time with different partners, and became a star throughout Europe. Her steady partner in the German original versions was Willy Fritsch, who was also popular in Latvia; in the French versions, on the other hand, the young, handsome Henri Garat took the part of her lover. The highly educated Olga Chekhova mastered all three versions of her films, while Renate Müller and Conrad Veidt played at least the English versions. Latvian moviegoers got to see only the German original versions, for in those days practically everyone in Riga spoke both German and Russian. It was not until later that the films were provided with Latvian subtitles.

In the years when UFA made multilingual versions of its films, a whole series of French actors could be found in Berlin, and some of them stayed at Mrs. Bergfeld's guesthouse. One of the most famous was Annabella, who moved on to Hollywood shortly thereafter. She came to Berlin accompanied by her second husband, Jean Murat, while Albert Préjean, Annabella's first husband, who had just starred in René Clair's *Under the Roofs of Paris*, used to turn up only occasionally to visit. Annabella and Jean Murat were among the few guests of the Pension Bergfeld who ignored me, and that hurt my pride. I thought Jean Murat was a very handsome man, but arrogant too, since he looked right through me. Many years later I encountered him again in Riga – on the screen in *The Possessors* (*Les grandes familles*, 1958) with Jean Gabin. Murat, by now a man of mature years, still cut an impressive figure.

A still unknown French actor, on the other hand, liked to spend time with Paulchen and me. Young and a little too thin for my taste, but incredibly clever and always ready for fun – today I'd say: artistic – he charmed us by joking, juggling, doing magic tricks, and teaching us all kinds of chansons. He gave me several portrait photos of himself with grandiloquent, histrionic dedications that I could brag about in Riga. The young man's name was Pierre Brasseur, and he was soon to become one of the best-known French theater and film actors.

Also among my parents' guests was Ossip Runitsch, the silent movie star from prerevolutionary Russia and one of the partners of Vera Kholodnaya in her famous melodramas. He lived in Berlin exile and acted in German silent films. Always elegant and dapper, he looked great in tails. Occasionally we used to meet him in Riga as well. He acted at the Russian Drama Theater and also in Yiddish-language plays at the Jewish Theater in Skolas iela. I was quite shocked when I saw Runitsch again not too long ago in Berlin at a festival featuring noteworthy silent films, in the 1923 film *Danton*. What a disappointment! He resorted to the worst clichés of pantomime. I couldn't believe that decades ago he had been an acclaimed and worshipped matinée idol.

That is how the cinema entered my life: with its problems, about which I learned fortuitously, and its personalities, whom I encountered in my daily life. This elementary interest, which would also extend to theater as time went on, never left me again.

In those days many of our family conversations revolved around the impending civil war in Spain. All sympathies were with the legitimately elected government: The opponents of the republic, Franco's fascists, were supplied with weapons by their like-minded supporters in Germany and Italy. Allied against these forces were people who had a broad spectrum of political convictions and were agreed that the endangered freedoms and democratic rights of individuals and citizens must be defended. From Latvia, too, volunteers went to Spain to support the Republicans, although their ranks included people with the most divergent views, for instance, social democrats and communists, whose parties were outlawed in

Latvia after the Ulmanis coup. Our family had no sympathy for the communists – whether they were Trotskyists or Stalinists – but I kept in mind that there are existential situations when such a joining of forces is imperative. One of Mama's young relatives also secretly went to the Spanish front to join the International Brigades. He was not a communist. At the time I had tremendous admiration for this Max, who, under the wing of his father, could have led a comfortable life. After all, he was doing the same thing as Ernest Hemingway, one of my favorite writers.

Even then, rumors were circulating about the USSR's double-faced role in this war. For propaganda purposes, the press and official representatives of the Soviet Union loudly proclaimed their support for the Republicans, but in actual fact the volunteers who were allowed to go and fight in Spain were arrested once they returned home.

I must confess that though I was aware of these events, I was at the time more fascinated with the history and literature of a bygone period than by contemporary politics and social problems. The unshakable feeling of security that had been such a blessing to me during my childhood had created something like a glass wall between me and an ever more menacing world, torn by contradictions and conflicts. I regarded the episode I am about to recount as just another amusing, satirical adventure story without giving much thought to the criminal cynicism – condemned by Father – in the face of a tragic, bloody conflict.

Hitler was already in power when my father received a lucrative offer he found hard to refuse. He rarely told us about his professional life, since much of it was subject to professional secrecy; but some stories were so amusing and instructive that he could not deprive us and our friends of them. Father was supposed to draw up a legally watertight, multilateral business contract taking into consideration the different currencies and legislations of several states. He was offered a fee of ten thousand pounds sterling (an enormous sum at the time, and this would only be the first installment). After he had familiarized himself with the offer, he rejected it, although the money would have been just what we needed for the move to Riga. I heard him say to Mama: "It's a dirty business." He told us the part of the story he knew.

Three entrepreneurs from Brussels, Paris, and Riga had decided to use the Spanish civil war to do profitable arms deals. The arms would be bought from the manufacturer in Czechoslovakia, loaded in a Mediterranean seaport onto a ship acquired for this purpose, and transported to Spain. Naturally there was plenty to do for a lawyer in a transaction of this kind. The freight had to pass through several countries, and the purchase of the ship, the hiring of the crew, and a lot more had to be settled by contract. The funny thing was that the three had managed secretly to enter into agreements with both sides – one and the same arms shipment had been promised both to the Republicans and to the Franco fascists after receiving hefty advance payments from both parties. At first everything went like clockwork; after it was loaded, the ship sailed from Genoa. Father said he had learned of this in all secrecy and had wondered himself who would ultimately receive the shipment. But even he could not foresee what happened then. Just before it reached the Spanish coast, the ship was wrecked for no apparent reason and sank. To this day, it is lying on the bottom of the Mediterranean, and the answer to the question as to whom the freight was addressed sank with it. Incidentally, there were no casualties as far as the crew is concerned – the lifeboats had not only been made ready in time, but were already completely loaded, and so the entire crew reached the land safely. The ship was insured for a large sum, and the three owners suffered no losses – on the contrary. Father added drily that in his opinion there had been no weapons on board; thus where and to whom these were ultimately sold – if they even existed at all – remains one of the secrets of history.

Of course, a machination of this magnitude could only succeed because in Europe everything was going haywire. The Spanish civil war ended, Franco was victorious with the help of the German and Italian air force, Hitler occupied Czechoslovakia, and no one paid attention to the three crooks who had made a fantastic amount of money. At least they had made sure the crew was safe – they were no murderers.

To me, all of this sounded like the script of a movie. Since Father was not involved in the affair, I could find the cynical craftiness and criminal energy of the protagonists amusing. It would have made a great gangster comedy. The fate of real countries and historical persons involved in the plot still did not seem real to me or appear to have anything to do with my life.

SCHOOL BEGINS

In the fall of 1929, I started school in Berlin. Even outwardly the comfortable villa not far from Schlachtensee, where a certain Professor Jensen admitted me to the first grade of his private school, was no ordinary educational institution. It was a long ride from the city center to school, and in those days I was still under Mademoiselle Speer's supervision. She brought me to school in a taxi; sometimes we would also take the underground and the bus. I particularly enjoyed taking public transportation, because I found it exciting to be surrounded by strangers, to observe them, and make up stories about them. While the governess waited for the end of classes, she would go for walks or read a book in the park.

Strangely enough I have almost no memories of this school. I can clearly visualize the motley company at Pension Bergfeld: dozens of people I met there, including lots of Berliners – servants, seamstresses, chauffeurs, and sales ladies. I can't recall my teachers and classmates, however. I didn't feel like making friends with any of them. Except for Steffi, whose mother worked at the department store, and Paulchen, of course, I had no real friends.

In Professor Jensen's school they were trying out new pedagogical methods whose purpose unfortunately remained unclear to me. At least the peculiar teaching techniques brought a breath of fresh air into the boring lessons, during which I ordinarily learned nothing new because I had long ago taught myself reading, arithmetic, and writing. They were trying to drum the curriculum into the children's heads with the help of sounds and rhythms. In class we handled various musical instruments: For instance, during arithmetic we beat on drums, and the teacher associated even the rules of grammar with the sounds of a piano, violin, and harp that in his opinion corresponded to them. In spring and fall, lessons were held in the garden if it wasn't too cold. By the last half of the school year in second grade I was already a student in the Luther-Schule in Riga.

A lot changed in our lives during that time. At the end of 1929 the entire capitalist world was shaken by the great economic crisis. We came to feel its effects about a year later. My father, whose activity was connected with international banks, the stock exchange, and large enterprises, received practically no more new contracts. Suddenly we had to tighten our belts and cut down on our expenses. Instead of two apartments, we could afford only one; also, there was no money for the expensive private school and the French governess. So my parents decided, without making a big deal out of it, to send me to school in Riga, where Oma's loving care and a big, bright room awaited me in Elizabetes iela. In Riga they would hire a less expensive and more modest German governess. Actually, nothing basically changed in my life – I had always commuted back and forth between Berlin and Riga. Only, so far I had lived with my parents in Berlin and visited my grandparents in Riga; now it would be the other way round.

In Riga Father picked a German school with a good reputation for me: The so-called Luther-Schule was a two-level private girls' school that consisted of the German Primary School No. 16 and the Luther Secondary School (called the Luther Gymnasium); both shared the same administration and teaching staff. In accordance with the principle of cultural autonomy within a national state, the parliamentary republic of Latvia with its consistently democratic constitution had not only schools where the language of instruction was Latvian, which of course represented the majority, but also schools for the numerically sufficiently large minorities – Germans,

Russians, Jews, and Poles – where teaching was done in the mother language of each minority while at the same time students were also given a thorough knowledge of the national language. Latvia and Estonia were considered exemplary in this respect, and until the mid-'30s parents were free to decide which type of school their children should attend. During the Ulmanis era a new law was passed prescribing schooling either in the language of the student's own minority or else in Latvian.

At that time I spoke Latvian only at a poor everyday level, so that it would have been difficult for me to go to a school where the language of instruction was Latvian. It was well-known that the Russian schools of Riga also provided a very good education. My knowledge of Russian was richer than my Latvian vocabulary. When the wave of white Russian émigrés swept westward, a considerable part of them, evidently guided by nostalgic feelings, remained in Riga, because here they felt nearer to their lost homeland. These people belonged primarily to the intelligentsia or to the aristocracy, which is why at the Russian secondary schools the teachers were often highly qualified, and even included former professors of the Moscow and Petersburg universities. Several Latvian schools also had a good reputation. By and large, in the period between the wars, Riga was blessed in having a multilingual intelligentsia – a rapidly evolving Latvian one, and that of the Germans, Russians, as well as Jews associated with these cultures.

The structure of the Jewish schools and particularly of the primary schools at the end of the '20s and the beginning of the '30s did not seem completely clear to my parents. In Latvia there were three types of Jewish schools, which is due to the peculiarity of the history of the Jewish people – schools with Yiddish, schools with modern Hebrew, and schools with Latvian as the language of instruction. In none of them was Father able to discover the principles of a classical education that were so important for him.

We didn't have to think long – we decided on a German school. After all, German was the primary language of my childhood. And why the Luther-Schule, of all places? It enjoyed the reputation of not lagging behind the boys' schools. We can hardly imagine it today, but in those days the prevailing traditional view still was that it was sufficient for girls to have a humanistic education – albeit an easier variant of one. For Father, of course, it was important that the Luther-Schule taught the classical languages. And there was another circumstance in favor of this school: The Walter brothers, mentioned above, worked as teachers here – the men who had taught my father at the German Classical Gymnasium before World War I. The Germanist Kurt Walter had in the meantime become the head of the Luther-Schule, and his brother Roderich Walter, Father's former history and Latin teacher, was still teaching these subjects. Father could thus be sure that his little daughter was in good hands. After all, I was barely nine years old – and so far away from my parents. At school, during the five years it took for my whole family to be reunited in Riga, I was, in fact, watched over unobtrusively yet conscientiously.

At the turn of the year, in 1930/31, in the middle of the school year, I moved into my grandparents' apartment, where I had always felt at home. In a partitioned-off alcove of my room slept Mrs. Mantz. She was German, her name was Regina, and she was the most vivacious and exuberant of all my governesses. A little over thirty, a divorcée, she was the only one of them who also had a private life, which I cheerfully welcomed. When Mrs. Mantz occasionally disappeared to meet one of her admirers, I covered her illegal absence. With the life experience I had gathered in Berlin, such things did not surprise me but gave me pleasure – only Grandmother mustn't hear of them on any account. I remember that Mrs. Mantz had one particular favorite; she told me how charming and witty he was and what a fine voice he had. He was an up-and-coming singer whose name was Aleksandrs Daškovs. Later – in one of my next lives – I occasionally ran into him; he had in the meantime ascended to become one of the great baritones of the Riga Opera. He implored me in jest never to mention these memories in the presence of his wife, the great soprano Elfrīda Pakule, who, incidentally, was discovered by Leo Blech during his Riga emigration years.

At age twelve, I was finally regarded as being grown up and was now rid of the governesses for good.

RIGA. ELIZABETES IELA 23

I always felt I was a child of Riga. Still, in retrospect, I realize how little I knew that city in the years before the war.

My walks usually took me to the adjacent Strēlnieku dārzs, the "Riflemen's Garden" (now Kronvalda parks) and its surroundings, but my favorite walk was to the City Canal with its swans and little Chinese pagoda, which I often remembered with longing in Berlin. Even then I was struck by how much the City Canal resembled the Landwehr Canal in Berlin, though the Berlin canal did not have the same spaciously designed park-like green space, and for long stretches commercial buildings, walls, and bricks often came right down to the water's edge.

What I liked most in Riga were the bookstores, for instance, Valters un Rapa near what was then the Hotel de Rome (now the Hotel Riga), or the one on Brīvības bulvāris owned by the Ettingers, a family that belonged to the Jewish intelligentsia. When I was ten years old, my father set up an account for me at this bookstore. I was allowed to buy there anything my heart desired without ever hearing a word of criticism, although some of the art books were quite expensive. There was also the famous music and instrument shop in the Old Town that everybody called "Julius Heinrich Zimmermann," the name of its owner. There, even we children were allowed to try out the instruments.

In my prewar rambles, I never walked as far as the outlying districts, such as the Moscow District or Grīziņkalns, Čiekurkalns, Zemitāni, or Mīlgrāvis. The part of town I wandered through – initially with my governesses and later with friends – stopped at the Daugava River and included the Ķeizardārzs (now Viesturdārzs), Strēlnieku dārzs, Vērmanes dārzs, the Esplanade, the Old Town, and the area around Krišjāņa Barona iela. I was also familiar with the villa district Mežaparks, meaning "Forest Park," where the part of our family that was later deported to Siberia on 14 June 1941 lived. Often I would stroll from Alberta iela toward the City Canal, on to Bastejkalns, over the little bridge and into the Old Town. There you could wander back and forth through the winding alleyways only to find yourself suddenly back on the banks of the Daugava, which in my earliest memories was still crowded with market stalls; the Central Market with its famous halls did not open until 1935. As a child I was passionately fond of historical novels, and during walks exploring past epochs of Riga the heroes of many different stories thronged my imagination. In Berlin, on the other hand, I was thrilled by the colorful, rapidly changing impressions of the moment; there was no time for dreams and fantasies – you could only grasp and commit things to memory with your eyes, ears, and mind.

My grandparents' apartment was shared by Uncle Žoržik. He had recently married lovely, gentle Raja, who was to become my closest friend. She was intelligent and highly educated, knew an impressive number of languages and fascinated me by her reserve, which, I suspected, concealed some mystery. My Aunt Cecilia, nicknamed Cilia, who was married by then, lived in Blaumaņa iela. Funnily enough, Raja was the sister of Cilia's husband Roman Pines: The two pairs of siblings had married "crosswise," as I put it at the time. The new relatives were also Jewish; however, the Pineses were Sephardic Jews who along with other so-called white émigrés had wound up in Riga. Half a millennium earlier their forebears had fled the Spanish Inquisition and had finally arrived in Russia.

The Riga Pineses, who had relatives in the Netherlands and in

France, were a cultured, wealthy, and tradition-conscious family who kept a certain condescending distance from the Yiddish-speaking "Eastern Jews." During the October Revolution they had lost all their property and had fled to Riga from the dangers in Petrograd. Passed down in the Pines family history is an anecdote that Raja's and Roman's youngest sister Genia told me twice. The first time she still had her maiden name. The second time I heard the story in 1989 in London, when Genia Pines had long been Mrs. Eugenia O'Hana and was sitting in the small drawing room of her villa on the Little Bolton under Renoir's unfinished painting "Nurse with Child." As she told the story, she occasionally interrupted herself to wonder aloud whether she should sell the painting for a million dollars or ask for more. This context was in comical contrast with the actual story.

In prerevolutionary Petersburg, Father Pines had a sizeable apartment building on Vasilievsky Island. The owner himself with his large family lived in a ground-floor apartment with many rooms and a spacious entryway that turned into a long hallway. In rainy weather the smaller children rode up and down the hall on their bicycles and tricycles. Mounted on the wall of the corridor was the telephone, at the time a luxury that could by no means be taken for granted. In emergencies this phone could also be used by renters who did not yet own this modern means of communication. If there was a phone call for a renter, Mr. Pines sent the *dvornik,* the janitor, upstairs to get him. The episode that elevated this hallway to the rank of a historic venue took place in June 1917, a few months after the February Revolution. The Czar had been overthrown, the war continued, the situation was tense. That day the children were once more riding up and down the hall. Genia was almost nine and Roman was ten. Their father comes out of the living room and picks up the receiver. He calls out the window to the janitor: "Go up to Mr. So-and-so's. He's supposed to have a friend staying with him. Tell the friend to hurry up and come to the phone. A Mr. Ulyanov." Summoned by the dvornik, the man soon appears, politely thanks Mr. Pines for being allowed to use the phone and picks up the receiver. The children go on riding up and down, and, curious as always, try to overhear some of the conversation. To no avail. Mr.

Ulyanov merely listens and concludes the conversation with the words "Thanks for the information!" After expressing his thanks again, he leaves the apartment. A short time later the children see him through the window as he hurries away with a large briefcase or traveling bag. Half an hour later the police arrive to arrest him. Too late. After reporting the event, Genia angrily exclaimed: "Why did Father have to send for him? If Lenin had been jailed at the time, the October Revolution wouldn't have taken place!" In dead earnest I chimed in: "Of course, it's all Papa Pines' fault!"

Around the time when I moved to Elizabetes iela, Raja and Žoržik's son Alexander, nicknamed Šurik, was born, and less than a year later the other couple, Cecilia and Roman – also had a baby, Jakob or "Jacky." Genetically they were like brothers – after all, they had the same grandparents – and they also grew up as brothers.

Cilia's family shared an apartment with Mother Pines, but whenever they could, they came to visit us in Elizabetes iela. Though they were different, the boys were inseparable. Gracefully built, sensitive, brown-eyed Alexander developed a literary talent unusually early. As soon as he was able to read and write, he started penning all kinds of things. When he started school, at the age of seven, he was already working on a family chronicle, taking on the role of a medieval monk. Later, too, he kept recording all his impressions and experiences in writing.

Jacky, strong and solidly built, with sky-blue eyes and his mother's black, seemingly lacquered hair, lived in the world of music. Even when he was a year and a half old it was clear that he had perfect pitch. He smiled shyly when spoken to and tended to be taciturn. It was impossible to get him away from the piano. Cilia was planning how to promote her son's talent and was ready to give up everything else for his sake. Still, she did not want to push the child and prematurely commit him professionally. She felt his character did not predestine him to be a virtuoso, but rather a composer. At the age of ten, or respectively eleven, when the two boys met their cruel death, Šurik already seemed very grown-up, while Jacky was still quite childlike. It was only at the piano that he felt entirely in his element.

In my childhood the Elizabetes iela apartment was the only place where I could enjoy the full range of traditional house and family rituals. It was here that my idea of the family as a clan whose members stand by each other in all respects and always support each other evolved, though critical feedback and frankness within the clan is absolutely mandatory, of course. My father, too, had quite naturally become part of this family, in which I believe he experienced more vitality and warmth than in his parents' house.

The men of the Lulow family were not big earners. During the years I lived on Elizabetes iela, Grandfather's professional life exporting wood was already behind him. While he did have the financial means to ensure a peaceful old age, they did not amount to a great deal. It's true that Žoržik was still working somewhere at some sort of job, but making money was not his strong point. On the other hand, he certainly knew how to enjoy life and give others pleasure with ease and charm. Everybody loved him, especially women, and people were willing to forgive him a great deal. In silence, Raja endured quite a few moments of sadness. Since there were no real prospects for Žoržik as a railway engineer in Latvia, my father tried to help him get established on an independent basis. He bought Žoržik and Cilia's husband Roman, who was also an engineer, a small factory that manufactured aluminum kitchenware so that they would finally grow up. At the time, aluminum was still considered to be a novelty with a bright future. The two likeable young men very soon steered the company into bankruptcy, and it was sold. They simply had no head for business and henceforth had to earn their living as salaried engineers.

Thus my father supported not only his mother and unmarried older sister Lonni, but also the rather extensive family of his wife. I never heard him complain about it or blame Mama's frivolous relatives, while it didn't escape me that Father's sisters turned up their noses and moralized that he could have had a large capital if his income didn't thaw like snow in the sun because of his wife and her family. It cannot be said that father took on this burden only because he idolized his wife. No, he dearly loved Mama's relatives, he felt wonderful in their midst, he liked their nonchalance, warmth, and joie de vivre, their relationships without envy, hypocrisy, or self-righteousness. And he was happy to make quite a few sacrifices for this small world.

My entire childhood, and especially the time I spent in Riga, feels like a series of uninterrupted holidays. I was surrounded by young, attractive, witty people who were always in the mood for fun and flirtation and knew how to turn an ordinary day into a festive occasion. At our house there were at least three times as many traditional celebrations as in other people's houses. Grandfather was fairly indifferent to the prescriptions and rules of Orthodox Judaism, but we adhered as a matter of course to the age-old traditions, and the connection with history and our forebears. But we also respected the beautiful and impressive rituals of other religions. My governesses alone represented a whole spectrum of Christian denominations: the first, a Russian nyanya, was Russian Orthodox, of course. Sister Olga, a German Balt, was a Seventh Day Adventist, while the Francophone Swiss governess was a Calvinist; these were followed by a Lutheran German, the English governess was a Baptist, and a few people close to us were Catholic. They took me to Mass, which my parents allowed them to do without a second thought. Mama was of the opinion that all religions share the same ethical quintessence, that there is a God for everyone, and that all of us can build our personal relation to him by following the traditions of our forebears or by finding an individual path of our own.

In Riga, too, my family's domestic circle of friends was diverse, although it was an accepted fact that in private Jews socialized with Jews, Latvians with Latvians, and Russians with Russians. Our friends were primarily well-to-do people from the Riga Jewish community, educated and cultured with the exception of a few nouveaux riches – in other words, what we now call the educated middle classes. My parents' circle of acquaintances also included Russians, so-called white émigrés, and German Balts – mostly Father's old schoolmates and fellow athletes, and the parents of my school friends. There were only a few Latvians.

Practically all the "indigenous" Baltic Jews – that is what we called the families rooted in Riga, Kurzeme, or Vidzeme[1], in contrast to those who came from Latgale, Lithuania, White Russia or Poland, or who had immigrated from Russia – practically all of them naturally spoke more or less fluent Latvian, German, and Russian, then still considered the local languages, as well as one or two foreign languages. In Berlin I used to boast: "Where I come from in Riga every cab driver speaks three languages." The last names of my parents' acquaintances were Misroch, Schalit, Minsker, Minz, Hoff, Herzberg, Lifschitz, or Herzfeld. I doubt if even one of these names can be found in the Latvian telephone directories today. Only a few far-sighted people managed to emigrate on the eve or in the first days of the Soviet occupation. Some fled east at the beginning of the war or fought on the front lines, but most of them were doomed – first, deportation to Siberia, from which some of them at least returned, and then the Holocaust, which swept away everything.

Thus we celebrated a threefold Easter, Christmas, and New Year: the Jewish festival of Hanuka, which to my mind not quite correctly was associated with Christmas, then the Christian holiday, and once more, two weeks later, the Russian Orthodox Christmas. The imposing fir tree in my grandparents' drawing room thus had to survive for a long time. For other children there was only one of these festivals, while for me there were all three.

It was the same at Easter. The Jewish holiday of Pesach, which I looked forward to especially, is celebrated in order to remember the Jews' escape from Egyptian slavery, when God parted the Red Sea and Moses led his people to the Promised Land. During this festival, at a sumptuous, richly laden table decorated with candlesticks, in the presence of the entire family and guests, a traditional dialogue of questions and answers takes place between the head of the family – the oldest man – and the youngest boy of the family. The latter asks questions about this event and the significance of this evening in ancient Hebrew: "Ma nishtana, halaila hazeh, mikol ha'leilot? – Why is this night different from all other nights?" From the patriarch, he receives the traditional answers, also in the language of the Bible. At

---

1. Vidzeme: German *Livland*, northeastern province of Latvia.

our house it was the grandfather who answered, of course, but since for a long time there were no boys in the family, it was the only child – I, a girl – who spoke the questions. Nobody had any objections – on the contrary, I was enthusiastically praised for diligently learning the ancient Hebrew texts. In an Orthodox family that would have been considered a scandal. The guests who sat at the endlessly long Passover table were also quite unusual. Among them were not only Father's former fellow student, the Polish Count Lubienski, a Catholic, but also his classmate Baron Korff, a German Balt, or the Russian Katya Nemirovskaya. They all celebrated together, and this became my lifelong ideal of open-minded social diversity.

I liked the Russian Orthodox Easter celebration, when everyone – even complete strangers – kissed in church. Because of the magnificent organ music, I loved to go to Catholic Mass. The members of the Baptist congregation, in turn, seemed very friendly and all appeared to know each other. However, I didn't find their church service particularly interesting, since I received no artistic impressions from it. Father told me: "You should go to America to the black Baptists, they are great singers and they even dance." I only got to see them in films, though.

As soon as my mama came from Berlin, social life at our house really took off. As a child and teenager, I was allowed to be present at the lively and stimulating intellectual gatherings, and particularly at the various parlor games. One of my favorites was called "The Literary Tribunal." It was played whenever a particularly interesting book had been published. One of those present represented the defendant, i.e., the book's protagonist or else its author, assisted by a defense counsel. Their opponent was the prosecutor, who almost malevolently tried to criticize the accused. The rest of the party appeared as witnesses who expressed their own point of view. Each of them supported their arguments not only with quotes from the book, but also dreamed up some of their own in the style of the author. This was far more interesting than merely discussing what you had read, it was exciting, witty – like a theater of our own.

And then there was the music! In those days it was almost taken for granted that an intellectual played an instrument. I've already mentioned that our Cilia was especially musical. Mama, too, played the piano, but was so self-critical that she didn't want to "annoy others with her din." Among my parents' friends there were two professional musicians, a violinist and a cellist. A few doctors they knew turned out to be particularly enthusiastic music makers; I got the impression that, for instance, it was absolutely essential that a surgeon should play the piano or violin to keep his fingers nimble. And so it happened that now and then, quite naturally, a kind of house orchestra would be formed that spontaneously gave a little concert.

I clearly remember my father's two old friends, whom I've mentioned previously. With Count Lubienski he shared memories of their mutual adventures in Petrograd. As a Polish diplomat, Lubienski was associated with the Riga embassy, so that he was an occasional visitor in Elizabetes iela, and my parents also visited him at his family estate in Poland. Count Lubienski adored my mother, something he demonstrated with the grandeur of a true Polish aristocrat: By diplomatic mail, he supplied her with seafood from Italy and France that was not available in Riga, and every year for her birthday on January 31st he had a blossoming white lilac bush in a tub airmailed to her from the Côte d'Azur. Another extravagant friend of my father's who dated back to his high school days was the German Balt Baron Korff, who introduced the writer and philosopher Count Hermann Keyserling to our home. While I didn't have the slightest idea what they talked about, I associate an important episode with Baron Korff: It was he who first made me think about the national question.

It may seem strange, but for a long time I did not experience any "special behavior" toward me as a Jewish girl. I knew all about the long history of the Jewish people, about the phases of glory and suffering. In theory I also knew about Judeophobia and antisemitism, about all kinds of deeply rooted, centuries-old prejudices. Still, during my sheltered childhood, I never came into direct and painful contact with them. I heard and observed that these prejudices were, among other things, profitably brought into play in order to get rid of capable Jewish competitors; that was why you had to study especially hard and know a great deal in order to gain recognition as an adult – that, more or less, was my conclusion. There was plenty of that kind of thing in Latvia, but Father surmised that among Latvians a prejudicial attitude toward the Jews existed in a latent and non-aggressive stage that was primarily expressed on a social level or when there were conflicts of interests. After all, even during the czarist era it had not been possible to motivate the Latvian population to carry out pogroms. Based on the democratic constitution and legislation that existed in Latvia, thought my father, mutual understanding could definitely be achieved. In my mind, for a long time, the issue of ethnicity did not seem to be a fateful problem, although it did cause me to think about it.

Even as a child I had been astonished how differently such concepts as ethnic origin, people, and nation were interpreted in the day-to-day life of Riga and Berlin. In the Berlin of my childhood during the Weimar Republic, and in the German books I had read, all the citizens of the German state were considered to be Germans. We had encountered a similar conception of nationhood in Paris as well. In the circles with which I came into contact, neither ethnic origin nor religion was considered particularly important: What mattered far more were culture and language, which created a common ground. Germany's Jewish writers, scientists, and artists also felt they were Germans; as the case may be, they were of Mosaic faith, just as other Germans were Protestants or Catholics. That was how I had come to believe that nationality was determined by the fact that one belonged to a state and its culture; on the other hand, one's ethnic derivation and ethnicity, like love and family ties, had to be a private matter. I knew there were other views, and I was already familiar with such terms as racism and nationalism; I had heard that there were occasional manifestations of hatred and brutal attacks. But I would never have imagined with what tremendous energy these poisonous seeds would one day come to bear fruit.

In Riga, the question seemed to be approached quite differently. I was constantly amazed by the fact that people were first and foremost defined by their ethnic origin, and only then by their individual characteristics, their convictions, or their social position. Wasn't it peculiar that the servant girl, after opening the apartment door, announced to Grandmother, "Ma'am, a Russian lady wants to speak to you," or to Grandfather, "Sir, there's a Latvian here to see you"? Sometimes she would add "gentleman" or "man," depending on the visitor's class. She did not announce Jews in the same way. To her way of thinking her employers' compatriots were self-evident guests, while the appearance of all the others seemed unusual to her. Here in Riga this a priori categorization was completely normal (later I realized that it was characteristic for all of Eastern Europe). It took me a while to understand to some extent the historical connections and thus the preconditions for this attitude. In my child's imagination I compared the differences between my two hometowns with two pieces of furniture: Berlin was a wardrobe, while Riga was a chest of drawers. In a wardrobe all the clothes hang next to one another and can be combined according to need and mood. In a chest of drawers, things lie separately in their drawers. It's true that they get along peacefully, but, once determined, their division into categories is maintained.

Naturally, in the public sphere of Riga, there were common economic interests, projects, and cooperative partnerships. In private life, however – traditionally and voluntarily – ethnic segregation was the norm. I was suddenly troubled by the idea that I might never meet the love of my life because he was in another drawer. Damn this predestination!

I still recall an incident that involved Baron Korff. During another visit by my parents at my grandparents' house in Elizabetes iela, he came to one of our family gatherings. He was said to be a modern-minded liberal who did not particularly regret the former privileges of the Baltic aristocracy; from the very beginning he had found National Socialism totally unacceptable. That is why we were all surprised at coffee one day when he remarked that it was a great pleasure for him not to have to sit at the same table with Latvians. Like most children whose education has not inoculated them with prejudices, I had a natural sense of justice. Baron Korff's words truly shocked me. What was that supposed to mean? In my grandparents' house, too, I'd always heard that everyone, whatever their origin, was first and foremost a human being. It was a good thing that Father, visibly dismayed, asked what the visitor meant by that. Korff said that working together with Latvians was perfectly all right, but privately, in company, he felt uncomfortable. They were still not socially acceptable, they acted affected and unnatural, as though they were trying to prove they had had a genteel upbringing. That was sometimes so oppressive, he said, that he preferred to avoid having social dealings with Latvians. Father mockingly inquired whether this was not the Baron's snobbishness speaking. At the time I was not yet really capable of following the rest of the conversation about history, the complexes of long-oppressed peoples, about individual and collective self-analysis, and other topics, but I thought about what Baron Korff had said for a long time.

Because the Latvians and members of minorities lived segregated from each other outside their work environment, there were indeed few of them among my parents' Riga friends and acquaintances. Paradoxically we met more Latvians in Berlin than in Riga. Naturally there were also Latvians among the guests of Mrs. Bergfeld, who came from Latvia – mostly people from Riga who always turned to my parents with questions about cultural and business life in Berlin. Occasionally the result would be relationships that verged on friendship, which did not really continue in Riga, however.

It was Emīlija Benjamiņa, the wife of the Latvian press magnate and millionaire Antons Benjamiņš, who spoke to Mama about this completely frankly. I no longer remember where the two of them had met; Mrs. Benjamiņa, whose sister, the actress Annija Simsone, was performing at a Berlin theater, showed up in the city fairly often, though of course she did not stay at Mrs. Bergfeld's guesthouse. I recall a melancholy conversation, as quoted by Mama: Mrs. Benjamiņa had said how much she regretted the fact that it was not possible for her to socialize with my mother in Riga. "You would be a true jewel at my receptions," she said, "but I have to consider my social circles. I have mine, and you have yours. That's just the way things are back home..." Both of them knew what she meant. "I consoled that intelligent lady who spoke so openly and cynically, but she felt ill-at-ease," laughed Mama. "I told her I had enough admirers and didn't mind leaving her gentlemen to their own ladies."

Experiences like these were not able to shake Father's optimistic faith in the Latvian state, which unified all its citizens. He held the Latvian constitution in high esteem and was firmly convinced that prejudices and mistrust would gradually disappear within a framework of freedom and national self-esteem. Why, in musical, sports, and medical circles, claimed Father, it was already possible to detect gradual and almost automatic changes, based on solidarity in the workplace, common interests, and a unifying culture. At the time, *rule of law* and *civic public spirit* were expressions with which I was quite familiar. With the Ulmanis coup and the dissolution of parliamentary democracy, the mood suddenly changed. After 15 May 1934, the healthy and commendable national self-confidence of the Latvians was increasingly inflated into a conceited, boastful nationalism.

Among our guests in Riga I remember two Latvian artists: Ludolfs Liberts and Sigismunds Vidbergs. Miraculously, a plate painted by Vidbergs is still in my possession today. The plunderers and thieves who plagued our later apartment in Vidus iela presumably left it behind only because it was cracked. Liberts usually appeared alone, for his wife, the opera singer Amanda Liberte-Rebāne, was on chilly terms with my mother. Other frequent visitors were Yury Yurovsky and his then partner, the actress Yekaterina Bunchuk of the Russian Drama Theater. Many people regarded the stage director and actor Yurovsky with suspicion, as he was one of the few prominent Russian cultural figures who liked to frequent Latvian artist circles privately as well.

Mama deeply despised national prejudices and narrow-mindedness. The Jewish community was also by no means free of such prejudices. It was unbelievable how many arguments against people of other nationalities we had to listen to when we visited Jews who did not share our views! Let me add at this point that in my view none of the ethnic minorities living in Latvia had as many factions in terms of culture, customs, and opinions as the Jews.

Another interesting person I remember well is the politician

Marģers Skujenieks. He was the representative of the Social Democrat fraction, belonged to its right wing and after the Ulmanis coup displayed a militant nationalism. Nevertheless he and my father had a relationship based on mutual respect. When I was in secondary school I was interested in his sociological research. At one point, in 1938, after being out of contact for a long period, Skujenieks called my father and came to see him in order to present him with his magnum opus, which had just been published: a comprehensive statistical survey of life in Latvia. Even then I studied the book with immense enthusiasm. To this day, it represents an indispensable source of information about the actual social and economic situation in pre-Soviet Latvia, unembellished by ideology. During the Soviet era I kept it in an inconspicuous place and lent it to people I trusted.

FATHER AND MOTHER

Surrounded by a large bevy of beloved relatives and friends, the first years of my life passed like an enthralling play, and I too was loved and spoiled. Still, even my childhood had its shadow side about which my relatives probably had no idea. Naturally I never doubted that my parents loved me; yet I missed their presence in my daily life – even in Berlin, where we at least lived together. Before falling asleep, I was sometimes tormented by a sorrow I could not confide to anybody.

In my family overt expressions of affection were not customary. A kiss, a hug were a relatively rare and thus quite extraordinary demonstration of love. Sometimes I would have wished for more cuddling and physical touch. The intimacy between me and Mama, between me and Father, which was actually very close, was chiefly expressed through conversations, understanding, and support. Often, however, weeks, even months would go by when I did not see my parents. The saddest moments were those when they left Riga or I had to leave Berlin. At times it seemed to me as though my whole life consisted of constant goodbyes. Then I would cry, although I had to do it in secret, in bed at night, for Mama could not stand tears and complaining.

I remember a time when she had again left on a trip. I took her pillow to bed, hugged it tight and breathed her familiar fragrance – it was "*Je reviens*" (I shall return), an expensive French perfume by Worth. Soon I grew calm again, but the sadness did not pass. With every new parting I managed to regain my composure more quickly and not to become maudlin. I didn't know that very soon there would come a time when there would no longer be a "Je reviens."

It may seem cruel to expect a child always to pull herself together. Yet I realize that it was precisely this that was invaluable training for me. In the eyes of others I was a spoiled, far too self-important girl who was never denied anything. In reality, while I was freer as a person and enjoyed more respect than the rest of my contemporaries, I was quite capable of setting limits for myself and got used to neither pitying myself in difficult situations nor expecting pity from others.

One of Mama's postulates was that there were only few things in life that truly deserved to be taken seriously: death, love, and all that was connected with them. Probably that was why she was so alarmed when a family member became ill. Indeed, at such times Mama could turn into a true guardian angel and give her whole attention to the "fortunate" person who had become bedridden. Sometimes I almost wished I was sick, for then Mama would drop everything – there were even times when she came back specially from Berlin. Then nothing else existed for her, and she would sit at my bedside, taking care of me and cheering me up.

My mother was a fantastic nurse, it was a special talent of hers. My father only rarely got sick, but when he did, he would be gravely ill. He once had a protracted case of meningitis; hovering between life and death, he was in danger of permanent brain damage. Mother insisted that he should be nursed at home at the Pension Bergfeld and not in hospital. A professional nurse was to assist her, the main caregiver. She did not leave his bed for an instant, spending the nights in a recliner in his room and trying to do everything herself. She believed that nothing could give a patient as much vitality as the sight of the beautifully made up and smiling face of his wife when he opened his eyes at any time, day or night. She wore a pretty light-blue-and-white striped dress, similar in cut to a nurse's uniform, and managed always to look fresh, fragrant, and radiant. Mother's calculation turned out to be correct, a fact also acknowledged by Father's attending physician, the famous Professor Sauerbruch, who, though with grave doubts, had authorized that the patient be nursed at home. Upon Father's successful recovery he was lavish in compliments – in this case, he said, the main credit must go to the selfless efforts of the charming lady of the house. On occasions like this, I realized how deep was the relationship between my parents; it was something one could easily miss in everyday life.

When I was fifteen, Mama and I once spent a few days at the new hotel-sanitarium of Ķemeri. I don't remember what treatments had been prescribed for her; at any rate, the main focus was the social life in the fine restaurant and the hotel bar. One evening I surprised Mama in her room in an unmistakable situation with a longtime admirer. After that we had a candid woman-to-woman conversation. Mother explained to me her concept of fidelity and steadfast love, which did not overlap with the prevalent one in almost any respect. She said that from her point of view a husband and marriage itself were a lifetime commitment, like the commitment to your father and brother; they were a part of herself – independent of anything that might ever happen as a result of various impulses or whims. The husband always came first, she said. True fidelity was, first and foremost, fidelity to a human being, not to a man in the erotic sense. She quoted a line from the British poet Ernest Dowson: "I have been faithful to thee, Cynara! in my fashion." I'm not saying that I adopted this view in later life, but I did make a mental note of it.

At times when my parents had to struggle with financial difficulties, I again realized how different Mama was from the other women around us in Riga, who experienced even a temporary financial setback as a heavy blow of fate. Mama accepted the situation without panic, let alone considered it a blow. It is easy to despise money when there is plenty of it, but she did not deviate from this attitude even when times were hard.

I still vividly recall a scene from my childhood: In 1931 my father actually was almost bankrupt, his entire fortune had melted away, and even the governess had to be dismissed. My parents intermittently came from Berlin to Riga to "lick their wounds," as my ironic mother put it. In Antonijas iela, we rented three small furnished rooms from an old lady, but still went to the grandparents' place in Elizabetes iela for the noon meal. I remember how Mother, laughing and with comical pathos as she played a melodrama in the style of a silent film, threw open the wardrobes and suitcases and flung everything on the bed: sable and ermine capes, the magnificent mink coat, the silver foxes; she shook pieces of jewelry from their velvet-lined cases so that Father could take everything to the pawnbroker's or sell them elsewhere. The only thing she would never part from was the famous green emerald. Like all women she loved to wear jewelry, but she was never seriously attached to things. They were merely a frame, beautiful but not indispensable, for Mama was sure of herself, whatever her role or costume. From my earliest age my parents had given me to understand: Only things that no one can take away from you have true value – heart, understanding, knowledge, humor, beauty too, as long as you are young and healthy, and, naturally, love in all its variations.

During this period in our lives, Mama and I once went to the station in order to go somewhere. We stood in front of a second-class carriage at the central station of Riga waiting to get in. A lady called out "Eva, Eva!", came hurrying over and gasped: "What? *You*'re traveling second class?" Without hesitation Mama replied, beaming a sunny smile at the lady: "Where *I* travel it's always first class!" At this point I'd also like to quote a much later conversation of similar content with another lady who wanted to get a rise out of Mama: "Did you know that your daughter was seen in bad company?" – "Wherever my daughter is, the company is always good," Mama retorted. I recorded this, too, on the tape of my memory.

Soon we were able to leave Antonijas iela. My parents returned to Berlin, and I moved back to Elizabetes iela.

In the winter of 1935/36, when my parents finally turned their backs on Hitler's Germany, there was a brief lean period. We had already moved into our own apartment at Vidus iela 9. Manya, our maidservant, was a pretty, cheerful, blonde young woman from Latgale, quick-witted and observant. When she told us how poor her large family was back home, she did not conceal the fact that she had decided she would lead a different life someday. She was devoted to my mother and imitated her way of dressing and behaving. Mama, too, enjoyed teaching Manya. When Mama's friends came to the house for five o'clock tea or a game of cards, they joked that Eva had created even her maidservant in her own image. Yet Manya did not forget her relatives, but tried to help them every way she could. Mama allowed Manya's goddaughter, Ženja, to stay in the maid's room while Manya herself often spent the night at her fiancé's place. In Riga, Ženja wanted to learn to be a dressmaker. The girl turned out to be talented, she had unfailing taste, and Mama's advice proved helpful to her. This was another time when Mama was unable to order expensive models from abroad, but we did have Parisian fashion magazines, so she drew her own original designs. Ženja was a quick study. In the kitchen, there was a sewing machine, a present from my mother, and she sewed several dresses that were so lovely that Mama's envious ladies did not have the slightest doubt they came directly from Paris. We fueled this legend with mysterious remarks and were fiendishly delighted at the success of our mystification.

At the time I wasn't particularly interested in clothes, let alone elegant clothes. It's true that I couldn't stand the frilly sweet-young-thing fashion prevalent in Riga at the time. And I could be capricious, even fastidious, when it came to color: To me, certain color combinations felt like a pleasant, or else unbearable, physical touch.

As a small child – I wasn't in school yet at the time – I was once engaged in a conflict with the French governess, a strict Swiss Calvinist, that I've never been able to forget. One morning she calmly picked out a pink undershirt and salad-green panties, and told me to put them on. Coolly, I refused. Mademoiselle Speer was dumbfounded. A child's silly notions, in her opinion, must be torn out by the roots. She sternly demanded that I should wear these articles of clothing, which absolutely did not go together. The combination of pink and green made me physically ill, which I told her. The governess lost her patience: "Nobody's going to see it!" I replied: "But I know what I'm wearing, I can feel the colors on my skin." We had to turn to a higher authority, and Mama immediately understood. Trying not to hurt Mademoiselle Speer's feelings, she tactfully explained that a child's taste in matters of personal clothing must be taken into account. The governess was so indignant she wanted to give notice.

Although ultimately I didn't spend very much time with my mother, it was she who had the most lasting impact on me. I loved her not only as my mother, but I also liked her very much, I admired her. I liked the way she was and who she was, but from an early age I had my doubts whether I liked how she lived. For myself, I had a different future in mind – one that was more self-sufficient, more active, more independent. At the time I was convinced that people must and should take their future into their own hands.

When I remember my sunny notions of what adult life is like, I am reminded of a scene from *Cavalcade*, which I saw as a schoolgirl. A ship's deck, a huge ocean liner, a starry night all around, and the peaceful expanse of the ocean; by the railing, a young couple, the audience knows this is their honeymoon. The two are happy and making plans for the future. The camera pans and in the frame appears a nearby lifebuoy, bearing the name of the ship: *Titanic*.

BOOKS. THEATER

My favorite room in Elizabetes iela 23, the so-called big salon, whose two bay windows faced the street, was both a sitting room and a library. The walls were lined with glazed but unlocked bookcases. This was my paradise. I was allowed to pick out and read whatever I wanted: novels in various languages; large-format, expensive art books thanks to which I became familiar with the paintings and sculptures of famous artists. In the Riga bookstores, in those days, you could get practically everything that was published anywhere in the world, and in the larger ones they had catalogues that helped you locate and order rare books. I had never been denied permission to buy books, though I realized that it would have been in extremely poor taste to show off my own ability to spend money at school, where my classmates came from families with different income levels.

At some point the books my parents purchased in Berlin also wound up in the Elizabetes iela bookcases, because there was no room for a large library at the Pension Bergfeld.

During the day, the salon was generally not used. Except for the bookcases, a leather couch, several armchairs, a coffee table, and a splendid desk in one of the bay windows, the room was empty. A huge Persian rug that was rolled up when there was an evening dance covered the whole floor. It was edged with wide bands of intertwined Oriental flower ornaments, while the rug itself shimmered in a wonderful, light, greenish-blue tone. I imagined this was an ocean with the six continents on its shores. When I had taken a book from the bookcase, I made myself comfortable in the continent where its plot took place, and read it there.

As soon as I had learned to read, at age four, I gave up being read to. The fact that I was allowed to take every book from the shelf was the first significant step on the path to independence, into a parallel world created by godlike demiurges, which seemed to me as real and tangible as the world around me. There I found people to talk to, friends, and teachers for all time. The experience I gained from books was no less important for me than what happened to me personally. I could definitely also divide my life into stages according to the books I read during specific periods.

As long as I was still a powerless little listener, the adults selected the reading material, but even in those days I voiced my objections. For instance, I couldn't stand most of the Grimm fairytales because they were cruel and bleak; besides, the protagonists often acted like mindless fools or else were downright reckless. Thus, for example, I speculated that the hungry wolf would not have devoured stupid Red Riding Hood if she had been the least little bit polite – let alone empathetic – and had offered him something from her basket. There would definitely still have been enough left over for her grandmother, and thus both their lives would have been spared.

Thus, when I began to read, I was immediately captivated by the Greek myths and epics, which took the place of the fairytales, so to speak. That was Father's doing, no doubt – with his unshakable love for the world of antiquity and its heritage he had already done his utmost to promote it. When I was little, a large number of German-language books were published in which not only Greek and Roman mythology and literature but also stories from the Bible were retold in a language children could understand, and which were wonderfully illustrated – with photographs of ancient sculptures and buildings, reproductions of drawings on Greek vases, etc. Because I was still so little and perceived everything as a real experience, classical culture was deposited within me completely organically like something that had happened to me personally. Added to this, there was Mama's legend about our alleged ancestors in ancient Alexandria. As a child I had the feeling I could communicate across the generations directly with the heroes and gods of those days.

It was no less important that these books laid in me solid foundations of criteria and notions of what literature is. That doesn't mean I read only outstanding books. As soon as I got a taste for literature, I devoured everything I could lay my hands on. My parents too were passionate readers: Mama was mad about so-called modern literature, from Chekhov and Pirandello to Proust, Joyce, Akhmatova, and Tsvetaeva; Father, on the other hand, in addition to his favorite stoic Marcus Aurelius and the German-language authors of the 19th and 20th centuries, preferred well-constructed detective novels, but also memoirs and historical works. Nothing, he claimed, guaranteed a deeper sleep than an elegantly solved crime.

Once in a while I would also come across the romantic and sentimental novels for teenage girls that were so popular in Germany, such as the Nesthäkchen series by Else Ury, which my classmates at the Luther-Schule loved to read; I found them boring. But the wonderful recent children's books of the period – Erich Kästner's heroes Emil, Pünktchen, and Anton – accompanied me through all the stages of my growing up and are dear to me to this day.

Pretty soon, even before I moved from Berlin to the Luther-Schule in Riga, I discovered historical novels. It was the beginning of my fascination for history, which to me seemed a vast reservoir of dramatic, tragic, and comic subjects from which you could draw knowledge about society and human beings. Books such as the *Short Novels of the Migrations* by Felix Dahn were never too thick for me. I began to read books in Russian, whose Cyrillic script initially caused me some difficulties. Again, it was a novel that introduced me to the history of the Russian Empire: Aleksey Konstantinovich Tolstoy's *Prince Serebryani*, a.k.a. *The Silver Knight*.

After classical antiquity and the Middle Ages, I discovered drama as reading material. My classmates were surprised, for the reading of plays was generally not popular. Through the reading of dialogues and stage directions I became accustomed to "my own mental stage," as I called it. It was there that I performed what I had read. In my imagination I was a stage director, not an actor. I empathized with all the characters rather than identifying with a single protagonist. This passion began on my tenth birthday, when Father gave me the complete works of Schiller. He sensed that Schiller's dramas with their passionate enthusiasm and ethical pathos were suitable for my developmental stage at the time. At first I read *The Robbers* and *William Tell*, which initially captivated me most, and soon thereafter all the rest. I could see quite a few of them in the theater, for instance, the productions of the Dailes Theater, where Schiller was often part of the repertoire.

At about the same time, in history books, I encountered the great German humanists. For some inexplicable reason all my sympathies were with Ulrich von Hutten (rather than with the wise Erasmus of Rotterdam), for he reminded me of Schiller's protagonists. I was so touched by Ulrich von Hutten's motto that I made it my own. Later I discovered that it was a quotation from Horace, which the poet borrowed from Seneca: "Si fractus illabatur orbis impavidum ferient ruinae" (If the world should break and fall on him, it would find him fearless). Why should an adolescent girl have memorized this sentence, of all things, for the rest of her life?

For my twelfth birthday I was given the complete works of Shakespeare – in the original and in German translation. I was not only studying English in school but also taking additional conversation lessons with an English private tutor. Naturally, modern colloquial English is different from the texts of Shakespeare, and yet it was he who helped me to get to know the flavor and the potentials of this language. I compared the German translation of the romantic poets Schlegel and Tieck with the original; I have kept this habit to this day when I encounter works in translation. That was how I discovered that the original and the translation never quite correspond. It is not without reason that the Italians say *traduttore – traditore* (translator – traitor). This motivated me to learn as many languages as possible at least at a reading level.

Once, in Mrs. Ettinger's bookstore, I purchased a comprehensive

English-language anthology, a collection of poetic masterworks from all over the world. I lugged the volume home with difficulty. Even the first pages were a surprise, introducing me to an entirely new sphere of interest: Akhenaten's Great Hymn to the Sun. I had read more than one book about the excavations in the Valley of the Kings and thought I was pretty well-informed about Egyptian history. Now I was stunned by the realization that thoughts and feelings that had been expressed several thousand years ago could strike me as completely familiar and accurate.

At the age of fifteen I discovered three French poets who have accompanied me to this day: Baudelaire, Rimbaud, and especially Verlaine. Evidently it is the melody of the language that most moves me in all poetry. This phase of discovering lyric poetry is also connected to my childhood friend Paulchen, our last meeting in Riga in 1938. Paulchen had started studying medicine in Switzerland and hoped he could remain there as a physician. Once, during semester break, Paulchen came to visit us in Riga. He was now a young man, and I too, at sixteen, was no longer a child, but our friendship was renewed as easily and quickly as if there had been no separation at all. Our immediate mutual understanding was based first and foremost on the realization that we shared the same literary tastes. It was Paulchen who introduced me to recent German poetry, and particularly to his favorite authors Rilke and Stefan George. I immediately acknowledged Rilke as my favorite as well; he made his way into my inner world to remain there forever. Soon after Paulchen left again, our ways parted, as a totally different life, full of great trials, began. We never saw each other again.

There is another book that has accompanied me since I was a teenager. For my fifteenth birthday Father gave me an anthology of the aphorisms and maxims of La Rochefoucauld. The little gilt-edged volume, bound in soft, red Morocco leather, from the Bibliothèque rose series, proved to be a source of philosophy of life – precise and sharp-witted ideas I wished I had expressed myself. Many Rochefoucauld maxims solidified a conviction, a principle of my own. For instance, "Il est plus honorable d'être trompé par ses amis que de leur méfier" (It is more honorable to be deceived by one's friends than to mistrust them) more or less corresponds to my attitude vis à vis those who are close to me.

When I was already attending secondary school in Riga, I discovered in a consignment of books, in addition to French writers who were well known in Latvia such as Mama's favorite author Marcel Proust, the novel of a still unknown young author: The title, *La Nausée*, was unusual und unattractive, but the book fascinated me and corresponded to my skeptical ideas about the world at the time. Many years were to pass until, in the late '50s, I gained access to Jean-Paul Sartre's later literary and philosophical work.

In recent years I have thought particularly often of a book that deeply troubled me as a schoolgirl and was branded on my memory: Franz Werfel's *The Forty Days of Musa Dagh*, written at the time of Hitler's seizure of power. It was probably the first literary work to address genocide in 20th century Europe – the genocide of the Armenian minority by the Turks in 1915/16, when Turkey was fighting on the side of the German Empire in World War I. The number of Armenians who were shot or otherwise lost their lives exceeds one million. The novel was based on the reports of two Armenian survivors and other eyewitnesses as well as rather meager documents. The most important evidence for this crime was still kept under lock and key at the time like a military secret, for which the moment of disclosure had not yet arrived. Today all the archives can be accessed, and it has become apparent that the accounts of the eyewitnesses and the author are absolutely in accordance with the facts. Revealed behind the dry historical dates and facts are the destinies of living human beings.

Both in Berlin and in Paris, my parents had Armenian acquaintances – nice people whom as I read I visualized in the roles of the victims described in the book. This novel resonated within me so strongly that for a long time I was unable to free myself from its effect but returned to the topic again and again in conversations with my parents and close friends; as far as it was possible for me, I researched the historical context, the reasons for the indifference of the international community, and the Turkish government's dogged policy of concealing the truth.

My earliest impressions of the theater, too, were so strong that later, more than once, I recalled them out of a purely professional interest. I had heard reports and discussions about stage productions and theater people since I was little. In Riga, we would go to the opera and the Russian Drama Theater; when it came to performances in Latvian, my parents preferred the Dailes Theater. We only rarely went to the German Theater, because we could of course watch brilliant German-language productions in Berlin. No matter how much of all this I might have understood – artistic impressions in early childhood do not fail to have an effect.

Thus, as a child, I saw onstage two world-famous actors who both left an indelible "snapshot" in my visual memory. One was a performance I saw in Berlin before I was of school age. I no longer even know the name of the play; in any event it was totally unsuited for children. Probably it happened to be the governess' day off, and because Mama did not want to leave me at home alone, she took me with her to the theater on the spur of the moment. Evidently it was a melodramatic light comedy – the great Fritz Kortner, whom the grown-ups around me knew from the famous expressionist silent films, played a cuckolded husband who decides to poison his unfaithful wife. I remember a single scene: In sight of the audience, Kortner pours something into a glass of wine, his wife comes in, the audience freezes – at any moment she will pick up the glass and empty it. Mama explains to me in a whisper why he wants to take revenge, I understand, but then something strange and inexplicable takes place onstage. I can see that the deceived husband is really terribly hurt and full of hatred, but at the same time he also radiates infinite love (at the time I did not yet know the term "passion"). And what was most puzzling was that Kortner stood with his back to the audience for quite a while. Without seeing his face, I read from his back alone how much he suffered when he had accomplished his vengeance. He felt no satisfaction on account of his victory, as I had expected – on the contrary, guilt and sorrow, but somehow no remorse.

At around the same time, when I was roughly six or seven years old, at the Russian Drama Theater of Riga, I saw *The Government*

Inspector – a play that can be understood on a number of different levels. Even for children it is interesting to observe what happens when people take a person for someone else. The role of Khlestakov was played by Michael Chekhov in a guest performance. I had the feeling as if he was not only incredibly short and thin, but also completely weightless. He literally floated across the stage, so that I said to Mama: "He is so light – his feet hardly touch the ground."

Many years later I had a good friend in Moscow – the theater critic Natalya Krimova (life partner of the theater director Anatoly Efros). Together with Maria Osipovna Knebel, a student of Stanislavski and director of the Central Children's Theater since the early 1950s, she edited a volume of the writings and letters of Michael Chekhov. For a long time, as an émigré, he was not allowed to be mentioned in the Soviet Union, but in the 'sixties the two women had hopes that their work had not been in vain. Natasha and I sat with old Mrs. Knebel, who lived with her sister (both seemed like relics from the Stanislavski era to me), and we spoke about Michael Chekhov. I told them that at home in Riga you could still meet Latvian actors who had been trained in his studio and had quite a few stories to tell. Michael Chekhov, who from 1930 to 1935 worked at the theater in Kaunas, Lithuania, often came to Riga. He was allowed to play his roles in Russian. I also mentioned my own impressions as a child. Maria Osipovna looked at me and began to smile, while Natasha pulled a page with the copy of a Michael Chekhov text from a stack of papers – part of a letter, I believe. When he was working on the role of Khlestakov, he wrote, he had cultivated a feeling of lightness and levity that would permit him seemingly to overcome gravity. His enactment of his role onstage had convinced even a small child.

The range of music available in Riga was virtually inexhaustible. I remember *The Barber of Seville* with two phenomenal guest singers, Feodor Chaliapin, who had come from Paris, in the role of Don Basilio, and Valeria Barsova, a wonderful coloratura soprano from Moscow in the role of Rosina. At home we said: "Where else in the world would it be possible to hear a brilliant basso emigrated from Russia and the Soviet opera star Barsova together on the same stage?"

I knew and admired local stars of the Riga Opera – Alida Vāne, Amanda Rebane, and Milda Brehmane-Štengele as well as Ādolfs Kaktiņš, Vladimirs Ančarovs-Kadiķis, Artūrs Priednieks-Kavarra, Nikolajs Vasiļjevs, and naturally Mariss Vētra, who also appeared in Germany and sang in musical films.[1] Just as captivating was the ballet with its soloists Osvalds Lēmanis, Edīte Feifere, Mirdza Griķe, and many others.

My parents' friends in Riga also included two Russian émigrés whose accomplishments in developing the Latvian National Opera and its ballet into a world-class stage are still honored today – the choreographer and educator Aleksandra Fedorova and the opera director Peter (Pyotr) Melnikov. He was the son of the legendary Russian baritone Ivan Melnikov, for whom his friend Mussorgsky wrote several opera parts. The Melnikov family was to be a support for me in later difficult times.

Among my parents' acquaintances there was one who aroused my particular interest: Mr. Becker from America, who had been a Baltic representative of the film production company Metro-Goldwyn-Mayer (MGM) since the mid-1930s. He lived in Riga on Elizabetes iela near Brīvības iela. In his spacious offices there was a film projection hall, quite a large room with a dozen comfortable club chairs to which more seating could be added when the need arose. It was here he invited my parents to private screenings of MGM movies. The invitation included me as well. I could come and go to my heart's content and get acquainted with Greta Garbo, Joan Crawford, and Clark Gable, with Broadway musical stars and their original voices – in Latvian cinemas, American films were mainly shown in a German synchronized version. Since these screenings usually took place in the late afternoon, I succumbed without resistance to the temptation to skip school. Also important was the fact that here the prohibition "Not recommended for children under age 16" did not apply to me. At the Forum, a large Riga cinema, a merciless Cerberus lay in wait. The

---

1. *Mariss Vētra* (1901-1965), actually Morics Blumbergs, was a world-famous Latvian tenor who also appeared in a few German musical films. His memoirs, written in Canadian exile, are very popular with Latvian readers.

entire flock of Riga's high school movie fans hated the scrawny lady with her tightly curled, gray permanent, and had nicknamed her *aitasgalva-maitasgalva* (sheephead-carrionhead). It was no use wearing Mama's high-heeled shoes and lipstick, or giving Father's hat to a fellow student to wear, for sheephead's eagle eye saw through every attempt at camouflage. Those who could not show some identification to prove they were over sixteen years old were ignominiously banished from the vestibule of paradise.

THE LUTHER-SCHULE

The Luther-Schule was located in the immediate vicinity of my grandparents' apartment – in the so-called Vorburg, a district that Riga Germans had once built for their own purposes but later rented to others. The Vorburg was between Eksporta iela, which ran parallel to the Daugava River, Vašingtona laukums, where the American Embassy had its seat, Ausekļa iela, and Sakaru iela. In this complex of buildings with its elongated, rectangular inner courtyard were located two schools, one for boys and one for girls.

I have warm and bright memories of my time at the Luther-Schule from early 1931 to the spring of 1937. In Germany, National Socialism was beginning to spread like a plague; I saw and felt it when I visited my parents in Berlin. But the German Balts with whom I came into contact at school – both the teachers and the students – remained immune for a long time to come.

The Nazis were quite simply despised both at home and in school by the girls in my class who often invited me into their homes. Although the adults did not speak with us much about political or ideological topics, I realized that the new masters of Germany were regarded as riffraff, barbarians, and aggressive loudmouths from Munich beer halls who were no credit to their country. As for their ethnic brothers, the German nationals who lived in the *Reich* itself, the families of my classmates looked down upon them rather disparagingly. My class at the time was a kind of miniature model of German society in Latvia.

While I was in primary school, there had also been several Jewish girls in my class. Well-to-do and educated Jewish parents generally strived to make it possible for their children to have a Western European education, particularly during the first years of school. After primary school the children changed over to Jewish or Latvian secondary schools, in accordance with a directive of the Ulmanis regime that people who belonged to minorities must attend either their own or else Latvian schools. Presumably because my parents still lived in Berlin and it was not clear whether they would head west or return to their native Riga, an exception was made in my case.

At the Luther-Schule none of us students felt even the slightest trace of Pan-German chauvinism, let alone antisemitism. In my class there was a single girl from a *reichsdeutsche* (Reich German) family. Good heavens, what rubbish she brought with her from home and expounded in school! But soon she realized that with us she would not get anywhere with her theories of the master race and of German superiority that she rattled off guilelessly. Most of the girls came from the families of the aristocracy and the city's patricians. Even now that their privileged position had ended, the customary atmosphere of affluence and of class consciousness still reigned in their homes. The former German landed gentry was still organized as a *Ritterschaft* (knighthood) whose social life took place in relative isolation. They kept themselves to themselves.

In my class there were several girls with whom I soon became close friends. Two of them – Renate Kühn, the daughter of a lawyer, one of whose forebears was Old Stender, and Regina von Sievers, the offspring of a once powerful Livonian noble family – located me in the late 1980s.[1] Around 1990, as soon as it was finally possible to travel

---

1. *Old Stender*/*Vecais Stenders* in Latvian, the name given to Gotthard Friedrich Stender (1714-1796), provost and pastor of the parish of Sēlpils, publisher of a *Lettische Grammatik* (Latvian Grammar), a collection of Latvian fairy tales and legends (*Pasakkas un Stahsti*), etc. "Young Stender" is the name given to his son, Alexander Johann (1744-1819), who also worked as a writer.

to the West without restrictions, I visited them in Bonn several times. Other friends were two students from abroad, Ilse Rörwich, who was Danish, and Svea Karlsson from Sweden.

My closest friend, however, was Marcelle Devillar, whose father, a Frenchman, was a representative of the Coty perfumery in the Baltic states. Her mother, a Latvian ballet dancer, had died young of consumption. Marcelle was raised by her godmother, her mother's unmarried sister, and Latvian was just as much her native language as French. In the Luther-Schule she mastered a third language, German. In her large apartment on Aspāzijas bulvāris, Marcelle, the only one of us children, had a movie projector, though only for silent movies. It served primarily the memory of her mother. I too, together with my friend, looked at her father's amateur films showing her enchanting and vivacious mother rocking in a boat on Lake Geneva or in a lush, blooming garden somewhere outside Paris. We also watched famous old silent movies, which in the mid-1930s the cinemas had long since stopped showing, although they could be rented as 16- or 8-mm Ciné films. There I got to know Charlie Chaplin, Buster Keaton, Pat and Patachon, Asta Nielsen, and other stars of the silent screen whose names and faces were familiar to me from old movie magazines and especially from movie posters I had seen in Berlin.

Obviously, at this school, diversity on a common basis of German culture promoted a sensible relation to national questions. I discovered that in German Baltic society the focus was primarily on whether one was well brought up, had a European education, and spoke good German. Yet I also noticed that subconscious feeling of superiority toward Latvians that had once surprised me in Baron Korff. Thus the parents of my classmate Astrid Breede were divorced, and at school we only knew her mother. There were rumors that her father was a Latvian by the name of Briedis; she herself never mentioned him, and we girls also knew that it would have been inappropriate to question her and to talk about it in the first place. Meanwhile, no one was bothered by the fact that Marcelle's late mother was a Latvian who could even be seen in an amateur movie. I wondered if the reason was that Marcelle was French, not German.

My years at the Luther-Schule were not yet overshadowed by antisemitism. The excellent general education I received there was to benefit me later, but in hindsight I must note that it was focused exclusively on acquiring a historical heritage. The contradictory intellectual currents of the first third of the 20th century, the historical cataclysms, the new scientific insights and artistic paradigms practically did not exist in this educational system. Fortunately that was all available to me at home.

We and the rest of our relatives spent the summer holidays, three whole months, in Jūrmala-Avoti as usual; at one time there used to be a railroad station by that name between Bulduri and Dzintari. Naturally it was my father who, every year from 1926 on, rented the same big two-story villa with a rambling garden, where my grandparents, my parents and I lived together with Mama's brother and sister as well as their families. Initially, before the birth of my two cousins, each couple, as well as I and my governess, was assigned a room of their own; later, the two boys got a separate room as well. People socialized in the spacious dining room or on the veranda and terrace. The house was open to everybody, everyone had friends who would come visit and made friends with each other; they were young, cheerful, and carefree. The children were free to mingle with the grown-ups, more even than in the apartments in town. Life in Avoti was so paradisiacal that it would never have occurred to anyone to travel to some fine foreign spa. There were occasions when my parents disappeared for a short period, but the general view was that there was no place where you could spend the summer as pleasantly as in the Riga resort area, Jūrmala.

Close by, in summer cottages that they mostly owned, lived a few other Jewish families we knew with their children, for instance, the owners of the Wolfschmidt Company, three brothers and their families, who were called "the rich Misrochs." One of them, Isak, was one of the few close friends my parents had in Riga. His cheerful, temperamental, and clever wife Lilly was Mama's bosom friend (her best friend in Paris was also called Lilly!), and her daughter Vivi, who was one year younger than me, became my substitute sister, as it were. Isak was the only impractical family member, unsuited for business, but to make up for it he was a charming and witty socialite, whom his respectable brothers rescued, like it or not, and pulled from the mire of debt. On the tennis and croquet courts in this family's vast park-like garden I also enjoyed exercising my inherently rather lazy limbs. What was nicest of all were excursions by boat and yacht on the Lielupe River to its estuary in the Bay of Riga.

BERLIN CHANGES – LIFE CHANGES

In the fall, winter, and Easter holidays I went to Berlin, sometimes for a whole month. Because my grades did not suffer, the school gave me permission to do this. The first years that I lived separated from my parents in Riga, the governess used to accompany me, but soon I took the journey alone. It never even occurred to anyone that anything could happen to me on the way. I clearly remember how Grandfather and Grandmother put me in the sleeping car and paid the conductor to bring me tea and keep an eye on me. I didn't go to the dining car, I brought my own provisions. I had a good sleep during the long night, and the next day toward noon my parents picked me up at the Bahnhof Zoo. In order to be able to travel without my parents, I received a fully valid Latvian passport at the early age of ten. I admit that I openly bragged about this document, for no other child I knew had one. Our country was a member of the League of Nations, and Latvian citizens were able to move freely within its borders without a visa or special foreign passport. You simply bought a ticket, got on the train, and set off – just as you do today within the European Union. Evidently railway trips were not too expensive, for many people from all walks of life took advantage of these opportunities. Practically all my teachers traveled in Europe during the summer holidays, especially to Germany and France, where they sometimes took advanced training courses, and so did the physicians we knew. Even our Elizabetes iela janitor came to us for advice as to what he should absolutely see in Berlin or Paris.

I very much enjoyed this life "on the move," as it gave me a chance to pursue my favorite pastime – observing people, comparing them with each other, and imagining their lives. Little by little I became aware of the alarming changes that were taking place in the world around me. I sensed that something was changing in people's behavior, in the way they interacted. At each visit, conversations at the Pension Bergfeld now focused on new, disturbing topics. In the city people suddenly no longer moved about as unselfconsciously as before. Rowdy "Brownshirts" roamed through the streets, rudely molesting people they thought looked like Jews. Every time I came to Berlin, they terrified me anew, although nobody wanted to believe they would stay in power for long. The grown-ups were worried and distressed. As Latvian citizens my parents and I were initially not directly affected by the race hatred manifested by ever new laws and by the violent political upheavals, yet Father lost one business partner after another. It became more and more difficult to maintain one's daily standard of living. It was agonizing to watch Jewish German citizens being increasingly humiliated, disenfranchised, and intimidated. Among our acquaintances as well, there was an increasing number of cases of arrests without a legal basis.

In this respect, Mama and I could have felt safe, for a fair-haired, slim lady who looked more like a northern European did not arouse suspicion. Even without completely understanding what was happening, I realized that many people had been pushed to the margins of society from their normal, secure lives and had become outlaws. The exodus of German Jews began. It's true that a limited number of emigrants were admitted, but no country was overjoyed to see them – whether people felt compassion for them or not, they were regarded as a burden, a nuisance. Little by little, events took on a character that was more and more unbelievable, almost surreal. Not only I, but people who were smarter than me were incapable of comprehending that a totalitarian power could dare to act not only cruelly and inhumanely, but also completely irrationally.

I was reminded of this stunned amazement a few years later, when the Soviet Union occupied Latvia. We couldn't imagine how something like this was even possible. In the West I still keep meeting people who simply cannot understand that with the blessing and even by order of the state, in the middle of the night, it was possible to break into the homes of defenseless people, drag them from their beds, cram them into cattle cars, and deport them. "Why didn't you protest? Why didn't you emigrate?" they ask.

We were initially just as naïve and blind at the time.

As I experienced personally, at the beginning in Germany many people felt the Nazis' rowdy behavior, their bellowing, their brutality were merely a kind of PR campaign that would ensure them the votes of the uneducated masses. This time even my father, an intelligent man who was normally capable of looking several moves ahead when it came to social and political developments, was wrong. He was of the opinion that once they came to power, the Nazis would not get anywhere with their extremist slogans; questions to do with management, with the economy, and many other issues would force them to cooperate with others and thus to make compromises. At the time we had no idea that a war was in preparation, that it was necessary at first to incite people to hate a mythical enemy called "the Jew," and to establish blind obedience to the Führer and to the principle of violence at every level.

At the time I learned what it means to be a Jew in an atmosphere of aggressive antisemitism. History is full of contradictions, and in my family in those days there were many discussions as to why this pathological Judeophobia had become virulent in Germany of all places – in the land of Lessing, Moses Mendelssohn, and countless others whose spiritual and moral values seemed to be an organic component of German identity, a land that, as many thought, offered the least fertile ground for it. Antisemitism, I heard, was primarily an Eastern European phenomenon; it had always been strong in Austria-Hungary, and especially in the Russian Czarist empire. There, pogroms against the Jews were a common occurrence, carried out with the support of the state. (The word *pogrom*, devastation, typically comes from the Russian.) From conversations at the time and later from books, I found out about the Beilis affair, masterminded for political motives in prerevolutionary Russia, and about the *Protocols of the Elders of Zion* and other provocations fabricated by the czarist secret police to which antisemites have been referring to this day. During major or minor crises, when people absolutely want to find a culprit, manipulators skillfully use these and other examples of "Jewish guilt" – ancient clichés stored deep in the unconscious – in order to corrupt weaker minds.

Some of our Jewish acquaintances had fought for the German Empire in World War I and had been awarded the Iron Cross. Mixed marriages were no longer the exception, and many writers and artists who were Jewish in origin contributed to the glory of German culture. I began to understand the saying that "being Jewish is not a nationality but a destiny."

Historical circumstances painfully compelled me to think about what the revival of these supposedly vanished atavistic instincts might mean for me and my family. I remembered the Middle Ages with its plague epidemics that suddenly triggered a wave of persecution and murder of Jews because fear and ignorance of the causes of the catastrophe focused the suspicion of simple-minded people on a specific group that could easily be accused of being to blame for it. Everywhere, and in every historical epoch, it is possible to identify the forces who use this phenomenon in order to gain power and manipulate the population.

Already during my last visits in Berlin at twelve or thirteen I observed with horror how quickly quite normal, kind people suddenly became enemies. To put it in a nutshell, the Jews are to blame for everything, and salvation lies in the Führer and a "pure-blooded nation." Later I was to realize that no totalitarian power can do without an exaggerated concept of the enemy: What the Jew was for the Nazis and other ultranationalists, the capitalist was for the Communists, for instance. And even if totalitarianism has been vanquished or has collapsed, the longing for simple solutions and a scapegoat, so convenient in so many situations, is still there.

The disgusting behavior of the Brownshirts in the streets of Berlin that I occasionally witnessed was to be only a taste of things to come. It became clear to me that the Nazis' slogans went hand in hand with criminality of the worst kind, rapacity, and violence. The sadistic gratification I observed as people were humiliated and tortured with impunity shook me to the core. As a result, during the years that followed, I began to study psychoanalytic treatises about the pathology of power and violence. As I had become accustomed to doing since childhood, I continued to observe and tried to understand what was happening to what seemed to be ordinary people – for instance, to systematically indoctrinated children. All of a sudden something that in civilized society had only recently been considered to be a sin, a crime, was permissible and even extolled.

As long as all German citizens still had a valid passport in their pockets and the German borders were not yet closed, the more sharp-sighted Jews, with heavy hearts, left behind their homeland and possessions and escaped abroad. Until the summer of 1939, it was possible to leave if you had a visa. All your property went to the German state. During these years almost all our acquaintances managed to emigrate. Those who insisted on their ownership rights were either immediately arrested or forced by brutal threats to sell their property seemingly legally for a ridiculously low price or to transfer it officially to "Aryans."

On the eve of the war, when our entire family had already gathered in Riga, Jews were allowed to leave Germany only in exceptional cases. How many conversations about emigration I listened to in those years – both at the Pension Bergfeld and later in Riga, where we deliberated about the fate of those who had emigrated or of friends who had remained in Berlin. Were we safe in Latvia? we wondered. I understood very well how cruelly people suffered at having to leave their home country where they were so deeply rooted, and where they had invested so much work and talent. The routes our friends and relatives followed as they went abroad were complicated and difficult, for after war broke out, they had to flee from Europe as well and seek refuge overseas. Thus, for instance, Father's youngest sister Jenny, who had moved to Königsberg upon her marriage, emigrated to Argentina in 1935 – a country totally unfamiliar to her, whose language she did not speak. There her husband, an engineer, found a halfway decent job, while Jenny managed to get a permanent position as a singer with the Buenos Aires radio station, and gave singing lessons. My little cousin Heini quickly learned Spanish and English. After graduating from secondary school and university in Argentina, he moved to the United States, where he made a career for himself under the name of Henry Raymont as an expert on Latin America. He was a journalist and wrote nonfiction. Today, after seventy years of separation, we have renewed our family relationship in Berlin, where Henry has regularly been a visiting professor at the Latin America Institute of the Free University of Berlin.

EUROPE CHANGES

How were my parents to act in this situation? Even if, as Latvian citizens, they did not suffer directly under the abuse of the Nazis, their life in Berlin became almost unbearable. Particularly Father, who had always assumed responsibility for the family, faced a fateful decision. In the endless nightly family conferences, my parents considered several strategies. Should they go to Paris, where everything was familiar and where there was no lack of friends and acquaintances? Or perhaps to Switzerland, where Father had business partners? Or overseas perhaps? They even considered Australia. But not far away, there was Riga, our haven of peace! As a neutral state, Latvia seemed to be as safe as Sweden or Switzerland. Mama was opposed to going to a distant country, she wanted to be able to go on visiting her parents and family in Riga whenever she liked. At that time you had to assume that a separation across continents was a separation that would go on for years.

That is why they decided to go back to their native city – and to a country whose citizens we were and whose citizenship meant a great deal to us. It was clear that from now on Father's professional opportunities would be severely restricted. Still, he did manage at least to renew his relations to Latvian export companies, and I cannot remember his ever lacking work during the four years before the

Soviet invasion. Father was able to come to an arrangement with the Ulmanis government, even if he made no secret of the fact that he condemned the coup as an illegal means of gaining power; he deplored the destruction of the successful and internationally respected Latvian parliamentarian republic in favor of an authoritarian, nationalist system headed by a "leader." In spite of everything, he valued Ulmanis as a competent economic policy maker, and invested his legal and business experience in the Latvian economy.

After the family moved to Riga, I too had to revise my plans for the future. My parents trusted me and let me have my way.

For a start, I decided to change schools. Back in the day, I had decided on the Luther-Schule because I intended to study in Western Europe one day. Now the situation was completely different, and I had to give up these ideas. In order to study history, which I had set my heart on, I would have to enroll at the University of Latvia, which fortunately enjoyed an excellent reputation. Since only conversational Latvian was offered at the Luther-Schule and the teaching of Latvian culture left much to be desired, I had to look around for a new school.

In this connection I am reminded of an incident that probably took place in the last year I spent at the Luther-Schule, in the winter of 1936/37. To replace our teacher of Latvian, who was unable to teach for a while, we had a young Latvian substitute teacher. Almost from the first moment I sensed that she felt insecure among the supposedly "high-born" German girls and made attempts to ingratiate herself with them. Once she came back to the classroom from recess while we were still chattering away and exclaimed: "What's this? You're German girls! You're not in some Jewish hovel here!" I got angry, but I managed to control myself. I still had 45 minutes left to consider what I should do. Toward the end of class I raised my hand: "Teacher, may I say something, please?" In a quiet, calm voice I pointed out that our parents, when they sent us to this school, were convinced that here we would be taught not only knowledge but – it went without saying – appropriate behavior as well. I remember word for word what I said: "You made disparaging remarks about Jews, although you know very well that I am Jewish. Like anybody else you have a right to your own opinions, which incidentally do not interest me, but I find it impolite and vulgar that you expressed them in my presence before the rest of the class. Please keep this in mind in future." I delivered my tirade formally with emphatic politeness – Mademoiselle Speer would have been happy. The teacher was speechless for a moment and turned red as a beet, but then composed herself and apologized, saying that she hadn't intended to offend me.

When the teacher had left the room, my classmates expressed their appreciation to me for defending my honor and self-esteem. They were true descendants of their knightly forebears in the good sense of the word.

After searching for some time, we decided on a somewhat expensive private school, the Esra-Gymnasium, where classes were taught in Latvian. When it came to the quality of instruction and Latvian linguistic culture, it was considered to be the leading Jewish secondary school in Riga. What was also attractive was the opportunity to take additional languages as electives, including Latin. At long last I would be able to familiarize myself with the modern version of ancient Hebrew, Ivrit. It had always seemed absurd to me that I was learning Latin and Ancient Greek, but had practically no idea at all of the language of my ancestors. Yiddish was not taught at this school, nor did I need it, because it was not spoken by those around us. I could understand it quite well, because Eastern European Yiddish is on the one hand related to German dialects and on the other hand rich in Russianisms.

Another fact that spoke for choosing the Esra-Gymnasium was that most of my former Jewish classmates had changed over to it from the Luther-Schule and that, last but not least, it was coeducational. After all, I was now fifteen years old; it was about time to meet some boys and to measure myself against them.

I devoted the summer of 1939 to the Latvian language and literature in order to reach the high school level. Theo Goldinger, my private tutor, had developed a special method of teaching a German speaker Latvian, different from the one he used with people whose mother tongue was Russian. During those three months I plunged so deep into the culture and history of this nation that in the postwar years Latvian would become the dominant language both in my working and my private life. I "adopted" it, so to speak. Or did it adopt me?

At the Esra-Gymnasium I met again my classmates from primary school, Nora Minsker and Riva Šefere (actually Schäfer). I was to remain Riva's friend until her death in the spring of 2014. In the student club I began spending time on studying film. The school was one of the few in Riga to offer working groups and optional elective subjects. Particularly in my senior year, my last year at school in 1939/40, when war had already erupted in Europe, I learned a lot about political problems and programs both in my regular classes and in discussions and conversations with classmates. Represented among the students were all kinds of different political and ideological views; they all criticized the authoritarian Ulmanis regime and preached various visions of the future, from left-wing Marxism to Zionism. Some of the boys were members of the illegal organization *Darba jaunatnes savienība* (Association of Working-Class Youth), which, as far as I can remember, included the entire spectrum of the left-wing opposition. My friends embraced the ideals of social democracy and were ready to take quite a few risks in order to restore the legitimate parliamentary republic and the rule of law based on the Latvian constitution. In the school there were also a few ultra-left communists who idealized the USSR and were to become active supporters of the coming Soviet occupying power.

In my class, it was the Zionists who met with more approval; their circles were active in all Jewish schools, because they were a legal movement. They not only dreamed of the Jews' return to the land of their forebears and the founding of a Jewish state, but also endeavored to acquire all the practical skills that were necessary to transform the neglected, economically backward territory of Palestine, which at the time was still controlled by the British colonial power, into a modern country. To this end they bought or leased farms where they offered so-called *hachshara* courses led by experienced Latvian agronomists. Their enthusiasm and determination as they set to this difficult task without the comforts of civilization impressed me a great deal, and I was also a little envious that they were able to believe in an ideal. However much sympathy I had for them, I did not join them for several reasons. An honest look into my inner world was sufficient for me to admit that I basically felt as a European and was rooted in European culture. Moreover, I have always been reluctant when it came to any kind of obligation to commit and submit myself ideologically and socially, to renounce critical doubts, and to march in step, as they say.

At the Luther-Schule there had not been so many political and social activities. Classes at the Esra-Gymnasium were far more challenging as well. The standards at the girls' school had been markedly lower, particularly in the exact sciences. Now I was suddenly able to be passionate about mathematics, this supposedly dry subject that so many of my classmates hated. As I solved the problems, I felt an almost aesthetic enjoyment, comparable even to the sensations aroused in me by music or films. Obviously so many new, complicated, and contradictory events had lately burst into my life that the flood of impressions was beginning to overwhelm me. The world and people proved to be far more incomprehensible than I had thought formerly. That is why mathematics – and specifically algebra, but also geometry and trigonometry – gave me great satisfaction. Here I could gain clarity on my own. The certainty that the result would be either correct or wrong, but clear and unambiguous in any event, was reassuring. The correct solution produced a feeling of happiness, a true catharsis. How simple and easy life would be if what was correct was always correct and what was wrong was always wrong, if everything was logical and unequivocal according to the laws. For a short time, I played with the idea of studying mathematics, but there came a point when I had enough of the abstract clarity. These exact solutions seemed just too simple. I returned to living, flawed human beings with their never completely solvable problems – in the hope that art and history would help me get my bearings – at least to some extent – in this jungle of civilization and the human psyche.

Only two subjects caused me problems: physics, which I did not like, and chemistry, which I did not like at all. My grades were barely mediocre, which surprised everyone, for as a rule these subjects and mathematics are considered to be a set – people who are good at one are also good at the others. But I loved only mathematics. Physics and chemistry bored me. Perhaps it was the fault of our teacher, Mr. Bermann.

At the Esra-Gymnasium, whose teaching staff consisted of highly qualified teachers, Mr. Bermann could stay on – which was no secret – only because he had served with distinction in the Latvian fight for independence in 1919/20. On national holidays he proudly wore his medal. Mr. Berman, a Jew who spoke perfect Latvian, was unfit to be a teacher. In the chemistry lab he only rarely succeeded in performing a successful experiment; every time, the students waited with bated breath to see what would go wrong this time. When Mr. Bermann announced he would produce a red substance by combining two liquids, the result was guaranteed to be green or something else that was non-red. One could only wonder how he had managed never to blow us up. But Mr. Bermann was such a good-natured and amiable man that neither the school administration nor the students or parents ever objected to his inexplicable teaching methods. Besides he had the laudable quality of giving average grades to all the failing students, so that anyone could pass without much effort. That's why I don't know beans about physics and chemistry.

One of my class' favorite teachers was the poet Pāvils Vīlips, who taught Latvian. We knew he had been one of the young Social Democratic intellectuals whose texts were no longer published now, under Ulmanis. Thus the poet became a teacher at a Jewish school. His teaching method was unconventional: He showed us that you could evaluate Latvian literature from a controversial point of view, and familiarized us with the criteria we needed to do that. He was quite frank about his personal opinions and expected us to be equally candid. His attractive wife, Elvīra Bramberga, was also an extraordinary person and popular with the public. She acted at the Dailes Theater and often supplied us with complimentary tickets. Vīlips, a highly educated man with liberal views, respected us students as intelligent, free-minded individuals. That was why we loved him. He was the only teacher we invited to our parties; there were even times when we had a drink together. He taught us the fundamentals for understanding the Latvian language and literature, while not adhering particularly strictly to the curriculum doctored by the Ulmanis regime, which represented the parochialism of the leader cult. Thus, for instance, Ulmanis' biography was placed on an equal footing with the life stories of the classical authors of world literature, while his patriotic effusions were equated with the best examples of Latvian literature. What is more, students were expected to memorize and quote entire passages from the texts of the *Vadonis* – the leader. Among us high schoolers this could provoke only sarcasm. The personality cult was simply ludicrous and tasteless, though admittedly authoritarian rule in Latvia, unlike in the great empires next door, was not accompanied by bloody violence and crimes on a mass scale.

For us, students at an upper-class private school loosely controlled by the state, it was difficult to understand how artists and intellectuals, too, could voluntarily take part in glorifying political power. We couldn't understand why a competent economist like Ulmanis allowed himself to be adulated in such a vulgar and tasteless fashion. After all, neither Roosevelt nor Churchill had any need of such veneration. When many years later I married the Latvian theater critic and publicist Valdis Grēviņš and got to know his family and friends, who belonged to the old Social Democratic intelligentsia of Latvia, I realized that the ideology of national self-importance had never been acceptable to a significant part of educated Latvians. While I was in secondary school, I had met only one of them, Vīlips, who in his classes discreetly helped us to preserve independent thinking and judgment. He even allowed us to have discussions about the work of Ulmanis' poet laureate Edvarts Virza, which would have been impossible in a public school.

The great poet and playwright Rainis was naturally also part of the curriculum, but the world of his ideas is so metaphorical that it is possible to interpret it in any number of ways. Mr. Vīlips, however, taught us to love Rainis not as a herald of nebulous ideas, but as a master of the word, a writer who explored the poetic potential of the Latvian language. I particularly liked that we read Rainis' plays in class with assigned roles and that during the reading of *Indulis un Ārija* (Indulis and Arija, 1911) Mr. Vīlips gave me one of the main male parts, that of Mintauts, the Lithuanian king. My fellow students were surprised, because there was no lack of boys in the class, but Vīlips said: "She has a man's brain."

From the first day that I began to discover Latvian literature in depth, the short-story writer and playwright Rūdolfs Blaumanis received a place of honor in my Olympus of world literature, next to Chekhov, Maupassant, and Katherine Mansfield. He was the only one of my newly discovered Latvian authors whose merciless and at the same time deeply perceptive gaze has never disappointed me to this day.

RIGA, VIDUS IELA 9

In the winter of 1935/36 we temporarily lived on Eksporta iela. Our future domicile in Riga, which was still being remodeled and furnished, was in a corner building at the intersection of Vidus and Vīlandes iela: a relatively new apartment building with an inner courtyard, in a middle-class neighborhood. The mezzanine apartment had five large rooms, four of them with doors to the corridor, but also connected by double doors. As was customary in Riga's so-called "gentry apartments," there was a maid's room next to the kitchen. The design of both the kitchen and the spacious bathroom was comfortable and modern, according to Mama's specifications. In Father's study, bookcases predominated, while in the drawing room, there was a combination of modern upholstered furniture and Chippendale. For my parents' bedroom, Mama ordered simple modern furniture in white and for the dining room in black high-gloss lacquer. My room was the farthest down the hall, which suited me perfectly.

We were destined to live in Vidus iela for only four peaceful years. During the Soviet occupation, half the apartment was taken from us. Then came the Nazis.

Compared to Paris and Berlin, my parents' lifestyle became quieter and more modest. It's true that they went out more often at night with friends to restaurants, bars, or social events; large parties, however, had become less frequent. Still, almost every evening, old friends would come and visit, new friends would join them, so that soon a retinue had gathered around Mama again. She still read a great deal and ordered scads of books, especially from Paris. For his part, Father missed hardly a single book published by German émigrés – Thomas Mann, Feuchtwanger, Werfel, Remarque. Our library grew visibly and could soon bear comparison with the beloved bookcases in Elizabetes iela. Mama was interested in everything that was happening in the world of art, which in Riga was colorful and varied; on the other hand, the city's society of middle-class, mainly Jewish, ladies bored her to tears.

Meanwhile I went my own way and became more and more independent.

It was during this period that Mama began to play roulette. In 1930s Latvia, gambling was illegal; the prohibition, which could be skillfully circumvented, made it all the more alluring. An attaché at the Argentinian embassy had organized a secret gambling den in his apartment at the corner of Elizabetes and Antonijas iela. That was where now and again Mama and her entourage used to lose considerable sums of money playing baccarat or roulette. Father disapproved, but Mama didn't care. In her opinion, he too was a gambler to a certain extent – at the stock exchange, which, as he admitted himself, gave him similar intense sensations. In his free time, he was a passionate bridge player, always pointing out that it is no ordinary card game but, like chess, a mental exercise. Apparently even the Catholic Church gives the game its blessing, at least I deduced this from the fact that Father Ādams Buturovičs could often be found at Father's bridge table, a highly educated and fine man who was soon to step into my life as a kindly genius. Father got to be such a master at bridge that he took part in international tournaments in Marienbad and Carlsbad. Twice Mama and I accompanied him there in summer.

Due to favorable circumstances, in 1938, Father earned an impressive sum of money in a big multilateral trade deal. A large part of his fabulous fee went to Mama, who, overjoyed, left for Paris, then

Italy, then Paris again. When she finally returned three months later, she announced laughing that she would have loved to stay longer, but unfortunately she had run out of money.

The year 1938 was politically crucial. In March Hitler's Germany annexed Austria. Six months later the European states caved in and ceded part of Czechoslovakia, the Sudetenland, to Hitler – in the hope that they could thus negotiate a lasting peace. This time even I followed the events. Father somberly told me that the decision had been a tragic mistake, which would only encourage Hitler's effrontery. He was to be proven right.

At the time many naïve and short-sighted people were pleased that peace had supposedly been preserved. During those days Mama was in Paris and later told us that after the signing of the accord people had hugged each other in the streets and cheered with joy. In Riga the prevailing mood was "What the eye doesn't see the heart doesn't grieve over," and initially life still went on as usual. A presentiment of the dangerous events beyond the borders of Latvia came with the first groups of emigrants, or rather refugees, who arrived in Riga after the anti-Jewish pogroms of the Nazis in Vienna. The Ulmanis government had agreed to accept them in Latvia – based on an agreement with the Jewish community in Latvia that undertook to provide for the material needs of these victims of persecution. The Latvian state granted them the right to work and guaranteed their safety and peace. This action did Ulmanis credit.

We housed two brothers from Vienna in Father's study. The older one was a craftsman, I believe a cabinetmaker or carpenter, and the younger had just graduated from high school. Quiet, taciturn, self-effacing people. From what they told us, we could see how traumatized they were. Many of their neighbors, acquaintances, and colleagues had been transformed overnight into followers of Hitler who were proud that they were the Führer's fellow countrymen.

After a few months, work was found for the brothers; they thanked us profusely for our hospitality and moved into their own apartment. I know nothing about their subsequent fate. Very shortly thereafter, the Soviet government, which had in the meantime occupied the three Baltic states, acted incomprehensibly and inhumanely toward these refugees. During the short phase of collaboration between the USSR and Germany, many of these emigrants were arrested and "handed over" as proof of friendship to the German security agencies, which meant certain death. Those who remained were suddenly considered to be Germans after Hitler's attack on the Soviet Union and were deported to the East. Hardly a single one of them survived either.

Mama was abroad. Father was busy, and so this autumn of 1938 I was left entirely to my own devices. For three months I practically never went to school; Father signed, without asking any questions, the notes saying I was sick. Both he and I had reasons for going our separate ways without bothering each other with our personal escapades.

Judging by certain indications, during Mama's long absence Father had taken a fancy to a lady who turned out to be the actress Lilija Štengele. Attractive and elegant, Štengele was *the* grande dame of the Latvian theater. When Mama finally returned home, she could not fail to discover the liaison, and now for the first time I saw that she was capable of being extremely jealous. During one temperamental scene she hurled a cigarette case with an engraved dedication that Štengele had given Father out the window. A tasteful, stylish case, silver covered with genuine snakeskin. Unabashedly, as was customary in our family, I began to tease Mama: Well, well – I said to her – she was accusing Father of exactly the same thing that she herself regarded as her indisputable right. Her answer surprised me. "There are people," she said, "who are so serious and truthful in their feelings that they had better not run the risk of a frivolous infatuation." And father, she said, was exactly such a person. With his sense of responsibility, his direct way of saying "yes" or "no," he could easily become entangled in complicated and, in the long run, painful relationships. "Our father doesn't play around, he is no Casanova. He takes everything he does seriously," she added. In that respect, she herself was different, she said.

There was a great truth in this. She demonstrated her love and fidelity to Father in her own way and with her entire existence to the bitter end.

In February I had celebrated my sixteenth birthday and had been transformed almost seamlessly from a child into a young lady. Up to that time the fact that my relationships with the male sex were purely friendly, like the one I once had with Paulchen, had never bothered me. Boys would talk to me, but only rarely ask me to dance at school proms. Growing up next to such a dazzling mother, I found it perfectly natural as a little girl that when it came to sex appeal (as the saying went then) I would never be able to compete with her. I accepted that, and it didn't cause me pain. It didn't even annoy me when as a child I would occasionally hear such tactful remarks as "Oh, that's the daughter of our lovely Eva? She doesn't look a bit like her mother ..." The world was full of thrilling possibilities, and I was constantly preoccupied with some interesting project. I dreamed of a different future for myself and had no intention to compete with Mama.

And yet: When, between my fifteenth and sixteenth birthday, the butterfly finally emerged from its chrysalis – no beauty, but still a pretty good-looking girl to whom people would pay attention, and not only because of the clever things she said – I was filled with something like euphoria.

One morning I took a closer look at myself in the mirror and realized to my surprise that I had undergone a total transformation that could not be overlooked. Mama was amused: "It's all there, everything a woman needs – not too much and not too little." Somehow I had managed to bypass puberty, which normally brings with it all kinds of problems. I had unexpectedly been transformed into a woman.

For a moment I completely lost my head. I enjoyed total freedom: Mama went to Paris, Father was up to his ears in work, and at the private school I attended, good students like me were not too rigidly disciplined – everybody knew the teaching material was not a problem for me. Thus at the beginning of the school year I hardly ever showed my face in class, devoting myself instead to an exciting "experiment."

From an early age I had read French novels and various psychological treatises, and felt perfectly equipped for anything that had to do with love and relationships between the sexes. As soon as I was granted unprecedented, intoxicating power over the young men around me, I immediately made use of it to try out certain aspects of my theoretical knowledge in practice. I did so with the thoroughness of a researcher, exactly as though I was carrying out an exciting investigation in the lab. I was really surprised how easy it was to manipulate the guinea pigs and how predictably they reacted when I applied the tactics I had learned from novels and plays. It was a period when I learned to despise the male sex (later I became more understanding). I admit that sometimes, as I engaged in this none too honorable pastime, I was disgusted with myself, for in order to twist somebody around my little finger I had to act a lot dumber than I really was. Since the girls around me were constantly falling in love, while I remained cool as a cucumber, it suddenly occurred to me that I was incapable of falling in love. It's true that certain feelings did stir in me; now and again I would prefer one young man to the others, I'd also enjoy dancing with him and exchange a few kisses. From this I concluded that I was reasonably normal, and that was enough for me.

    I divided the young men I knew into two categories. With some of them I would have fun, we'd go out together and have a good time, but there wasn't really much I could talk to them about. I couldn't imagine a relationship on equal terms without the exchange of ideas, without lively interests. That's why I had friendships in the true sense of the word with a totally different type of young men, who, on the other hand, were not particularly entertaining, since they were usually neither good dancers nor elegant cavaliers. However, I was attracted to both kinds of men. At times I thought to myself how great it would be to meet a man who embodied both sides. Then, no doubt, I might finally experience the true love extolled in literature. Meanwhile, though, time was passing, and nothing happened. Probably I would always have a divided (or double?) life. In my relationships with the "spiritual" or soul friends I could also discern certain romantic and even erotic stirrings, which I instinctively did not encourage, however. Even then I valued a dependable and trustful friendship far more than a crazy infatuation.

Thus in that period between my fifteenth and seventeenth year I enjoyed my newly discovered power until I got bored with these little games. I came to the following conclusion: Any woman who is not pathologically repulsive (which happens only rarely) or absolutely stupid (that, too, happens more rarely than people think) can "get" virtually any man. The crucial question is, can she keep him? – and is the cunning, deception, and trickery even worth the trouble? As I expanded my "experiments," I could see for myself that a man lured by means of some special strategy lost the last little bit of appeal for me as soon as I had him on the hook. Once and for all, I realized that in love (and not only in love) the only thing that has true value is what you are given as a present, an unexpected gift. I was fed up with playacting and decided to be only myself – then we'd see whether I meant anything to anyone.

In the late 1930s, great changes took place in the thinking and planning of the daughters of upper middle-class families. As recently as in my mother's generation women from these circles for the most part wanted nothing other than to be their husband's decorative wife at home and in society, and to enjoy life. Women like my beloved Raja, who were bored at home and longed to put their sharp intellect and their outstanding education to good use, tended to be the exception. The girls of noble birth at the Luther-Schule also got no further than the ideal of an educated society lady when they thought about their future. During my last years at school, however, the girls in my class at the Esra-Gymnasium already had different ideas about life. Together with the boys we not only discussed what we would study at the university, but also what kind of work we would do, although many of the girls apparently had no need to worry about making a living. The most popular fields of study both for the boys and the girls were medicine and law. Those whose parents had big companies and enterprises tended to favor economics and engineering. Frequently my classmates decided on the professions of their fathers, because an established office or medical practice was waiting for them, and also because from an early age they had developed an interest in this career.

Secondary school students were not allowed to visit nightclubs or evening events for adults, but their families had large apartments. That is why we gathered at house parties, for which we had a Russian name – *vecherinka*. In the circles where I moved every apartment had a large salon with a parquet floor and an upright or grand piano, plus a "pataphone," of course, as well as a collection of dance music and shellac records. Sheet music of the latest songs and hit tunes with the original text or Latvian translation were immediately available in the music stores; many could play the piano reasonably well, so that one or the other of us at once sat down at the keyboard, which we appreciated more than music from the gramophone. Sometimes there'd even be enough players for a small orchestra. In the last years before the Soviet occupation we fell in love with South American dances like the rumba, samba, and carioca, or the British Lambeth Walk. That was when swing first came into vogue. We knew the famous dance orchestras of Glenn Miller and Tommy Dorsey, and loved Louis Armstrong, Bing Crosby, and other popular crooners. They were also familiar to us from American musical films, which were tremendously popular in Latvia. Enthusiastically we watched the movies with Fred Astaire and Ginger Rogers or from the Broadway Melody series with Eleanor Powell and other stars. We loved the music of Gershwin, Kern, Berlin, and Porter. Immediately before the outbreak of war a new star appeared in the musical firmament: young Frank Sinatra with his seductive voice, who in those days could only be heard on the radio and was not appearing in movies yet. We danced till we dropped. In the last two years before graduation, we girls hardly danced with our classmates anymore. The admirer of a self-respecting high school girl traditionally had to be a university student.

When there was a forcible shortage of living space in the Soviet period, such house parties would soon disappear for half a century.

The prohibition against secondary school students visiting nightclubs and restaurants challenged us to ignore it. Actually, nightclubs or restaurants did not tempt me, but I could not stand prohibitions and had to gain admittance to said establishments for that reason alone. A degree of caution couldn't hurt. To go to a nightclub like the famous Alhambra would have been unwise, because there I could run into friends of my parents and even teachers.

Usually we would agree to meet at a less distinguished but safe place, for example, in some pub in Mežaparks. In the clique that took me with them to adult venues I was the youngest: university students, a few of my girlfriends, who were a little older – five to seven of us who would gather around a big table.

The center of our group was the university student Jāzeps (Joseph) Pasternaks, who had just returned from studying abroad. Everyone called him Ossi. He was extraordinarily good-looking, witty, and very musical to boot – I believe there wasn't an instrument Ossi couldn't play. He flirted with one of my classmates who was two years older than the rest of the class. Dora's parents had managed to leave the Soviet Union, something that was considered to be practically impossible in the '30s. They had received the authorization to visit their relatives because of some urgent matter, a severe illness, I believe, and had remained here. In other words, they were among the above-mentioned *nyevovrashchentsi*, the ones who did not return home, several of whom we knew in Berlin and Riga. Since the curriculum at the Soviet school Dora had been at before was completely different, she had to repeat two grades and joined us sixteen-year-olds at age eighteen. She was a pretty brunette with cornflower blue eyes, and hurled herself into the vortex of pleasure even more enthusiastically than we. Dora was the first person from whom I heard directly about the horrifying, almost incredible things that were happening in the Soviet Union. Life in Riga surprised and delighted her. A romance developed between her and Ossi, and the two of them took me with them everywhere as an alibi with her parents.

Many years later, when Pasternaks had long since been married to the great actress Lidija Freimane (while I was now married to Lidija's school day friend Valdis Grēviņš), I used to remind him that he was the first to lead me astray by dragging Dora and me through many a den of iniquity.

At the end of the '30s our circle of friends no longer included only Jewish young people; gradually we were joined by a few Latvian and

Russian boys and girls, especially from university student circles. Common interests, mutual sympathies, but above all erotic attraction cannot be stifled by national prejudices. The standards according to which I had been raised had become established in Riga as well: namely, that people's value and attractiveness are determined solely by their personality and not by factors over which they have no influence.

At the university, students were clearly divided into fraternities and sororities. Probably the reason my attitude toward student associations was reserved was that I had read so much about the virtues of the German "dueling fraternities." Perhaps I still recalled the grown-ups' opinions of the Latvian fraternities. Without doubt these organizations are primarily typical of Germany, although in my childhood in Berlin, during the Weimar Republic, modern young people already regarded them as outdated and conservative, indeed, even as breeding grounds of a reactionary mentality. In Riga, on the other hand, where the Latvian University did not yet have centuries of tradition behind it, this imitation of the rituals of the former masters of Latvia seemed like protracted growing pains to me.

My new acquaintances and admirers included two members of Jewish student associations whose code of behavior was not very different from that of the Latvian ones. The guys said my opinion was biased. I'm sure that was true, but still I couldn't stand the overblown local patriotism of the fraternities, their arrogance, and particularly the excessive drinking.

The bar at our house was always filled with resplendent bottles, and at our family celebrations or when there were visitors, guests were always offered French cognac or a wine that went with the meal. Mama liked martinis with gin and vermouth. I too soon learned all about various types of alcoholic beverages, though it would never have occurred to me to drink more than a few sips. I can't remember ever seeing anyone who was drunk in our home, let alone someone who could no longer stay on his feet or didn't know what he was blathering. I was convinced that this only happened to vulgar, uneducated people who didn't know how to behave. Until the postwar period, I did not know that alcoholism is an addiction. That's why I was literally shaken when, at a student dance, I saw intelligent boys transformed beyond all recognition. At the time I thought: No matter how much I may like a man – if I saw him even once with an ugly mug like that, I'd find him repulsive forever afterward.

The fraternity brothers were my last guinea pigs. The ones I knew not only used to get drunk, but also stupidly dueled with rapiers. That was another thing I couldn't get excited about – it seemed like the vulgar aping of the customs of the vanishing estate-based society. That was why I took the liberty of participating in their game in order to find out how far stupidity can go. Thus, just for fun, I egged on two "cockerels" against each other, for instance, by making them jealous, whereupon they challenged each other to this kind of senseless duel. Naturally this no longer took place in the early hours at the edge of the woods, as it did in Pushkin's time, but in a gym – and it wasn't a fight to the death. I'm not proud of the way I behaved at the time and admit that I did not perform the "experiment" only so as to make fun of the stupidity of the duelists. To a certain extent, their posturing also flattered me.

The following episode also belongs in that frivolous and egoistical phase of my youth. In 1937 a family I knew had a visitor staying with them, a man no longer young from Australia. Evidently his father had emigrated from Riga at the end of the 19th century, had managed to become a "sheep millionaire" (that is, the owner of a huge herd and factory for meat products), and the heir of all these millions had now traveled to the homeland of his forebears. He was probably around 35 years old, in other words, as old as the hills in the eyes of a fifteen-year-old. There was a rumor among our acquaintances that he was looking for a bride, since he had taken it into his head that his wife must absolutely be from Riga. Once or twice he also visited us. I didn't even take a good look at the millionaire from overseas because I had dismissed him at first glance as a completely commonplace avuncular type. When he was done visiting, he went back to his Australia, and Mama told me, laughing, the behind-the-scenes story of his plan. It kept us amused for a long time to come.

It appeared that the Australian's choice had fallen upon me, although he had hardly spoken a word with me. He had discreetly turned to Mama, who was in turn supposed to acquaint me with the scenario of the future he had worked out for me. He was convinced, he had said, that I totally met his requirements, for he had decided to change his life fundamentally, which he was now wealthy enough to do. He intended to leave that half-savage continent and to settle in London. It was his ambitious plan to be presented at the British court, and for this purpose he needed a suitable wife. He would pay for me to have three years of education at a renowned Swiss girls' finishing school, which I would then leave at eighteen as a perfect high society lady. Luckily, he said, I was already fluent in various languages, but there among other things I would be instructed in such essential subjects as arranging receptions, being in charge of a large number of servants, tennis, golf, and riding, participating in fox hunts, and playing bridge. He would see to the finishing touches himself, giving shape to his Galatea exactly like Pygmalion. Finally the prospective suitor added that this way he hoped to prove to me that he was worthy of being loved. He was not pushy, he said, and wasn't trying to rush me since he was aware I was only fifteen years old. Mama, he added, should prepare me for the decisive conversation.

Mama and I almost died laughing. There was such unanimity between us that it didn't occur to either of us even to begin to take this fantastical proposition seriously. Only much later it crossed my mind that this was after all a proposal of marriage that in any other family might have been welcomed as a gift from heaven. The reason I tell this story here is that it's always interesting to imagine how your life would have turned out if at a certain moment you had acted differently than you did in reality.

I recalled this comical episode a few years ago when I spent some time in Francophone Switzerland. Quite near to where I was staying, there were two of these world-famous private boarding schools, one for boys and one for girls. A lot had changed since the 1930s, except for the insanely high school fees perhaps. What had also changed was the concept of what constitutes high society; somewhat to my surprise I learned that at present large numbers of the children of the

"New Russians" were being polished there. I observed two groups of students walking along the shore of Lake Geneva led by their teachers. The younger pupils were speaking Russian, while the older teenagers spoke only French. My Swiss friends and I were agreed that it was unlikely that all these well brought-up heirs of oligarchs would ever return to Russia.

FIRST LOVE

My first great love came when I was seventeen. All the theories I had so neatly arranged in my mind collapsed. This time it did not even occur to me to use my artful strategies and tactics.

We had already known each other superficially since I was ten and Dima fourteen. His name was Dietrich Feinmann, but in the Feinmann family and among friends he was called only Dima. His mother, a member of the Russian intelligentsia, was one of the white émigrés. She had baptized her son Dimitri. But in October 1918, when toward the end of the war and at the beginning of the revolutionary upheavals occupiers changed constantly, a German was in charge of the registry office. He would not accept a Russian name and tacitly replaced the name with the German "Dietrich," which he found more suitable. Dima's father, a dentist who was much in demand in Riga, was of Jewish descent.

The Feinmanns lived near my grandparents, and three rooms of the large seven-room apartment in Elizabetes iela 63 were used as a dentist's offices. When I had to see a dentist in Riga, I was brought to Dr. Feinmann. I still clearly remember the waiting room, also the treatment room, which in my eyes looked like a medieval torture chamber. I found even the reproduction that hung over the sofa in the waiting room horrible. Arnold Böcklin's "Isle of the Dead" was extraordinarily popular in Riga and adorned countless living rooms of the solid middle class. For me the painting's symbolism is fused for all time with toothaches and a fear of coming torment. No less repugnant seemed a boy I encountered almost every time in the hallway or the treatment room. As far as he was concerned, I didn't exist. As soon as the dentist began to drill, he would come in, usually to ask his father for money.

Our families were not so close that they would ever visit each other. Dima's name kept coming up years later in the circle of students I knew. Among his fellow students he enjoyed the reputation of being someone people could rely on.

Dima had graduated from the First City Gymnasium of Riga, an elite school that emphasized classical education, with Latvian as the language of instruction. I had heard that he had begun studying medicine, although music was his true passion and the Riga Conservatory attracted him at least as much. What tipped the scales was that he wanted to make his father happy. Finally the two of them agreed that after finishing his medical studies, when his "livelihood was assured," as Dr. Feinmann put it, he could do whatever his heart desired, even become a pianist. So Dima studied medicine and continued to take piano lessons on the side with a concert pianist, Sergey Tager, who also taught at the Conservatory. At a party in the home of mutual acquaintances, life brought Dima and me together again. That was in the spring of 1939.

I enter the salon. Sitting at the piano is a young man who looks familiar. He's playing Chopin. I come closer, fascinated by the way the music is reflected in his face, in his eyes, and even more, by how gently his fingers touch the keys. We look at each other and smile. From that moment on, we belonged together.

Even though my girlfriends prophesied all kinds of complications, our relationship developed perfectly naturally. Admittedly at this time Dima was involved with two very different women, everybody knew about it – and so did I, of course. I was not particularly bothered by the much-discussed rumors of his affairs. After all, I knew that there can be a huge difference between a beloved woman and a mistress. Besides, his private life had begun long before we met.

Our relationship developed carefully and cautiously. Dima did not pressure me, he treated me with the utmost respect, and it took an unusually long time before we really felt we were a couple. Incidentally, the two above-mentioned ladies disappeared from our lives quite soon without a trace.

I've always loved music, and Dima brought it even closer to me. He even taught me to read a score. When he came to visit me, he would sit down at the piano, ask me for a motif that corresponded to my current mood, and improvise so wonderfully that I thought I would melt like wax. We began going to the opera and to concerts together. At the time, Leo Blech had been invited to the Riga Opera for three seasons, and he fired musical life in the city with his enthusiasm. Somewhat self-mockingly I noted that love is even more rapturous when it has a musical backdrop. In turn, I was able to surprise Dima with many discoveries in the realm of literature and film. There seemed to be no question that a common future awaited us – we had no need to even talk about it. We spoke about our career plans and how we could juggle our different interests. Dima had not made a firm career decision yet. After he appeared in public as a soloist with Chopin's Piano Concerto No. 1 in the winter of 1940/41, he again began to ask himself seriously whether he should make music his profession after all.

I planned to study history and toyed with the idea of continuing my education in London at a famous institute of archeology. The art and philosophy of antiquity had always fascinated me, but I was convinced that one should first know the course of human history before immersing oneself in art history, since history is the foundation of the life of the mind. At the university I wanted to discover new horizons. That was how I had the perhaps extravagant idea of beginning my studies with something that was relatively unfamiliar to me: an introduction to economics and its history as taught in the first semester of the economics program, after which I would switch to the history department.

Towards the end of my senior year in high school, the Latvian government issued new regulations that students in the final years of school must spend part of the summer holidays doing farm work. Not all secondary school students were thrilled about it, but I was. My beloved Rūdolfs Blaumanis and other Latvian authors had awakened my interest in rural life. Now I had the opportunity to explore it for myself. I did my first "field studies" in the summer of 1939.

Father's sister, Aunt Edith, lived in Kurzeme. Her husband, David Glinterniks, was an officer in the Latvian army, a physician. After barely one and a half decades serving in Liepāja, he and the military hospital were moved to the county seat of Saldus. His family – Aunt Edith and the two daughters, who were in secondary school – temporarily remained in Liepāja. In Saldus Uncle David met a capable farmer whose land was beautifully situated on the shore of Brocēnu Lake, and he it was who agreed to have me work for him as a summer help.

I was amazed that I immediately felt like a member of the family. Everything seemed so familiar. The oldest son was already enrolled in the Saldus high school, while the two younger children were still in primary school. To my surprise they did not have permanent hired hands; for certain jobs, people were hired temporarily. The farmers themselves were busy from morning till night. In summer the children helped too. Yet nobody tried to overwork me particularly. "You're not to go into the cow barns," laughed my host when we first met. He was probably sorry for his cattle. "Don't you worry, we'll find a job for you."

Naturally on a sizable farm, especially in summer, there is no lack of work, but my main job was instructing the two children, especially in German. They had a few gaps in other subjects as well, for instance, in Latvian spelling. I remember I kept having them write dictations. Thus I was now in the country, but without coming in contact with actual farm work. I felt great in Brocēni. I had my own little room, was surrounded by pleasant, friendly people who were interesting to talk to, and the fabulous natural landscape around me cheered both my body and soul.

In the family's bookcase I found the same books – including

recent publications – that were read and discussed by my acquaintances in Riga. The farmers and I enthusiastically exchanged views about Scandinavian authors such as Hamsun, Lagerlöf, and Undset, who were especially popular at the time. Many in the community sang in the choir, played amateur theater, and went to see performances in Saldus, Liepāja, and Riga. Both at "my" farm and at that of the neighbors in Broceni the rooms were furnished with tasteful arts and crafts objects. I had the impression that there was no provincialism in the Latvian province. I felt drawn to the country people because I found them authentic. In Riga I was often annoyed by the way people conformed to cheap modish clichés and the aesthetic models favored by the movies or the weekly magazine *Atpūta*.

Later, already during the Soviet era, when I was working in the editorial office of the Liepāja daily *Komunists* and moved around Kurzeme a lot, I noticed that in many respects the vibrant intellectual life and deeply instilled cultural traditions had successfully been preserved – even under the conditions of Soviet leveling. We who live in Latvia are often not aware of this ourselves and do not appreciate it because it seems so self-evident to us.

That late summer of 1939, Dima came and visited me for a whole week. We spent unforgettable days together. He charmed my hosts by sitting down at the piano in the parlor or playing the accordion. "We haven't heard such good music in this house for a long time," said our delighted host. We tried as much as we could to do our share of the garden and field chores, and still had plenty of leisure time to go on long excursions by bicycle, to swim in the lake, or simply to enjoy each other's presence.

I returned to Riga with wonderful memories. School would begin again on the 1st of September. In the world around me, as far as I could tell, everything was fine. My classes, all the way to the finals, went like clockwork. At my side, daily, I felt a person who was close to me.

The feeling of safety, the certainty of being loved and protected that my family had given me from earliest childhood was even intensified: by my first serious relationship, which never caused me the least pain or disillusionment.

Of course, we all anxiously followed the news of the Soviet Union's invasion of Finland and the devastating Winter War that followed. We hoped that the Mannerheim Line would hold until the Finnish David would finally – although with immense losses – foil the plans of the Soviet Goliath. A Finnish Soviet republic, whose future government was already prepared to take office, was to remain Stalin's pipe dream. Now we all wanted to believe that everything was in order.

Admittedly what was disturbing and uncomfortable were the Soviet military bases that had been established in Latvia, Lithuania, and Estonia on a contractual basis. Now and then, you'd meet a Red Army officer on the street in his unattractive uniform; but the garrisons kept a low and disciplined profile, so that naïve faith in Latvia's neutrality and our government's competence, and confidence in the inviolability of the recently signed bilateral mutual assistance pact between the USSR and Latvia were maintained.

For me the winter of 1939/40 and the spring that followed passed in a euphoria of self-delusion. I had never experienced so many intoxicating all-round successes.

LIKE SOMETHING OUT OF PUSHKIN

The Feinmanns were a middle-class Baltic Jewish family who spoke both German and Russian. As I mentioned earlier, Dima's mother was Russian. One of the brothers of Dima's father was also a medical man, a lung specialist. He had served as a front-line physician in the Imperial Russian Army in World War One. Working as Red Cross nurses in the military hospitals were many young women of noble descent (including the daughters of the Czar himself), who used to dine together with the doctors and officers at a special table. During one meal a high-ranking officer took the liberty of making a disparaging remark about Jews. Dima's uncle, a man who had plenty of self-esteem, stood up, boxed the offender's ears, and added that he was willing to give him satisfaction. The officer merely shrugged and said that he certainly was not going to have a duel with someone who was not a proper officer and who was a Jew to boot. One of the nurses was so thrilled at the young Riga doctor's behavior that she fell in love with him and married him. Two decades later I was to meet her.

Dima's aunt, Ludmilla Dmitriyevna, née Buturlina, was descended from an old family whose roots went back to the mythical era of the Varangians. In Russian history the Buturlins are known as an old Boyar dynasty. It was a pleasure to hear Ludmilla Dmitriyevna speaking, with a touch of contempt in her voice, about "those upstarts the Romanovs," from whom her forebears would never have accepted a title because they did not serve the throne, but Russia, and Russia alone. About her ancestors on her father's side she spoke with pride and respect, while things were a little more complicated where her mother's lineage was concerned. Her mother was born Countess Bobrinska. The first Count Bobrinsky, Aleksey, was the illegitimate son of Katherine II and her favorite, Grigory Orlov. In addition to the title of count, huge estates and various privileges were also bestowed on Aleksey. Thus I sat in front of a direct descendent of Katherine the Great and listened to her tell me regretfully that her mother's origin had nothing to do with historical merits, but rather with a kind of bedroom service. But there was no altering that.

Ludmilla Dmitriyevna was a personality who contradicted every stereotype of a lady of noble birth. She loved and deeply respected her husband and continued to work as a nurse at his side in Riga as well. In her youth, as the Czarina's lady in waiting, she was said to have been a beauty. I met her as an older lady who captivated me by her calm and kind dignity. She was somewhat gaunt, gray-haired but full of vitality, with a sober view of life and an incredible sense of humor.

Dima's uncle, who had acquired the reputation of being an outstanding specialist, bought a large property in Priedaine.[1] One of the buildings was renovated to become a beautiful home. A second building housed a pulmonary sanatorium, which thanks to the competent management and loving care of the two Feinmanns enjoyed a good reputation. The uncle died in 1932, and according to her late husband's wishes the widow transferred the sanatorium to the Jewish hospital Bikur Holim while continuing to work there. The sanatorium treated patients of all ethnicities.

Since her marriage was childless, his aunt looked upon Dima practically as her son. She accepted me, too, without reservation and confided to me stories from her remarkable life. During the Soviet period the sanatorium was nationalized, and a municipal medical office and labs of the city of Jūrmala were installed in the residential

---

1. Residential area of the city of Jūrmala (Transl.)

building. Here Ludmilla Dmitriyevna was employed despite her advanced age. Until her death in 1951, she was allowed to keep two small rooms on the top floor of her former villa. Since I had moved to Liepāja in 1950, I was no longer able to visit her during the last year of her life.

In the postwar years, a son of her brother miraculously surfaced in Moscow. She had always assumed that all her relatives had been killed in the Revolution. However, her brother's family had survived, but probably for reasons of caution had not wanted to contact their relatives abroad. Ludmilla's nephew, the son of this brother, had become an officer in the Red Army during the war; he followed the family tradition of defending his country in the event of war – regardless of who was in power. In our last conversation at the end of the '40s Ludmilla Dmitriyevna said it had been the duty of every Russian patriot to overcome, in this war against Hitler's Germany, his hatred and righteous anger against the communist regime and to defend his fatherland against the aggressor. A time would come when the Russian people would find a way to a commendable life. This was also the view of most of the white émigrés, for example, in France, who for the most part had joined the Resistance or General de Gaulle's army.

I shall never forget the winter evening when she invited us to come to Priedaine, promising a surprise. Somewhere she had managed to scare up a real Russian troika sleigh with bells, drawn by three horses, with a fur lap robe and fur-covered cushions. Dima and I sped across the snow-covered beach along the Bay of Riga – like the lovers in an old Russian painting. Ludmilla Dmitriyevna wanted to give us the gift of an unforgettable, romantic experience, one she had also experienced in her youth in Russia.

At the time, I listened entranced to the fantastic stories of Dima's aunt. They, too, were memories of *her* Atlantis, engulfed for all time. Like other noble young ladies, Ludmilla Dmitriyevna had graduated from the Smolny Institute in St. Petersburg. Cadets and officers of the Imperial Army were invited to the splendid balls as partners of the young girls. At one of these balls, young Ludmilla met a brilliant officer, Count O'Brien de Lacy, the descendent of an Irish-French noble family that had entered the service of the Czar and resettled in Russia. It was love at first sight, but the parents would definitely not have allowed their sixteen-year-old daughter to marry. So O'Brien de Lacy, with the help of some of his officer friends, secretly eloped with his beloved one night, and in a troika, to the sound of sleigh bells, they sped out of the metropolis across the dark, snowy plains of Russia. That same night they were married in a country church by a humble Russian orthodox priest. Ludmilla's parents agreed that it was more sensible to give in.

But soon bitter reality irrupted into Ludmilla's paradise: Her mother died, and so shortly thereafter did her father; a little while later, one of her brothers followed the parents. Then only Ludmilla Dmitriyevna and a brother were all that remained of the family. Her brother finally became suspicious...

The murder trial of O'Brien de Lacy became the talk of all Russia and went down in history. Ludmilla's husband was accused of the murder of her brother. With the help of a doctor named Panchenko, he is supposed to have infected him with cholera bacilli in order to get his hands on the considerable family fortune. The father's death also seemed somewhat suspicious, but there was no evidence. The accused was defended by one of the most famous attorneys in Moscow, nicknamed Goldmouth, which was why the trial had wide resonance. O'Brien de Lacy was sentenced to life imprisonment.

Even when she described this terrible crime, Ludmilla Dmitriyevna kept her sense of humor – suddenly she gazed dreamily into the distant past and sighed: *A vsyo taki – kakoy bil muzhshchina*! (And still – what a man he was!)

The atmosphere of a bygone era surrounded me particularly when old women friends from the days of the Smolny Institute gathered at Ludmilla Dmitriyevna's home – including the great character actress Lydia Melnikova from the Riga Russian Drama Theater. Logs crackled in the fireplace of the large salon, the table was laid with antique china and silver, the cozy, warm room was filled with the sound of hushed voices, the fragrance of French perfume, and the aroma of good coffee. I felt I was in a 19th-century Russian novel or at a theatrical performance. I can still picture a moment that seems like a scene from *Eugene Onegin*. The servant opens the door, and in comes a tiny, shriveled old man. Ludmilla Dmitriyevna introduces him with the words: "Monsieur Dubois, our good neighbor!" Monsieur Dubois turned out to be an ancient Frenchman who at some point in the 19th century had wound up in Russia. From there, the wave of emigration had later washed him up in Latvia, where he lived out his long life in Priedaine.

At the time none of us knew that we were living the last months in a world that would soon cease to exist.

PHOTOS

Esther Lulow, the grandmother in Libau (modern-day Liepāja), end of the 19th century.

The father, Leopold Löwenstein (Lēvenšteins), as a high school graduate, 1912.

The mother, Eva Löwenstein (Lēvenšteina), née Lulow, shortly after her marriage. Petrograd 1919.

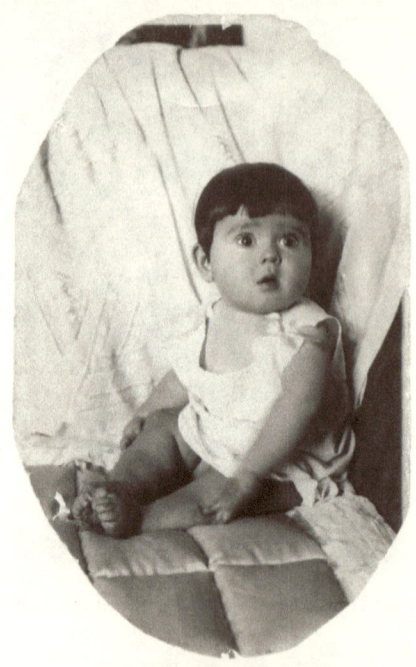

Life begins!

First steps through the park. The proud father is in the background. Paris 1923.

"Madame Charloff," the Russian nyanya *[nanny], with "Vally" on the balcony of a hotel. Nice 1923.*

With Sister Olga, the German governess.

Valentina and her parents, 1925.

At the beginning of the Berlin period, 1927.

The house at No.9 Meinekestraße in 2011.

Anny Ondra, the nicest of all the "movie aunts."

Anny Ondra in Hitchcock's Blackmail, *1929.*

Oscar Dancigers in Jūrmala, in the late 1920s.

"They resembled my mother to a T": Brigitte Helm and Jeanette MacDonald.

At the Christmas market in Riga.

With Cilia, Valentina's Aunt Cecilia, at a Midsummer Night's Eve celebration in Jūrmala.

One bicycle, two cyclists: Valentina and Uncle Žoržik.

Leopolds Lēvenšteins, 1930.

With the Lulow grandparents and the fox terrier Topsy.

Cecilia, nicknamed Cilia, Valentina's favorite aunt.

Bosom friend Raja, married to Uncle Žoržik.

Raja's brother Roman Pines, Aunt Cecilia's husband.

Eva Lēvenšteina, Valentina's mother.

Valentina's mother with Cilia, Žoržik, Raja, and the Riga friend Lilly Misroch at a Jūrmala beach, late 1920s.

The parents with relatives and friends in Jūrmala. Front row (from l to r): Raja, two Misroch ladies, Valentina's father, Genia Pines (lying down), Cilia; back row: Žoržik, Oscar Dancigers, Valentina's mother (5th from the left), and Roman (2nd from the right).

Leopolds Lēvenšteins in Vidzeme, ca. 1930.

Costume ball in Elizabetes iela. Seated: Cilia and Raja with two unidentified gentlemen; standing: Žoržik, Jurijs Jurovskis (director of the Russian Drama Theater), Roman, Valentina's mother with two other friends, early 1930s.

A happy child.

The cousins: Alexander, nicknamed Shurik, and Jakob, nicknamed Jacky.

Valentina aged 16.

Music lesson.

At the first class party at Esra Gymnasium.

With girlfriends Vivi Misroch and Ira Levit, 1937.

Just a flirtation, nothing serious.

Ira, Valentina, and a classmate as a pillow, summer of 1938.

Eva Lēvenšteina in the spa park of Ķemeri, 1938.

In front of the new hotel sanatorium "Ķemeri," 1938.

New Year's Eve 1939/40, the last in a free Latvia: Valentina's parents and three admirers.

The last summer in Jūrmala: Eva Lēvenšteina, 1940.

Dietrich Feinmann, Dima, as a university student aged 22.

Dr. Paul Schiemann.

Emīlija Gajevska, with the little daughter of the Karčevskis family, who sheltered Valentina in their home.

The first photo for the new Soviet passport, end of October 1944.

PART II

THE SECOND LIFE

Those who forget the victims
murder them for the second time
and permanently.
Paul Celan

SHOCK WITHOUT THERAPY
THE FIRST SOVIET YEAR

I still clearly remember the day on which the Soviet tanks rolled into Riga. Father impressed upon us that we should stay at home. He said that without doubt there were people who were happy now: for instance, those who hoped for greater social justice; or those who rejected the illegitimate dictatorship of Kārlis Ulmanis and naïvely believed the parliamentary republic would be restored; and finally some of the Jews, because they hoped the Soviet tanks would protect Latvia from the Nazis, who represented an even greater danger for us. It was well known that in August 1939 a nonaggression pact had been concluded between Germany and the USSR; no one had a clue that there was a secret additional protocol. If you go through the newspapers of this period, with the hypocritical Soviet promises of democratic freedoms and elections, you'll realize how the illusions were fueled.

For the entire time that my father still had left to live, he tormented himself with self-reproaches. He had always had an extraordinary sense of responsibility toward his family, and his profession gave him insight into political events. But in 1940 we encountered a phenomenon that was inconceivable to us as Westerners: All the agreements and declarations whose validity is contractually guaranteed in a democratic society and that are therefore taken for granted became ineffective. Of course we knew that laws in the Soviet Union were radically different from those that applied to us. However, we were not prepared for a situation in which the Soviet power trampled all over laws and agreements it had enacted itself.

My own situation was beyond strange. Many people in Latvia experienced a "summer of horror" (*baigā vasara*), while for me these months were the most beautiful and happiest of my life. It sounds hard to believe, but I can testify that it is possible, and I am not ashamed to admit it. My euphoria attenuated the shocks, as the life we had lived up to this point completely collapsed. I found refuge in a minuscule world that was almost hermetically sealed off – it was like being in the eye of the storm. In our self-centered landscape, overwhelmed by a love fulfilled, only the two of us existed: Dima and I.

We spent the summer in Jūrmala. Dima proved to be a fantastic sailor and rower. For days on end, we'd go tacking back and forth on a yacht or in a rowboat on the Lielupe River, where we had discovered a tiny island that henceforth belonged to the two of us alone. The escalation of events, the degrading spectacle of the sham elections in the occupied Baltic states, and finally the grotesque entry into the "fraternal community" of the Soviet republics, the anxious conversations in my family, Father's self-reproaches, the radical rearrangement of our daily life: all this happened before my eyes and affected me as well, yet my consciousness could merely register it; it was beyond the power of my imagination that I would be not merely a spectator of the unfolding historical tragedy, but also one of those affected by it.

When I remember the year 1940 today, it takes great effort to separate my actual impressions at the time from the way I see things now. One thing was certain: private property was going to be expropriated and nationalized. But the Jews had no alternative. They hoped that in the Soviet Union they would escape with their bare lives. For people like my parents, losing their worldly possessions was not the greatest tragedy. Father told me: "If this regime sticks even partially to its own principle 'From each according to his abilities, to each according to his needs!' then neither you nor I need fear for our livelihood."

I eyed the principles proclaimed by the communists with wariness. Still, in the years to come, I was to realize even in extremely adverse circumstances that knowledge and skill actually do help one to survive in every situation, because they are useful to others as well.

Father no longer had access to his bank accounts in Switzerland and in the U.S., not to mention what he had lost in Latvia. Nevertheless, compared to other people from our social circles, he still had a modest income. I remember Mama joking: "Your sisters always accused me that because of my thoughtlessness and extravagance you never got to have any factories or other properties. Now it's becoming obvious that we were right to live the way we did, and have nothing to regret."

In fact, the material loss was the least important reason for our negative attitude toward the new ruling powers. It was incomparably worse to lose one's freedom, human and civil rights (although these had already been violated during the Ulmanis era) – and the hope that the Baltic states might continue to be a neutral and democratic buffer zone between the aggressive major powers and ideologies, like Sweden or Switzerland.

Several of my girlfriends now became completely helpless, at a loss what to do. For them a future in the security of their family's wealth – big real estate properties and considerable bank accounts – was part of the unshakable order of things. And now an avalanche swept everything with it within a few days and weeks.

My mother faced the changes in our daily life with equanimity and irony. After a tearful farewell, Manya, the maidservant, stopped working for us, and Mama took care of all the household chores with ease and as a matter of course; she was an excellent cook and prepared culinary surprises for us. She scornfully brushed off the complaints she heard from other ladies in her situation.

When I look back today, I have to admit that during the year of the first Soviet occupation my family and I got off comparatively lightly. My father could have been arrested or even murdered, as were many others. He was wealthy enough, had lived in Western Europe for years, and was in contact with influential international financial circles. All of this must actually have made him look suspect and "unreliable" in the eyes of the powers that be.

When, in the fall of 1940, I began studying at the university, I came into contact, for the first time, with Soviet forms and their interminable catalogues of questions. The trickiest question for me referred to hypothetical stays abroad, which in the new social order were considered to be a great sin. I was accused of having spent my childhood not only in Riga, but in Berlin as well.

A detailed account of Father's work could have proved to be another danger. We agreed we would only list two companies for which he worked as a regular consultant: the chemical giant I.G. Farben and the German film company UFA. I suspect that the readers of the form, low-ranking officials of the Riga branch of the NKVD, did not quite know what kind of companies these were, or simply did not consider them to be particularly important. Of course, we couldn't entirely conceal the fact that I had spent my childhood abroad in Western Europe, though I did keep quiet about part of this period. According to my concocted curriculum vitae, I had been in Berlin only as an infant, and had spent my entire school days with Grandmother and Grandfather in Riga. Paris was not mentioned at all.

The strongest shield that protected my father in 1940/41 was a sheet of paper. What a tragicomic paradox! It was a consultant's identity card of the resettlement agency UTAG that dealt with all property rights related to the resettling of Baltic Germans. The first "Back to the Reich" wave had begun in October 1939, directly after the signing of the Molotov–Ribbentrop Pact; nevertheless, a certain number of Baltic Germans who were critical of Hitler had remained in Latvia until the imminent occupation of the Baltic States by the Soviets became a reality. Then – almost without exception – they too left.

Since a nonaggression pact had been concluded between Hitler's Germany and Stalin's Russia, the resettlement could take place peacefully, almost up to the German attack of the USSR in June 1941. A number of Latvians also succeeded in leaving the country after they had somehow managed to produce evidence that they were allegedly Germans.

UTAG remained in operation for a long time during the first Soviet year. It registered the Baltic German properties and settled questions relating to their handover and compensation. The Soviet government did not interfere much in the affairs of Hitler's future subjects and did not prevent them from emigrating. Since the Baltic German lawyers had for the most part already left the country, my father's former schoolmates asked him to advise UTAG on issues of finances and liquidation. His work was based on a private agreement, but the friends arranged for him to get a seemingly official certificate – admittedly one that had not been entered in the German records – that represented an extremely weighty document in Soviet eyes and that the NKVD people respected without further ado. After all, Hitler was considered to be a friend of the USSR and was not even allowed to be publicly criticized at the time.

Latvia's "entrance" into the USSR marked the beginning of the arrest and assassination of all known, including potential and even presumed, political opponents of the Soviet Union. In conjunction with the extermination of Latvia's political elite – not only the supporters of Ulmanis but also his opponents, the supporters of parliamentary democracy, and particularly the Social Democrats – the first merciless blow was directed against the white émigrés. One after another, the editors of the Russian émigré newspapers *Segodnya* (*Today*) and *Segodnya Vecherom* (*Tonight*) – both Russians and Jews – who were good friends of Mama, disappeared. The men were already arrested in the first days and several of them were shot. Mrs. Kharitonov, the wife of the deputy editor-in-chief of *Segodnya*, was a good friend of the family, so I clearly remember the tragic events. Similarly, Sergey Tsivinsky, the paper's famous cartoonist, who used the pseudonym Civis (Latin for citizen), vanished without a trace.

What shocked me no less than the repressions and expropriations were the social changes that went hand in hand with the change of power, the abrupt transformation of people's words and behavior as they unscrupulously conformed to the demands and style of the new rulers. Even at the time I wondered how much of this was lies and hypocrisy and how much was the almost incredible ability to talk oneself into believing one had a different biography. I'm not talking here about dedicated Communists, whose jubilation and belief in a better future I have never held against them. After all, their utopian faith was sincere and honest, even though it did no one any good.

What I did find convincing was the thesis that the six years of Ulmanis' authoritarian rule had indirectly prepared the ground for totalitarianism. The citizens had already grown accustomed to the curtailment of freedom of speech and of opinion; they had come to terms with the creeping abolition of democracy. I also remember muttered discussions about whether it was right not to offer any resistance to the occupation. Hadn't the Finns demonstrated how you resisted a Soviet invasion? Admittedly no one claimed that Latvia's fate could have been averted by armed resistance against the Soviet giant. The situation in Latvia was radically different from conditions during the so-called Winter War of the Soviet Union against the Finns. We were talking about something else: If there was no resistance on the part of the government, even if it were only in the form of an internationally voiced protest, it might appear that the republic of Latvia freely accepted the course of events and recognized their legitimacy. If a Latvian parliament had still been in existence, letters of protest and diplomatic measures at the very least would not have failed to materialize – as they would have elsewhere in the world in similar circumstances.

Of course, at the time I lacked the political knowhow to be able to participate in such conversations. Yet it would become clear that all of us knew far too little. By clinging to the hope that things would not turn out that bad, we did the only thing that was possible: We noted the fact of the Soviet occupation and practiced endurance and survival.

The obtrusive political propaganda, which took on grotesque forms, was repulsive. But there were also artistic and educational initiatives that were very popular with the younger generation. For instance, interdisciplinary circles of amateurs formed at the university that – particularly in the realm of music – were barely politicized. For me, becoming a member of the Komsomol was out of the question; but in order to be active in the cultural field, I joined the student union. We flung ourselves into a life of music, which played an important role at the university as well, and were thrilled when a student orchestra was founded, with which Dima performed piano concertos by Chopin and Liszt; on those evenings I was in heaven, able to forget everything around me.

I can still see the Riga concerts and opera performances during the years from 1939 to '41, without the fateful break in the summer of 1940 – thoroughly enchanting and untouched by the adverse events of the real world. The standard of the singers and instrumentalists, which was already considerable, had been raised even higher by Leo Blech. Blech, a German Jew who was persecuted in his own country, had found refuge in Latvia, where a rich field of activity awaited him. In a conversation with my parents – they had already met Blech briefly when we lived in Berlin – he praised the wealth of talent present in the Latvian music scene in no uncertain terms. Among my most blissful art experiences during those years were the Verdi operas *Aida*, *Il Trovatore* and *Un Ballo in Maschera* conducted by Blech; his crowning achievement was an unforgettable production of Mozart's *Magic Flute* in the beginning of 1940. In this production, in the role of the Queen of the Night, Blech introduced to the surprised audience – which included Dima and myself – the phenomenal coloratura soprano voice of the young Elfrīda Pakule, who was still relatively unknown and to whom opera directors had so far not paid much attention.

Music in those years determined how I felt about being alive. I felt as if the structure of sounds became the protected space in which I lived with the person whose presence had in the meantime become indispensable for me. A highlight was the evening at the end of 1940 when Blech conducted Beethoven's Ninth in the Great Hall of the opera house. We young people sat glued to the balustrade of the third balcony, clutching the thick score in our hands. Never again have I experienced this absolute triumph of the human spirit over the menacing reality that surrounded us as I did in this concert.

It was impossible to shield ourselves totally from real life; every day brought some new event I could not immediately adjust to. Thus, while I had of course already heard that upper middle-class apartments must now be turned into so-called *komunalkas* (communal apartments), I couldn't imagine what it was like being forced to live with total strangers.

Again we were lucky. We were allowed to keep three of our five rooms; a Red Army major and his wife were quartered in the other two. The Noshchinskys came from Leningrad. The major, who was Polish by birth, was an army doctor and, as he emphasized, a professed Catholic. His wife Elisabeth, who was Finnish, came from Karelia and worked as a military hospital nurse.

Immediately after his arrival, when he had put away his luggage, Noshchinsky knocked at our door. My mother opened the door. He mentioned his name and apologized. "I'd like you to know," the major explained, "that in my opinion it is not right to come barging in and take up residence in someone else's apartment. But it is not our own decision, and that is why I can only offer my heartfelt apologies."

The Noshchinskys turned out to be extremely pleasant flatmates, and our relationship was uncomplicated right from the start. We never experienced the enforced closeness as an ordeal. Mother often invited the two of them for coffee, Father occasionally offered them a cognac, and we talked to each other a lot. The conversations soon became quite frank. Noshchinsky's candor did not particularly surprise us at the time. It was not until later that I realized how great a risk he had taken by trusting us and relying on our decency.

The major warned that now, shortly after the invasion of the army, everything was still comparatively peaceful. Repressions without a trial would, for the time being, be directed primarily against politicians, former government officials, and large-scale manufacturers. But the time of mass repressions would inevitably come. "You have no idea what lies ahead," said Noshchinsky.

Around the spring of 1941, when the atmosphere had indeed become much more tense, Major Noshchinsky had already worked out a kind of plan of further action.

"When they come for you, here's what you must do: As soon as there is a knock on the apartment door, your daughter must come into our rooms. We're members of the army, our living space is under the control of a different agency. Without a special order they have no right to search us. You can put jewelry or other valuables that you want to leave for your daughter in our rooms. Initially we shall hide Valentīna, and later we'll say she's our relative. When the mass deportation took place in Leningrad, a certain number of children were saved this way – neighbors took them in."

My parents understood that the major was telling the truth and believed him – though somewhat theoretically, for they were incapable of imagining that it would really come to this.

A seemingly insignificant incident has remained in my consciousness as an eloquent sign of the times. A distant acquaintance of my parents, a well-to-do Riga Jew, was an active Zionist; his wife, Nelly, a quiet, friendly woman, came from Vienna and at twenty-six was considerably younger than he. They had a three- or four-year-old son. The husband was immediately arrested. The family's apartment went to an NKVD officer. He said they should pack as many belongings as they could carry, and clear out.

Nelly spoke no Russian and could also barely understand Latvian; apparently she had no relatives or friends in Riga, and in this situation she and her child were totally helpless. I was asked to accompany her to the housing administration. She had only one request: that she be allowed to keep at least the smallest little room in her apartment, because otherwise she and her child had nowhere to stay. I was her interpreter, and thus, for the first time, I got to visit a Soviet agency. It had been set up in a hurry just recently; it was run by several women who looked and were dressed markedly differently from our women.

One civil servant, obviously local, who as far as I could understand had been in the underground until recently, listened to what we had to say. I saw she was Jewish just like Nelly and I. While I tried to translate, she started yelling: "What is wrong with you? It serves you right, your husband had it coming to him!" She used a number of hackneyed political phrases that had just come into fashion.

And suddenly this Soviet civil servant turns toward the child, who stands before her totally intimidated by the loud, incomprehensible verbal exchange, and says with undisguised hatred, squeezing the words through her teeth, sneering: "Boy, are you in trouble now, *burzhuichik*!" The frightened little boy hid in the folds of his mother's skirt. I still remember this sight as a symbol of that time. Many brutal and cruel things happened in that first year of Soviet rule, relatives and friends were arrested and deported to Siberia, but my most vivid memory is of this little boy, whom I scarcely knew and who hid his face so the hostile world would vanish. At the housing office I directly perceived for the first time how a base soul succumbed to the temptation to enjoy its power over people who had no rights.

When I later heard about the accusations that Jews were primarily responsible for the wrongdoings of 1940/41, accusations that had become dogged clichés, I recalled this scene. The little boy was Jewish just like the screaming civil servant, like his mama and I. What was significant was not the ethnicity or religious affiliation – it was the ideology, the system of power, the allure of impunity that made people into monsters. In many people, the layer of civilization turned out to be alarmingly thin, it was no more than a kind of glaze. Under it lurked base instincts, reined in neither by law nor by education, neither by culture nor tradition nor religion. I clearly saw how people of no account were intoxicated by unexpectedly acquired power, how they enjoyed humiliating others, deciding their fate and even their life and death. As long as I did not yet feel the threat of physical extinction, what most depressed me were the tragicomic changes introduced by the new powers that be, both in cultural life and at the university. The institutions of higher learning were flooded with semi-illiterate, self-opinionated people sent by the Party, who stood at the lectern proclaiming primitive dogmas. I was tormented by anger and regret for this senselessly wasted time, as we were not allowed to skip these "lectures." Incidentally, I would have listened with interest if someone who had scholarly competence had expounded the doctrine of Marxism. I was interested in the structural analysis of capitalism, although I have never been fascinated by the political utopia of communism. But what was offered to us in the Marxism-Leninism course at the university never went beyond the level of "politinformation" at a collective farm.

No doubt other former faculty members also gave lectures, but I remember only Edgars Dunsdorfs, with whom I studied the first two semesters of the history of political economy. He did not disappoint his students, and I became very attached to him.

Until the night of 14th June 1941, many of us had nurtured the hope that the repressions would cease as soon as those whom the regime regarded as hostile or dangerous elements had been taken into custody. After all, they had to end someday. Those who had been spared, though with bitter losses, would begin a halfway normal life in the new circumstances.

June 14th put an end to this illusion.[1] Of course, we had heard about the mass repressions in the Soviet Union, but it was unthinkable that anything similar would happen in our country as well. We also kept clinging to the naïve hope that Vyshinsky's promise and similar promises that in the Baltic states much of our usual way of life would remain unchanged carried weight – for instance, that no collective farm system would be forced upon us.

The first to be affected was Aunt Frieda. Frieda, that merry, witty redhead, was my mother's favorite cousin, and they even looked somewhat alike. Frieda, who had lost her parents early, had before her marriage been a frequent visitor of ours in Elizabetes iela, where she sought refuge in our family nest. To everyone's surprise she finally married a goodhearted, even-tempered, and very much older widower, to whose teenage daughter Frieda became a beloved second mother. Later, the couple had a little daughter, Noemi, who was now four years old. Luckily the stepdaughter had left for Italy on the eve of the Soviet occupation to study art; she remained there and married

---

1. On June 14th a total of 15,424 Latvian citizens were deported; 11.7 percent of them were Jews. At the time the Jewish share of the population was 4.8 percent. Thirteen percent of those arrested during the whole "Year of Horror" were Jews (Source: Marǵers Vestermanis).

one of her professors. As for Frieda's husband, Mr. Finkelstein, he owned a small textile factory, a stable foundation for the small family.

The evening of that fateful June 13th, the Finkelsteins were celebrating a birthday at their villa in Mežaparks, or maybe it was some other kind of celebration (I can't remember exactly). Among the guests was Uncle Žoržik, my mother's brother. The celebration lasted well into the night, and Žoržik spent the night in Mežaparks.

Out of breath, he appeared at our doorstep early the next day. At dawn, a truck had driven up to the Finkelsteins' house, the family was crammed inside and taken away. Žoržik had managed to prove that he was merely a guest, which was also confirmed by the maidservant; after all, his last name and registered address were different.

The deportation of Frieda's family was a shock. At the same time, we were glad that our beloved Žoržik had been spared. Had we known what would happen to him a few weeks later, we would have been sorry that he had not been deported as well.

The bad news followed each other in quick succession.

Among those deported were several girlfriends, and a number of former secondary school and university classmates. We had no doubt that the same fate awaited us. That night in June had changed everything. There was no official information, the newspapers and radio said nothing, the authorities acted as though nothing had happened.

Instead, a word-of-mouth network of information functioned at full tilt. People who were in the know claimed they had found out that once the cattle cars had been emptied at their destinations in Siberia they would return and then the next wave of deportation would follow. In the meantime, such things no longer seemed unthinkable. Major Noshchinsky became even more insistent – we must get ready, he said. In the first place, he said, I must spend the nights in their side of the apartment.

But Dima and I had a different plan. We would get married. Up to that point we had not spoken about this concretely yet; we were so sure of each other that we were not interested in having a stamp in our passports. Now, however, we had to prepare for a totally new situation. We had understood this much: Only if you had a marriage license could you hope, when deported, if not to stay together, then at least to locate each other later on. We were told that in prisons, too, only officially registered family members were given information.

Getting married was very simple in those days: You would register in the morning, produce your "clean passport" (that is, one without the annotation that you were married), and by the afternoon you were married, or rather registered, as this prosaic marriage ceremony was now called. We hadn't told anyone – not until we came home from the registry office that evening did we announce to our parents that we were officially man and wife.

At the registry office we had been given a marriage certificate with which we had to go to the passport office to get the appropriate stamp. Yet we were unable to do so, which was to become unexpectedly important later on. The marriage took place on June 16th. Two months later – in the meantime the German occupation had taken the place of the Soviet one – we got married in a Catholic church.

There was no proper wedding reception, but still a sort of honeymoon: Ludmilla Dmitriyevna invited us to visit her in Priedaine.

In those days, Father again had to stay in bed on account of his old kidney ailment. He was treated by a very good urologist, Dr. Goldberg, whose life partner was a real beauty, a German woman called Margarethe Klaus. Her mother was Latvian. I still remember how terribly afraid she was of being deported, she fervently hoped that Goldberg's reputation as a doctor would save them both from suffering this fate. Not a month later she was to save her Jewish partner – this time from the Nazis, by hiding him and providing him with everything he needed. After the war they were finally able to marry and stayed together the rest of their lives.

The week of June 14th to 22nd passed in chilling expectation. Day after day, the list of deportees we knew about became longer and longer – from the really rich families to merchants and craftsmen and even blue-collar workers. What was most confusing were repressions against working people who simply did not fit the category of bourgeois. Very many of them were Jewish. Their offence, for the most part, was that they had formerly sided with the Jewish Bundists or the Latvian Social Democrats, for which they had already been penalized under Ulmanis.[2] It's a well-known fact that the Bolshevists hated the leftist non-Communists no less than the class enemies. Here again was an expression of the new rulers' strange logic.

It was perfectly obvious to us that the Jews of Riga and of all Latvia were especially hard hit by the actions of June 14th. Soon thereafter, the Nazi propaganda proclaimed that the Jews were responsible for all the atrocities of the NKVD; and in the state of shock at the time, when Latvian society in its pain and despair sought for culprits, many people clung to such manipulative lies.

Until the independence of the Latvian republic was restored half a century later, we were unable to gain an accurate picture of the specific dimensions of the mass deportations of June 14th, 1941; it was gradually assembled from reports and encounters with those who managed to come back. In 1958, Aunt Frieda and her daughter returned from Siberia. Noemi had grown up in the meantime and had graduated from secondary school. Uncle Finkelstein, who had to do heavy labor in the camp, had died there of starvation and cold. Frieda had been lucky enough to meet an acquaintance in her cattle car, Mrs. Nukša, the French wife of a Latvian diplomat. They were taken in by Russian peasants, without whose help they would have perished on the godforsaken collective farm.

In the general confusion and despair after June 14th, only a week passed before the next blow: Hitler attacked his ally Stalin – presumably unexpectedly, although one could draw the conclusion both from the newspapers and from other sources that the love affair between the dictators was nearing its end. Naturally they had a lot in common and had learned a lot from each other or, as the expression goes, compared notes. Nevertheless, their imperial ambitions and economic greed prevailed.

We were to spend only a few days in Priedaine. At the end of June,

---

2. *Bundists:* Jewish organizations advocating socialist goals that went back to the General Jewish Labor Bund (Alliance) in Czarist Russia.

Dima was summoned to Riga: his draft papers had arrived. As a medical student in his last semester, Dima was considered to be fit for military hospital service, although, because he had had infantile paralysis as a child, he was exempted from the regular service. He had overcome the consequences of the disease, except for occasional relapses, by intensive training in various sports. From time to time, he had severe leg cramps. This was considered to be a sufficient reason to exempt him from military service, and as it turned out, it was taken into consideration now as well.

Dima called me from Riga to tell me this news; he said I should get on my bike and come home. It no longer made sense to stay in Priedaine. In the few days that remained until the Nazis occupied Riga, we had to make a decision.

THE LAST ACT BEGINS

When I later thought back a hundred times to the events of that time and tried to figure out what would have happened if we had acted differently, it became clear to me: In order to reach a sensible decision, we dramatically lacked the time. It's true that our minds were not completely paralyzed; and dispassionately they kept telling us only one thing: As Jews we need to escape!

My family should have realized this all the more – after all, we had seen the aggressive antisemitic attacks in Berlin with our own eyes. And since that time the situation, as far as we could judge from a distance, had only gotten worse. But we, our relatives, and friends were virtually numbed by the thought that we should now go of our own free will to the place to which, only a few days ago, our nearest and dearest had been deported – a country about which we had no more illusions, indeed, which to us looked like an anti-world.

The omnipresent loudspeakers simply denied the retreat of the Soviet troops; the radio broadcasted constant requests that people should remain calm, while chaos reigned in the streets. The Soviet government agencies along with their employees and the latter's families fled in panic, and the Red Army, which the propaganda extolled as invincible, beat a retreat, caught unawares and unprepared, disoriented, and disorganized. (During the years of the Great Terror it had lost its most competent leading cadres.)

Although our reason kept warning us that it might be far more dangerous to remain in Riga, we found ever new pretexts for not allowing ourselves to be evacuated to the East together with the fleeing Red Army. We tried to persuade ourselves that things would surely not be that bad. Father did not doubt for a single moment that the U.S. would enter the war and the Allies would jointly overcome Hitler. Until that time, we must wait and endure insults, humiliations, and repressions.

There were also a few existential obstacles to our escape. Our grandparents encouraged us to go, but they themselves refused to leave Riga and move to a menacing foreign country. They said they were practically at the end of their life's journey and therefore didn't have a lot to lose. Mama in turn could not and would not leave her family even now, while it was impossible to organize the evacuation of at least nine persons. What is more, Father was still bedridden because of his kidney problems.

Later, I thought: If there had been merely a two-week interval between the attack on the Soviet Union and the occupation of Riga by the Germans, we would have realized that the point was not whether the Soviet Union was acceptable for us or not. We would have realized that what threatened us was annihilation plain and simple. That in the eyes of the Nazis all Jews, regardless of whether they were rich or poor, of Mosaic or Christian faith, were vermin that must be exterminated.

Dima's family, too, stayed in Riga. After all, his mother was a white émigrée and furthermore had a "suitable" family tree. Two of her brothers lived in the Berlin diaspora. The elder, Alexandr Ozup (Otsoup, as he spelled his name in French exile), was a well-known writer with the pseudonym Sergey Gorny, which became his official name; his daughter was a ballet dancer in a German theater. This uncle of Dima had been living in Berlin since 1922 and publishing his work in the émigré press; he was highly respected in the Berlin Russian Orthodox congregation. Dima's other uncle, Sergey Ozup, had graduated from the czarist military academy and risen to the rank of lieutenant-general of the Czar's Guard, though he was also considered an authority on iconography research. He owned the largest private icon collection in Europe. Both brothers had moved from Berlin to Madrid with their families on the eve of World War Two and remained there the rest of their lives. For the last forty years an old monastery near Madrid has housed an icon museum named after Sergey Ozup (*Exposición de iconos – Colección Sergio Otzoup*).

As soon as Hitler's army had marched into Riga, the Ozup brothers sent Dima and his mother "strong papers," copies of documents that made them secure in regard to both their national and religious affiliation.

Thus we all remained in Latvia: Dima's and my family and most of our closest friends. Almost all of us had lost family members on June 14th, and that was why it was so difficult to cross the fateful threshold – the decision for evacuation to the USSR. Of my schoolmates at the Jewish secondary school and of my fellow students at the university, only a few left the country with the Soviet military. Several classmates joined the army in order to go to battle together with the Western Allies against the criminal Third Reich. People hoped that under the influence of the Allies quite a few things would change in the Soviet system as well... Many members of the Jewish community who had been rooted in the Baltics for centuries stayed in Latvia and paid for their shortsightedness with their lives.

We heard that in Riga and elsewhere in Latvia armed, so-called self-defense groups were proliferating, established on their own initiative. On the highways of Vidzeme, these groups were firing not only at the last Red Army soldiers who were fleeing in chaos, but also at civilians traveling eastwards on trucks, bicycles, or on foot. A year later, one member of such a group, under the influence of alcohol, was to boast in my presence – without knowing who I was – about the "heroic deeds" he had performed at the time. There were also reports about them by individual unsuccessful refugees who had not managed to reach their intended destination. After the fugitives had escaped the "acts of revenge" of the armed units, they returned to their starting point, making their way stealthily alone or in pairs.

In the streets, many Latvians celebrated the arrival of the German troops – under the ludicrous illusion that the Latvian republic would directly be restored. As though the clock would be turned back by a year when the Soviets retreated, as though their former life could be resumed. The new occupiers were supported because they were the adversaries of the previous ones. Later it dawned on me that at the time the Latvians – or at least a part of them – for the first time in their history, were cheering the Germans. Centuries of experience, up to the open rejection of the Hitler state by Ulmanis, had been wiped out by the shock of a single year under the Soviets. Others, however, in a Riga vacated by the Soviet army but not yet occupied by the Germans, were overwhelmed by a feeling of terrible helplessness and the presentiment that our decision to remain here had been a fatal error. The last act in the lives of our families and many like them had begun.

UNDER THE YELLOW STAR

The registration of the Jews of Riga began on July 25th, 1941. They were all issued a special registration card along with the instruction that they wear a six-pointed yellow so-called Star of David, ten centimeters in diameter, attached to their clothing on the left breast. This regulation must be complied with in full by July 28th. At the same time Jews were forbidden to use the sidewalks. On September 1st this was followed by an additional regulation: yellow stars must be attached on the back as well.

Father and Dima did everything in their power to protect Mama and me from direct contact with violence and humiliation. In the months that followed, our freedom of movement ended at the apartment door. Since Father took care of the necessary outside errands, he wore the yellow star like all other Jews. Dima, on the other hand, was not affected by these and subsequent regulations directed against the Jews; as someone who was half Jewish, or "half Aryan," he continued to be a free man.

From the two of them, Mama and I learned what was going on outside. For the most part, in the ensuing months, everything that was happening beyond our four walls reached me only indirectly – as information from a reliable source and from the publications of regulations and laws. I never saw the new rulers and potential murderers face to face. Thus, among other things, I knew that the police (*šucmaņi*, as we soon called all of them, even when they were strictly speaking various units of the Latvian auxiliary police) were expanding their activities and had already become an organized force. They were beginning to plunder the homes of Riga Jews. It became apparent that in Latvia, too (as in Germany), one of the driving forces of antisemitism was plain old envy and greed. The Jews were quite simply declared to be outside the law.

In preparation for a possible deportation, Father had, in the last days of the Soviet occupation, invested all our liquid funds in jewelry and gold coins that could be bartered for food if we were deported. These were predominantly smaller items – rings, chains, bracelets – and watches. Together with Mama's jewelry, they were sewn into two wide leather belts that we women could wear around the waist under our clothes. A kind of secret safe had been installed in the big armchair. This is where, a few weeks later, when she left for the ghetto[1], Mama hid her talisman – the ring given to her by Emanuel Nobel. She hadn't been without it even for a moment for the last twenty years, for she believed that it protected her and brought her good luck. Although I am not particularly superstitious, I did have something like an irrational premonition that this was a portent of bad luck. Perhaps Mama would have done better to take the ring with her.

Even in the first days of July, Latvian police forced their way into my grandparents' apartment in Elizabetes iela. They said they were there as "avengers" – they would now pay the Jews back for the deported Latvians. They swaggered about, called my grandparents communists, and seized a number of valuables. And they took with them my uncle, Žoržik, who had only recently managed to escape deportation.

He was the first in our family to be killed.

The Jewish men, as we found out gradually, were for the most

---

1. The boundaries of the so-called Big Ghetto in Riga ran along Carl Schirren iela (the former and present-day Lāčplēša iela), Jēkabpils iela, Katoļu iela, Lazdonas iela, Lielā Kalna iela, Lauvas iela, Nirzas iela (formerly Žīdu iela, now Ebreju iela), Jersikas iela, and Latgales iela.

part brought to the Latvian prefecture or to the headquarters of the Latvian auxiliary police unit of the German Gestapo (SD) at the corner of Valdemāra and Elizabetes iela. They were beaten up and humiliated. During the first days they were also forced to disinter the hastily buried corpses of the victims of the NKVD, who were then identified and buried in the cemetery. Such scenes were photographed and published, for instance in the Latvian daily newspaper *Tēvija* (Fatherland). This rag was one of the most odious organs of the Nazi collaborators that in its particularly fanatical anti-Jewish propaganda surpassed even the German press, which I was also reading. I remember one caption: "Žīdu bendes pie savu upuru kapiem" ("Jewish executioners by the graves of their victims"). The fate of the gravediggers had been sealed even before the murdered people were identified – they were mostly shot on the spot – and tossed into the pits they had dug themselves or elsewhere. Presumably that was what happened to our Žoržik as well.

From Paul Schiemann, who later hid me, I heard that practically all the bodies of people killed in the last days by the Soviets could be identified – not only those that had been buried but also those that had simply been left unburied by the hastily fleeing Chekists.[2] In the official lists, however, the notation "Unknown" frequently appeared. The reason: The identified Jewish victims of the NKVD must not be named lest the myth of Jews as culprits, as originators of the Soviet crimes, should be shattered. After all, this myth was perfectly suited for manipulating the shocked Latvians and for making them into accomplices in the crimes of the Nazis.

It was at that time that my father – and Mama and I along with him – experienced a sad disappointment. At the end of the 1930s Alfrēds Valdmanis, the then minister of finance of independent Latvia, had consulted Father on legal matters. He was a very pleasant, polite man who brought my mother flowers and paid her compliments. He had a lot of respect for Father, admiring his keen

---

2. Paul Schiemann: *Zwischen zwei Zeitaltern. Erinnerungen 1903-1919*. Bearbeitet und mit einer Einführung von Helmut Krause. Schriftenreihe der Carl-Schirren-Gesellschaft, vol. 3. – Lüneburg: Verlag Nordland-Druck GmbH 1979, 216 pp., with numerous illustrations, soft cover.

mind and skill. Admittedly he asked him apologetically several times not to tell anyone about his visits – if these were made public, it would damage his reputation as a minister. Those who were eager to take his post would use them against him and claim that he took advice on affairs of state from a Jew.

In the Soviet year, 1940, Valdmanis managed to escape the worst. Father, who never discussed at home the information confided to him by his clients, merely mentioned briefly that he'd been able to help his colleague in some way when he went underground. I didn't know any details.

After the Nazi invasion, the ex-minister immediately resurfaced and took up a high-level position in the Latvian self-government established by the Germans. Father decided to have a talk with him, not to ask him for concrete help, but in the hope that Valdmanis was possibly aware of what lay in store for us Jews and thus knew how we should best proceed. However, when Father called him, Valdmanis could ostensibly only vaguely remember him, refused to talk to him and asked him not to bother him in the future. After their years of working together and the former minister's avowals of respect, this was something Father had not expected.

In 2010, in a publication by the Latvian historians' commission, I happened upon a memorandum addressed on 11 July 1941 to the "Leader of the German Reich" by the conference of representatives of Latvian organizations. The 13 points of this paper are a pledge of allegiance and at the same time a request for a certain degree of independence and for incorporation into the Greater German Reich. Under point 9, there is a demand for the "liberation of Latvia from all Jews and fundamentally from Russians and Poles as well." One of the spokespeople of this conference was Alfrēds Valdmanis. He even forestalled the German wishes and anticipated commands. In this context I am reminded of something Hannah Arendt once said: "The problem was not what our enemies did, but what our friends did."[3]

---

3. Quoted from "Was bleibt? Es bleibt die Muttersprache." Günter Gaus in conversation with Hannah Arendt. ZDF, series *Zur Person* of 28 October 1964. Full text: http://www.rbb-online.de/zur-person/interview_archiv/arendt_hannah.html

Another significant episode from the first months of the German occupation is etched in my memory. As I mentioned above, the Latvian so-called auxiliary police, under the pretext that they were looking for suspicious persons and weapons, searched Jewish apartments. Even more, however, most of them were interested in unexpected opportunities to snoop around in the private homes of well-to-do people and to take whatever their hearts desired. As a pretext they used the national struggle, which had taken the place of the class struggle proclaimed during the Soviet period, i.e., the expropriation of the bourgeoisie – though only the Jewish bourgeoisie this time. It was not for nothing that Hitler's Party called itself "socialist."

Among the looters there were quite a number of primitive folks who perhaps had formerly felt they themselves were marginalized. With particular relish they taunted intelligent, well-to-do, and educated Jews, not forgetting to insult them by calling them communists, who they said were to blame for the deportations and shootings under the Soviets.

One evening our doorbell rang. Father opened the door: Outside stood two uniformed men with red-white-and-red armbands. One was slightly drunk, a middle-aged man, from Latgale judging by his dialect, the other maybe a few years older than me. They came into the apartment. The younger man said nothing, but the older one talked without interruption, and made himself pretty comfortable: "Hey, boss, how about some refreshments?" Father went and got a bottle of cognac and Mother prepared a snack. The policeman was not in an aggressive mood, and in his tipsy condition he didn't feel like making the rounds of the rooms. After helping himself to more cognac, he demanded: "And now cough up what you stole from the Latvians!" And as though this was a first-class joke, he added with a laugh: "In any case, you won't be needing your gold jewelry anymore!" Father brought a couple of watches and rings. The older man seemed satisfied and turned back to the cognac. The younger one had held back all this time, which is why the other man had a sudden idea: "Listen, have the young lady show you the other rooms!

If there's anything that takes your fancy, help yourself!" he said with a suggestive wink.

Girls and young women were especially vulnerable, since the robberies were often accompanied by rapes. This had recently happened to my classmate Angelika, a pretty redhead, who had been raped in a gateway by three drunken policemen and almost lost her mind as a result of her experience. She too was later killed in the ghetto.

I felt uneasy. Dima was not at home, but at his parents' house. I got up and went with the younger guy. He closed the door behind us and said: "Don't be afraid, miss, you have nothing to fear from me. Please excuse what's happening here." I sensed that he was unhappy, in despair even. We started talking.

On June 14th his whole family had been deported. When the Germans invaded Latvia, he immediately rushed off to join the auxiliary police as a volunteer, out of his mind and filled with hate and thirst for revenge. Now, a couple of weeks later, he had realized with horror what a huge mistake he had made by participating in the unjustifiable "punishment" of people who had not the slightest thing to do with the Bolsheviks' crimes. It was obvious that he detested his companion, who was acting like a common robber. But the young man also knew that he could not correct his misstep all that easily, for paramilitary units of this type do not simply release their people; if he quit, he would draw suspicion to himself. That's why he had decided to volunteer as soon as the Germans began sending Latvians to the front. There, he said, they would be facing armed soldiers, not helpless women and children.

This meeting meant a lot to me. It helped me to remain confident that salvation can beckon even in seemingly hopeless situations. During the next three years, when I had lost everything and anybody could have betrayed and destroyed me if they had wanted to, I experienced for the first time in my life what it means when people keep compassion, courage, and decency in their soul. It sounds like a paradox, but during this inhuman period, of all times, I was to learn that humaneness, too, is a reality. The young guy whom I encountered by chance at a critical moment – I know neither his name nor what became of him – contributed in his own way to my keeping this faith alive despite everything.

EMĪLIJA

About two months after getting married at a registry office, Dima and I had decided to get married in church as well; at the time we were still hoping this would protect me from persecution. We were married in the Mater Dolorosa Church near Riga Castle. Immediately before the ceremony I was baptized as a Catholic: The godmother-cum-witness was Emīlija Gajevska, who devoted herself to her new duties with an enormous sense of responsibility and seriousness.

Emīlija, my guardian angel.

We had known each other since my childhood. Back then she was the housekeeper of the lawyer Andrzej Blankenstein, Father's colleague and erstwhile business partner. My mother was his ideal, the love of his life, on whose account he had remained single. He became a close friend of our family and often came to visit us. Blankenstein, the offspring of a Jewish-Polish family, was the Swiss honorary consul in Riga during the last years of Latvian independence. It was to be hoped that even during the German occupation he would not be at particular risk.

Between Blankenstein and Emīlija, an unusual relationship had come to develop. The elderly woman, who had had a primary school education at best, proved to be so charismatic a personality that she not only had a profound impact on her employer but on everyone else who met her. Emīlija was a holy person in her love and humility – and in her unshakable conviction that God had sent her to serve people. You could always sense that she stood above the hustle and bustle of daily life.

Since Blankenstein often visited at our house, it was quite natural that she came with him. In Vidus iela my parents were no longer able to give big parties, but on the rare occasions when a larger number of guests had to be invited, Emīlija came and helped our Manya. She became very fond of our family and especially me. She had no children of her own.

Gradually, Emīlija told me her life history.

As a girl she had dreamed of becoming a nun and joining a convent, but it had been God's will that she was born as the oldest daughter of a poor family with many children, and this meant that she started working early to help raise her younger siblings. Like many other girls from Latgale, Emīlija had come to Riga to find a job and had later brought one of her younger sisters, Marija, to join her; this sister later got married and had four children. Marija's husband, Juzefs Karčevskis, also came from Latgale and worked as a janitor in a large apartment house in Riga's Old Town. This family, too, was to play an important role in my life later on.

Blankenstein was well-to-do and paid Emīlija a handsome salary, which for the most part was sent to Latgale and also supported Marija's large family. As the years went by, Emīlija's wardrobe hardly changed; only when an item of clothing was completely worn out was it replaced by one that was like it or very similar. She had everything she needed: a winter and summer overcoat, a woolen dress for winter and a cotton one for summer, most of them black, and she always wore a headscarf, also black, but with white dots. Emīlija was gaunt, small in stature, had a dark complexion and dark hair that was already turning gray. Her voice was soft and soothing. She spoke Latvian with a strong Latgalian accent.

In her free time Emīlija did amazingly lovely embroidery work, especially for the decoration of her church. Once I saw a cover she had made to be placed under a small statue of the Virgin Mary – a real work of art.

Emīlija loved and felt pity for all people, but there were some who were especially dear to her heart. One of them was Mr. Blankenstein, whom she apparently treated almost like her own son – she felt his frivolous lifestyle very keenly. He had never married, but occasionally had women friends who would disappear again without further ado a while later. Once a beautiful Hungarian dancer took up residence in Blankenstein's home for a longer period; she had remained in Riga after a guest appearance because of this love affair. Emīlija liked this young woman and tried to convince her employer to marry her.

"It doesn't matter that she's a dancer," she said, "apart from that she's a nice Catholic girl." Emīlija was very indignant that Blankenstein, in her opinion, was leading women by the nose but had excluded the idea of founding a family from his life program.

For Emīlija everything was clear and simple, she knew the difference between good and evil, and there was indeed great wisdom in her worldview and conviction.

It was Emīlija's dearest wish that I should be baptized. She wished this for everyone she loved and considered to be a good person.

When Dima and I got married, I did not want to play the hypocrite, and openly admitted to both the priest, Ādams Buturovičs, and Emīlija that it was only circumstances that had led me to get baptized and married in church, and that I would not observe the rituals.

"I believe there is a God," I said, "but people come to him in different ways, and for each individual the relationship to God is deeply personal."

The wise priest, Emīlija's father confessor, received my words favorably, and she herself did not seem especially disturbed. Later too, after all the trials we faced, I unmistakably sensed Emīlija's conviction: "So what if the child doesn't go to confession and pray – she's suffered so much that God will forgive her."

When, before the marriage ceremony, I entered the empty church, I discovered a man in Wehrmacht uniform in the farthest corner. I was startled. Father Buturovičs reassured me: "Don't worry, he's a military priest, you have nothing to fear from him. He will neither say anything nor report this." Later, too, I got the impression that the Catholic Church, with whose representatives I came into contact several times, made every effort to follow God's commandments and not the demands dictated by the regime. Although the Vatican gave in to the pressure of fascism to a certain extent (half a century later, Pope John Paul II was to apologize for this), many Catholic priests in Europe did not obey the Nazis; it was not just a few who, within the limits of their possibilities, supported those who were innocently persecuted and doomed to die. In Latvia, too, the Catholic Church, with Bishop Jāzeps Rancāns at its head, did a great deal to save individual Jews during the German occupation. That is my personal experience. It is the moral courage and decency of individuals to which people like myself owe their idea of the power of faith.

Among Riga Catholics, Emīlija's voice carried weight. I sensed that she was an intermediary between the Church and those who needed help. Already during the first Soviet occupation Emīlija had helped people who were persecuted; it was she who had found our acquaintance and her little boy a place to stay after the two were thrown out of their apartment by the Soviet authorities. When the Germans occupied Riga, Emīlija immediately came to our house.

As I recalled this later, it occurred to me that she was, as it were, taking up a post that she did not leave until the moment when I could again move freely in the streets. Without Emīlija I would not have survived. And I'm not the only one. Since Emīlija never spoke about it, I can only speculate how many people she helped; among those I knew were my classmate Riva Šefere, her mother, and brother.

Naturally Emīlija's first priority was Mr. Blankenstein, but since at least initially it seemed he was in no danger, she took our family, in addition to other people, under the wings of her unremitting care. In the first months, together with Father and Dima, Emīlija spared us having to leave the house and being exposed to humiliation and jeers on the street: she ran the necessary errands and brought us news that became more and more horrifying. Every day Jewish citizens were deported from their homes or picked up on the street, only to vanish without a trace. Everybody understood what that meant.

Even before the Riga Jews were forced into the ghetto, a boy named Boris Kliot showed up at the house of acquaintances of ours who had managed to escape from the prefecture. His shocking report reached us as well. I barely knew him; he had been a student at the Esra-Gymnasium, one grade below me. He had been able to escape because one of the guards at the entrance happened to be a student at the ballet school where Boris was attending a class. At the first opportunity, the guard took him aside, opened a back door and hissed at him: "Beat it, as fast as you can!"

Particularly shocking was a scene described by Boris that I can still visualize as if I had seen it with my own eyes: Old, gray-haired Jews were forced to sweep the floor with their beards and to lick it with their tongues. Later I read that similar sadistic methods were also documented during the power orgies of German and Hungarian, Romanian and Croatian Nazis.

HUSBANDS AND WIVES

In the spring of 1941, the Soviet authorities had started replacing the passports of the Latvian Republic with Soviet passports. As in most European countries, there was no annotation regarding ethnic affiliation in Latvian passports, while the passport holder's religion was recorded unless the holder expressly objected. Baptized Jews who according to their passport were considered to be Catholic, Russian Orthodox, or Lutheran would thus potentially have had a chance of surviving under the Nazi regime. In the new Soviet passports, the ethnic nationality (i.e., even Jewish ethnicity) had to be recorded. For Jews this was tantamount to a death sentence.

When the National Socialist occupation succeeded that of the Soviets, only part of the population had new passports – and many were left completely without papers because they had handed in their Latvian passport in order to be issued a Soviet one, but hadn't received it yet. In Riga, however, the process of passport replacement had by and large been concluded. Dima, according to his Soviet passport, was Russian. As I mentioned already, circumstances for him were favorable, and he was left alone. In fall he could continue his studies at the university in peace.

For mixed marriages there were special laws. In Germany, Jews who were married to "Aryans" were persecuted less radically almost until the end of the regime. Initially the Jewish spouses had to stay at home quietly and unobtrusively. After the beginning of the war, they often had to do heavy forced labor, mainly for the arms industry. German men with Jewish wives were excluded from public life and could not hold leading positions. Quite a few men separated from their wives in order to keep their social standing. In Latvia, however, from the start, much more brutal regulations were in effect: Women categorically had to separate from their Jewish husbands, and they had no choice but to obey the order – or to hide their husbands. A relatively large number managed to save their partners; I know several such families. A Latvian or "Aryan" husband of another ethnicity, in turn, could officially keep his Jewish wife only if she got sterilized – otherwise she had to go into the ghetto and thus to her death.

The procedure was quite regularly done in hospitals and documented in their files.

This cynical law, which promoted blatantly immoral actions, could change people's destinies for the rest of their lives.

Just before the war, when I visited Aunt Edith in Liepāja (renamed Libau during the Nazi occupation) I met a classmate of my older cousin who was a student at the First City Gymnasium. Marija or Mura, as she was called, came from a middle-class Jewish family. Even while at school she was head over heels in love with a young physician, a Latvian, and during the first Soviet year the two got married. Under the Germans Mura's husband, who worked as a doctor at the Liepāja hospital, was compelled to agree to the forced sterilization of his wife in order at least to save her life. Mura's entire family was murdered, she was the only one to survive. The war ended, the Soviet power returned, and life went on.

I met the two again in the early 1950s. They were working successfully in the medical field and despite their enforced childlessness were a harmonious couple. It looked as if together they had managed to overcome the severe trauma. But Mura confessed to me that the pain of her humiliation and mutilation had never let up. As the years went by, her husband's irrepressible desire for a child of his own had grown. A young nurse bore him a son. He officially divorced Mura, but without separating from her, and married the child's mother. From then on, they lived as a family in the doctor's large apartment. Mura loved her husband's little son with all her heart and looked after him while his mother went to work. It was admirable how selflessly she rose above her fate. The nurse knew that her husband had been divorced only on account of the child.

Initially she seemed to be reconciled to this situation, but very soon she began to resist. One can understand her as well. It wasn't difficult for her to make Mura's life unbearable by treating her like a servant and ordering her around. What was most painful for Mura was that she was soon forbidden even to come close to the child. Finally she realized that it was up to her to take the decisive step.

In our conversations Mura never complained, but rather worried about her husband, who had become depressed in this monstrous situation. Yet more important to her than everything else was the child's welfare. She decided to withdraw from her former husband's life altogether, and went to Riga. Soon thereafter, she had the unexpected opportunity to emigrate. How she managed this is another story and a scenario for an adventure film.

Now all the protagonists of this sad story are dead, which is why I have taken the liberty to recount one of the protracted, quiet dramas caused by an inhuman regime.

When Mura's story began in the summer of 1941, the question of marriage was an urgent concern for me as well. Admittedly, Dima and I didn't have to rack our brains: According to the provisions of those who fought for "racial purity," there was no alternative for so-called half-Jews – everything was strictly and unmistakably regulated. If a half-Jew married an "Aryan" woman, he was from that point himself considered an "Aryan"; on the other hand, if he married a Jewish woman, he lost his own rights and was considered to be a "full-blooded Jew." I was overwhelmed by a grave responsibility. It was clear what was in store for Dima if anyone found out we were married. But he didn't even admit the thought that for the sake of his own safety he would break off all contact with his "wrong" choice of a wife. What should I do? I offered to go to the ghetto when the time came. Dima regarded this offer as an insult.

Faithful and chivalrous, without wasting words, he consciously chose inescapable danger.

Fortunately, only very few people knew of our marriage. At the university, nobody was aware of it. It hadn't been entered in the house book but existed only in the records of the registry office. Thus there was nothing left for Dima to do but to continue to keep his marital status secret. He was prepared to protect me to the last.

In the meantime, the building at Vidus iela 9 stood almost vacant. A few German Baltic families had been called "home to the Reich" back in 1939 as "Baltic Germans," other residents had been deported by the Soviets, and others again had been evacuated to Russia. The officers of the Red Army, who had confiscated some of the apartments, had also disappeared, to be replaced by members of the German Wehrmacht. In the two rooms of our apartment that were closest to the entrance – Father's study and the salon – a captain, a middle-aged man, took up his quarters. His orderly was housed in a basement apartment.

At about the same time we took in Mr. and Mrs. Babst and their twelve-year-old daughter Natasha. Because the family had by chance been visiting in Riga on June 13th and 14th, they escaped deportation. The Russian-born Andrey Babst had fled from the USSR and was one of "those who didn't return home." Many years ago he had come to Liepāja for what was to have been a short visit, only to remain there for good. He had married a Liepāja woman, Vera Michelson, the daughter of an old established, wealthy Jewish family. She had been the first wife of Cilia's husband, Roman; the two had been divorced amicably after a short marriage.

The night of June 14th, Vera's entire family was deported – her parents, her brother, his wife Lucia, who was Italian, and their little son. Thus the Babsts remained in Riga. At first my grandparents gave them a place to stay at Elizabetes iela 23, but later, shortly before my parents went to the ghetto, the Babsts came to Vidus iela.

The whole house was officially under the charge of the Wehrmacht, although local people still lived in some of the apartments. Unexpectedly, the captain turned out to be a quiet, polite, and honorable man. He never even mentioned our being

Jewish or referred to the situation resulting from this fact. That could have been interpreted in various ways, yet his emphatically polite conduct, especially toward us women, indeed his behavior in general, testified to the fact that he was no ardent supporter of Hitler. Since the entire apartment was considered to have been handed over to the Wehrmacht, the Latvian auxiliary police we called *Schutzmänner* and the Latvians called *šucmaņi* were not authorized to enter it during their raids without a specific order.

The Hauptmann, as we all addressed him without mentioning his name (which has therefore not remained in my memory), worked for the economic organization for Eastern Europe, whose mission was the exploitation of the Ostland (or Baltic region): It was in charge of transporting food and other goods to Germany. The fruit of the land and of labor streamed into the Reich by the trainload, and the Hauptmann accompanied these transports, being responsible for their safety. He took no notice when the Babst family appeared in our apartment.

The drivers of the high-ranking officers quartered in the house, who lived in two basement apartments and with whom Dima sometimes used to chat, said that the Hauptmann came from an East Prussian military family and adhered to the traditional custom of not fighting civilians. He spared the people who had found refuge in our home that summer additional suffering and humiliation.

GHETTO

Already in early August 1941 work began in Riga's so-called "Moscow Suburb" setting up an enclosed zone, referred to as a "ghetto" modeled on the separate, though by no means hermetically sealed-off residential quarters of the Jews in many medieval European cities. On August 23d, 1941, there was an official announcement that a ghetto had been formed. All Riga Jews were notified that they had to move there; they were allowed to bring as much as each of them could fit into a suitcase or cart, all the rest had to be left behind in their homes. I wrote down the orders and regulations issued after this date, which, with German thoroughness, documented the ordeals of Riga Jews – and thus of my family as well – in a little notebook, with tiny letters, so that I could use it as long as possible. Together with my later notes, I kept it like a treasure in a pocket of the linen belt I mentioned earlier. The notes were in a shorthand I had invented myself. I managed to preserve these inconspicuous papers until the autumn of 1950. During a search by the KGB of what was then my apartment in Riga, an old canister I kept in a desk drawer was confiscated; its contents were of inestimable value for me – they consisted of these copies and notes, but also of the last short letters and notes from my family. These relics, which were so important for me, were thus lost forever, but they have remained in my memory the rest of my life.

On October 23d, the area was fenced with barbed wire by order of Mayor Hugo Wittrock. Its only connection with the rest of the city was a single gate, which was guarded by the Latvian auxiliary police.

My own connections to the outside world were Dima, whose university vacation had just begun, and Emīlija (and, to a lesser extent, Andrey Babst and individual visitors), who walked around town a lot and saw what was happening. They had observed the following: Public opinion had gradually perceptibly changed. For many people, enthusiasm regarding the supposed liberators had given way to disillusionment, for those who did not indulge in self-deception realized pretty soon that the Germans had not the least intention of restoring Latvian independence. Latvian self-government agencies were formed, and a new social elite emerged that made common cause with the leading German cadres.

While the front had moved farther east, war is war, and life had become incomparably more complicated. Only few goods were freely available; the bill of fare of the townspeople became more and more meager, while farmers were burdened with heavy tithes. Latvian foodstuffs rolled toward the eastern front and to Germany. A new expression appeared in people's vocabulary: *black market*. In order to supplement their sparse rations, the townspeople began to roam through the countryside, exchanging all kinds of objects of value for food. This was prohibited but continued all through the German occupation. Emīlija and her sister, too, occasionally took this risk; it was not possible to stop the barter trade, they said.

Coexistence with the Germans gradually became routine. On the whole, life went on as usual, people got accustomed to the fact that somewhere farther away there was war.

People had a roof over their heads and went about their work. Some had found a job with civilian organizations or continued to work in the factories that were now under German management. They crammed for their exams or studied at the university, celebrated modest holidays, allowed themselves to have fun and entertainment. Cultural life resumed, after the summer break concert halls, theaters and museums reopened their doors, and a few publishing houses also resumed production.

But in the very center of Riga, as though in another dimension, there was a group of thirty thousand people, isolated like lepers, with whom all contact was taboo. The majority, which lived a normal life, tried not to notice them. The Latvians had their own problems.

Emīlija said that many people consoled themselves with the thought that things wouldn't be that bad. So what? Let the Jews with their yellow stars walk in the gutter, lock them up in the ghetto, that's simply Hitler's policy, what can you do ... Let them live in the ghetto, they'll get used to it. In the countryside, meanwhile, all the Jews had already been murdered. And later, when the mass murders had taken place in Riga as well, most citizens behaved like the three famous monkeys: See no evil, hear no evil, speak no evil.

To be sure, neither Dima nor Emīlija were in contact with fervent supporters of the Nazis, for instance with members of the Pērkoņkrusts movement[1], which had been forbidden under Ulmanis – fanatical supporters of fascism in its worst – i.e., German –version who had briskly started up their activities again and profited by cooperation with their new masters.

When, after nine months spent in hiding in Vidus iela, I came into contact with the life of the "normal" people again, I was surprised how exactly the idea I had formed based on the accounts of Dima and Emīlija, plus what I had read in newspapers and magazines, corresponded with reality.

And then came the day when my parents had to go to the ghetto. Naturally I too was on the list, and thus the decent janitor, Oboļēvičs, entered into the house book: "All three have gone to the ghetto."

I remember the last conversation with my mother. We sat in the kitchen, and I wept uncontrollably. Mama could not stand such emotional outbursts, and I had learned long since to control myself. But at that moment I was incapable of doing so.

---

1. *Pērkoņkrusts* (Latvian for "thunder cross," a traditional symbol in Latvian folklore, known elsewhere as a swastika): an organization founded on 12 May 1933 that merged with the Latvian National Association (*Latviešu Tautas Apvienība*), which had been outlawed one month previously.

My mother had never seemed as beautiful as she was on the day I saw her for the last time. Completely calm, she sat on the kitchen chair like a queen on her throne. She was forty-two but looked much younger. Those who didn't know often thought she was my older sister. Father was older than she, at the end of his forties, a man in the prime of life.

Mama's Russian émigré friends had offered to hide her temporarily in their summer house in Jūrmala. It seemed one had a better chance of not being discovered there than in the Riga apartment buildings, where there were eyes and ears everywhere. Nevertheless, a certain number of Jews did survive in the anonymity of the large city. But Mama categorically refused to hide. As always, she justified this with clear, simple, downright archaic principles. As though it were today, I can hear her calm words: "I've lived as I liked and have gone my own way, sometimes even separate from your father. But we should go to our death together." At that moment I understood that Mother cherished neither hopes nor illusions – while Father was still trying to maintain optimism.

She concluded this conversation, our last, by repeating her unshakable decision: "I forbid you to come with us. I'm going with my husband, and you must stay with yours. He wants to prove he's a real man. You can't refuse him that. For Father and me it will be easier if we know you're alive."

I didn't know what to do. It felt like betrayal to stay while my parents left, but I also realized Mother was right. She sensed, no, she knew that both of them would die. Father was still speculating – the U.S. would enter the war and the armed forces of the USSR would rally, Hitler's defeat was inevitable, and until that time we must keep on going. Put up with humiliation, hunger, forced labor, whatever – but at that time (like many others) he couldn't imagine that everybody without exception would be killed. Father continued to think logically and reasonably. But the time of reason had ended long ago.

Mama left the house elegantly dressed, as beautiful and proud as ever. Only the yellow star bore witness that nothing would save her from human infamy. Father hugged me tight, and with a smile, gave me one of the stoics' favorite words of wisdom as a parting gift: "*Perfer et obdura!*"[2] And as I forced myself to control my face, which was contorted by crying, I responded in the same spirit: "*Superanda omnis fortuna ferendo est.*"[3] Talking in quotations had always been one of our favorite amusements in the old days, in a time that now seemed like a blissful dream.

Dima's parents were struggling with problems of their own. It seemed they were hopelessly at loggerheads; for a while they had even divided the apartment into two halves. But in reality they loved each other dearly, only the father was constantly getting entangled in some sort of love affairs, while the mother was insanely jealous, suffered from depressions, and occasionally had nervous breakdowns. Yet it did not even occur to either of them to get divorced. In the face of mortal danger all their disagreements and quarrels were forgotten.

Yevgenia Osipovna herself was basically not in danger. After all, her brothers had sent her "Aryan" family documents. But, panic-stricken and impractical as she was, it was too much for her to find a hiding place for her husband and to protect him. It seemed easier for her to sacrifice herself out of love. This was a decision that was fully in keeping with her fatalistic Russian nature. She did not even exploit the trump card of her documents. Dima's father, on the other hand, naturally objected to his wife – who of course did not have to go to the ghetto – accompanying him there. Thus they argued once again and then left together after all, never to return.

It was in those days that all the rest of my relatives also moved to the ghetto. My grandparents and Raja with eleven-year-old Alexander (whose father Žoržik had already been murdered) left the apartment in Elizabetes iela 23, the cozy nest of my childhood. Cilia joined them with her husband, Roman, her ten-year-old son, Jacky, and her mother-in-law. There, in the cramped space of the ghetto, all of them – including my parents – lived together in a tiny apartment and supported each other.

---

2. Be patient and tough (Ovid).
3. Every misfortune can be overcome by endurance (Virgil).

Father's relatives also complied with the order. Grandfather had died long ago; living at Oma Rebekka's were Father's brother, Max, who looked so incredibly like him, and his disabled older sister, Lonni. I've already mentioned that Mama and I were not particularly close to this family. Father's mother was a good person, she had devoted her whole life to the family, the children, but we found her views unacceptable. She also interfered massively in my uncle's life. Unlike my mama's family, Rebekka had a whole series of bourgeois prejudices, including against members of other ethnic groups. Uncle Max was officially considered to be unmarried and had a room in his mother's household, but every one of his relatives knew that at the same time, for years, he had been living with his woman friend, or common-law wife, as she was then called. As the mother saw it, there were two important things wrong with her: One, she was Latvian and two, she was divorced, and on top of everything she had a little son from her first marriage. The family of Max's woman friend was also opposed to this relationship. As soon as Max began to speak of getting married, his mother would get a heart attack, and finally the topic of marriage disappeared from the agenda. Later I wondered whether Max's girlfriend might have been able to save her husband, as many a Latvian wife of a Jewish husband managed to do.

Later, when my parents were no longer alive, a strange period began when I found it difficult to order my emotions and thoughts. Our apartment, too, seemed alien to me. It no longer had any of its former character, even the remaining furniture seemed to have lost its familiarity. The apartment was now divided into three: Two rooms were inhabited by the new owner, the Hauptmann, and two by the Babst family. The back room officially belonged to Dima, and I also lived there illegally. For nine claustrophobic months – until May 9th, 1942 – it was transformed into my hiding place.

Riga janitors had been instructed to deregister all residents who had moved to the ghetto by entering the annotation "moved – destination unknown" in the house book. Even then, the powers that be made sure they would leave as few traces and evidence of their crimes as possible. Our janitor, Aleksandrs Oboļēvičs, however, clearly and legibly entered: "Went to the ghetto." When in October

1949 my legal existence resumed, it was owing to this entry in the house book that I got my papers and a place to stay. Incidentally, Oboļēvičs had initially believed I had actually gone to the ghetto; when he realized very soon that I was still living in Vidus iela, he was as silent as a grave. Not long ago Marģers Vestermanis, the tireless researcher of Jewish destinies in Latvia, told me that our janitor Oboļēvičs had later hidden the musician Salomon Ostrowski in his home for a while before taking him to Žanis Lipke.[4]

We had nothing to fear from the Hauptmann. It was obvious that my parents' fate had affected him. He said to Dima: "If you need any concrete (and he emphasized this word particularly) help, let me know without fail." When we occasionally met in the hallway, he casually said hello. As though it was a matter of course that I was still here. Unfortunately, the Hauptmann was usually away on business; if he had stayed in Riga more, we would have felt safer – and perhaps some of what happened later would have turned out differently.

Dima continued his studies as though nothing had changed. Daily he met people with very different views and attitudes, which is why he had to be constantly on guard and practically trained himself to hide his true thoughts and feelings. The last semesters of medical school are no bowl of cherries. Illnesses and their treatment are not subject to politics, and the students and professors had neither the time nor the desire to think about political doctrines. That's why Dima's studies were bearable from a moral point of view as well.

Life without papers was extremely dangerous, so that anyone who was at all able to do so tried to obtain some. Because the passport exchange had been discontinued at the beginning of the German occupation, many people asked local authorities to issue them replacement IDs. These were valid for six months. That meant that there was a chance of acquiring such papers for those who were persecuted, like Jews or escaped Soviet prisoners of war. Dima tried

---

4. *Žanis Lipke* (1900-1987), a dockworker in Riga who smuggled many Jews out of the ghetto and, supported by his family and two dozen helpers, saved them from being murdered by the National Socialists. In 1977 he was honored as one of the "Righteous Among the Nations." A memorial was opened in 2013 in the house in Riga where he had lived.

every way he could to contact the appropriate people, which was not simple because rules of secrecy had to be observed.

During that period a man who knew Dima's mother, a naturalized older Russian émigré, visited us from time to time. Ivanov worked for a Latvian local government agency where issues of citizenship and ethnicity were settled. He was not a supervisor, but just an ordinary civil servant. He told my husband he could get papers for me. Ivanov constantly kept saying that security demanded large expenses, and we gave him money without a murmur. Over time, Ivanov wangled a sizable sum from us. What is more, he repeatedly offered to hide our valuables, which he would return to us once the danger was over. Dima trusted him – after all, this was an old acquaintance of his mother – I, on the other hand, felt uneasy. Ivanov bragged that thanks to his connections with the Latvian police he could protect me perfectly... But he didn't even get me a replacement ID. It was others who did that.

They too were Dima's acquaintances – several young guys who worked at the Latvian prefecture. They had managed to get hired to work directly in the department that was responsible for temporary IDs – with the secret goal of providing false papers for people who were at risk. The group was headed by Yuriy Perov, a lighting technician at the Riga Russian Theater. His lovely wife, Irina Zoppi-Perov, was a Russian actress who originally came from Italy. The Perovs were close friends of the Babsts.

According to the false genuine document I kept my first name, but borrowed the last name of Major Noshchinski, whom we held in good remembrance. Besides, this name could also be found in our house book. Now I was Polish – Valentina Noshchinska. At any rate, for at least a few months there was hope I would safely survive whatever inspections there were. Soon thereafter, the underground group was discovered, in April 1942, I believe. They were all arrested and shot.

During this period Emīlija became irreplaceable for us. She had acquaintances everywhere, even at the Central Prison and in the prefecture. Conscious that during this time of trials God had given her the task of saving human lives, Emīlija felt so strong that she feared nothing and no one. It's almost a miracle that nothing actually happened to her. That was when I learned that it is primarily fear that makes you vulnerable and destroys you. Countless times, Emīlija took a risk on my account, but I did not torment myself with self-reproaches that she had to suffer fear – she was quite simply fearless.

Emīlija came to us, told us what was going on in the city and in the ghetto, and sometimes even brought little letters or notes from my relatives. I myself had no direct contact with the residents of the ghetto. I only received occasional news and heard the reports of people who had escaped. In my thoughts, in my imagination, I lingered with them, but could not share their cruel fate. I was spared the humiliations and physical pain, blood and deadly terror that those who were nearest and dearest to me were doomed to suffer.

The short letters our intermediaries were able to bring us now and then reported that the Jews did not let themselves be beaten down and even in this situation did not sink into a chaos of despair, but endeavored to maintain order and cleanliness. The Jewish Council (*Judenrat*), which had been set up in the meantime, had organized a medical service headed by an acquaintance of our family, the legendary surgeon Professor Vladimir Mintz.

Dima, in turn, had heard something about the Jewish ghetto police who were in charge of keeping order there – among them there were said to be young men who were secretly organizing a center of resistance in the Riga ghetto. Later they planned an armed uprising, knowing full well that there was no question of victory, but at least they wanted to drag down as many opponents as possible into death with them. The plan failed, and I have great respect for these fearless men who had the courage to rise up against a vast superior power. I did not learn about all this until much later, however.

The news became more and more alarming. It was clear that something terrible was imminent. Emīlija had found a few trustworthy people – devout Catholics, men of conscience – even among those who had been detailed to guard the ghetto. Through them we were able to send our people food and twice even valuables.

Every morning the able-bodied Jewish men were led in columns to various work assignments at the request of different Wehrmacht units. The luckiest were the "barracked" Jews, that is, those who worked in Wehrmacht workshops and spent the night there. The army needed not only shoemakers and tailors but also various other master craftsmen. Men who had previously learned no trade tried to acquire the necessary skills in order to work. Women were employed as cleaners and seamstresses. Among others, my classmate Riva Šefere together with her mother and brother had been assigned to a Wehrmacht barracks. They too, were later helped by Emīlija; Riva's brother even hid for one day in the home of Bishop Rancāns, who subsequently found him a long-term hiding place.

Emīlija or her brother-in-law Juzefs Karčevskis had found out the route along which the men were taken to work and back; they waited for them to pass and, pretending they had met them by chance, were able to exchange a few words with them and slip them small packages. My father and Cilia's husband, Roman, had been assigned to a group that was taken to work outside the ghetto in the mornings and therefore received somewhat larger food rations.

It became more and more difficult to give anything even to those who were marched through town as forced laborers – not to mention those who were penned up like lepers behind barbed wire. Signs posted in many places showed how dangerous it was even to approach the ghetto. In German and Latvian, they read as follows (I've copied the inscription from a historical photograph): "Persons who climb over the fence or attempt to communicate with the inmates of the ghetto will be shot without warning." Daily, Emīlija told us about this problem. We had agreed that Dima must not show his face near the ghetto; he must outwardly display the same indifference and ignorance that the Latvians of Riga had adopted as their normal behavior. What happened behind this façade was undoubtedly very different for each individual.

Through the grapevine, Emīlija had heard a few things about my mother: that even in the ghetto everybody looked on her as on a miracle; that despite everything that was happening she radiated peace and equanimity to the very end. In her presence people were able to draw strength, she was a model of how to endure without falling into despair, of how to preserve one's self-respect and dignity. Those who saw her gained new confidence themselves. Mama's family stayed together. Even in the almost intolerably crowded space of their apartment the atmosphere was peaceable and loving. Later I was told that people visited her in order to gain courage.

We knew that the ghetto was under the administration of Mayor Wittrock; it was guarded by a company of Latvian assistant police headed by a certain Lieutenant Danckops. This is what conditions were like from October until the end of December 1941, when the extermination of the Jewish citizens of Latvia in Riga – the so-called "action" – was concluded. It was in the intervening period that the fateful events at the end of November and the beginning of December took place. Again, I had no direct contact with what happened, but only received news and occasional copies of printed announcements and orders.

On November 29th, Dima came home from the university and reported that the able-bodied men had been interned in a separate part of the ghetto, while women, children, and the elderly had been led away in long columns.

Soon we received more detailed information as to what exactly had happened.

The first order was to the effect that all able-bodied men aged 18 through 60 had to line up in columns on the morning of November 29th. They were taken into the fenced-off part of the ghetto grounds, called the "Little Ghetto." There the men survived for a prolonged period, and from there they were led to work to meet the needs of the Wehrmacht units. The second order was in my view so cruel that I didn't want to imagine what the inmates of the ghetto must have felt when they read it. It said that all men and women who were not capable of working, as well as all children, must get ready to be transferred to another camp. Each person was allowed to take up to twenty kilograms of luggage. Verbally they were told that the ghetto had to be vacated, and that was why they would be moved to another camp where they would be given easier work. Nevertheless, as survivors later told me, many realized that this meant death. Those who had remained in their apartments were driven out on the street, and feeble and old people who were unable to march in the column were shot without further ado. In historical sources I later read that 800 dead bodies were collected and removed from the streets of the ghetto.

Admittedly we did not learn all this until the days that followed. At the time, the end of November, we knew nothing specific – except for the fact that no one had returned to the ghetto. On December 8th, the second "action" took place: During this action, those ghetto inmates who had survived November 30th were also shot. The only ones who were left were the workers in the Little Ghetto – the men whose families had just been exterminated.

Both times the columns had been driven south through the streets of the "Moscow Suburb" completely openly and visible to all. Soon the rumor spread in the city that the inmates of the ghetto had not been taken to another camp but shot on the outskirts of town, probably in the Rumbula forest. I found it significant that the authorities did not even try to deny such rumors. Everyone seemed to have agreed to remain completely silent about what had happened. Over time many people probably began to believe they had not known about it. It was as if these thousands of people had never existed.

In the meantime, the ghetto did not remain empty, but began to fill with Jews who had been "evacuated" here from Central Europe. This, too, was known to everyone who wanted to know. As early as November 30th, the first train from Berlin arrived. Since the ghetto had not been completely vacated, the more than thousand Berlin Jews were the first to be shot in Rumbula. Then, gradually, transports of Jews from Germany and Austria began to arrive. By the beginning of 1942, their number had increased so much that the elderly among them would be shot as soon as the trains arrived at the Škirotava station. Today we know how many people were shot or sent on to other concentration camps. It is said that a total of 25,000 people were deported to Riga from Germany, Austria, and Czechoslovakia.

Eleven thousand of them were murdered; a few more thousands came from Hungary and Lithuania. Several transports also went to Estonia. The last people to have been deported to the Riga Ghetto, empty by now, are said to have been Jews from Cologne.

Dima and Emīlija brought horrifying eyewitness reports. The luggage the ghetto inmates had brought with them was taken from them, and at the edge of the pit they were forced to undress completely. After shooting children, women, and old people all day long, the shooters, who were drunk, threw the clothing on trucks and brought it back to town, where it was distributed or sold.

In some European countries the citizens tried to defend their Jews in an organized manner, which was successful in Denmark and Bulgaria. The Jews themselves put up armed resistance, although they knew that their struggle was futile. The most famous example of this is the 1943 uprising in the Warsaw Ghetto. Neither one nor the other happened in Latvia. The majority of our Jews resigned themselves to their fate, as though paralyzed.

In the two "actions" on November 30th, almost all my family members lost their lives – my mama and her parents, my paternal grandmother, Uncle Max, the families of my aunts and my little cousins – a total of seventeen of my closest relatives. Evidently they were already taken from the ghetto with the first column, though I shall never know for sure.

Those who survived were Aunt Edith and her two daughters, who were evacuated to Russia together with the field hospital in which Edith's husband, David Glinterniks, was working, and Mama's cousin Frieda and her daughter, whom the Soviets had deported on June 14th. Both Edith's as well as Frieda's husbands were killed, one at the front, the other in the Gulag, but the women came back. Father's younger sister Eugenie – Aunt Jenny, the singer – survived in Argentinian exile along with her husband and son.

Among the men interned in the Little Ghetto, who had to do forced labor some time longer before they too were murdered, was my father. By a bitter irony of fate, my parents were separated on their last journey, and Mama could not go to her death together with her husband as she had so firmly resolved to do. The same was true of Dima's parents. I don't know where Mama and all my loved ones are buried – in Rumbula, in Biķernieki Forest, or elsewhere. None of us survivors know where exactly they could linger for a sad moment of remembrance to lay down flowers or a pebble. We have only symbolic sites of commemoration.

PEOPLE. DESTINIES

At that time, in late 1941, I lost almost all sense of reality. I lived and acted as if in a nightmare. Something within me switched off, a dead zone spread further and further. I did not cry and felt no pain, as can happen after severe injuries when one initially feels numb from the effect of the shock. I remained in this state of icy torpor all through the German occupation, and it persisted for some time after the war. I tried with all my strength not to thaw because if I did I would have been totally incapable of doing what it took to survive.

My brain, on the other hand, worked as lucidly as before, my thinking was surprisingly sharp, and my ever-present desire to understand the world became an obsession. In my head, a kind of machine was constantly working away, I kept constantly thinking, thinking, thinking: How is it possible that the world has suddenly turned into a place where there is no longer any orientation, where things are happening that actually cannot be happening, that human beings are acting in a way human beings should never act. I forbade myself the luxury of mourning. I was filled with a furious defiance I had never experienced before, a burning, icy contempt for those who – whatever their motives – had forfeited the right to call themselves human beings.

The only thing that still kept me sane was love. Dima and I had nobody left in the world but each other. We clung to each other with a strength unknown in peaceable day-to-day life. Being together was happiness despite everything. As far as I myself was concerned, I was afraid of nothing, under either occupying force. But at the thought of people I was close to and loved, I turned into an irrational creature obsessed by worry whom only her strong self-control helped to conceal the panic. All this time I had been thinking and worrying about my parents, my grandparents, and other relatives. I had lost them. Now I was afraid only for Father and for Dima, for whom I myself posed a threat.

Dima continued attending classes at the university, while I stayed confined at home. He and I did everything to maintain the illusion of a normal life. We read, discussed the news we had heard on the radio or elsewhere; now and then one of the few trustworthy friends we had came to visit, and to our joyful surprise every once in a while someone who had been able to flee during the "liquidation" of the ghetto would resurface.

On the stairs, Dima had started a conversation with a German sergeant-major who lived in the basement apartment directly below us. Dima saw that he was a man of honor, and he was not mistaken. The two made friends in spite of the difference in their ages, and I too made Otto Wiechmann's acquaintance. He served as the driver of a major who was quartered in one of the upscale apartments. Very soon our conversations became quite candid. Otto told us he was actually a typesetter and had worked in a Leipzig print shop; the employees, traditionally Social Democrats, had been persecuted by the Nazis. He too had been in a concentration camp for a while, from which he was released when he agreed to join the army, although he had already passed the draft age.

We instinctively felt we could trust him. He often came to see us and naturally knew about me. Occasionally Mr. Wiechmann helped Dima when he had to deal with the Latvian local government agencies, which were taken down a notch or two as soon as a German sergeant-major appeared before them.

During that first winter of war on the eastern front, we became close friends with the conductor Arvīds Jansons and his wife Ida.

They lived quite close by, in Eksporta iela. This was the only place we sometimes risked going to together, despite all the danger. We'd go to their house in the evening, stay the night, and return to Vidus iela in the early morning, for during the night there was curfew. We talked, we made music. Ida, an enchanting redhead whom I had known at a distance for a long time, had a pleasant, though not a particularly big voice. I remember her role as Siébel in Gounod's *Faust* and especially her title role in Offenbach's *La belle Hélène*, a part that seemed to have been written for her. During the last years of Latvian independence Ida worked at the Liepāja Opera, which was where she met Arvīds. He had initially been a violinist in the orchestra before his talent for conducting was discovered. The first time I met this couple who lived for music was during a visit with my relatives in Liepāja, the Glinterniks. At the time they were very much in love, but they did not marry until Arvīds was appointed as conductor of the Riga Opera. That was in the first year under the Soviets. Ida so strongly believed in her husband's talent that – it can be said without exaggeration – she dedicated her whole life to his work, as she later did to that of her son Mariss.

The Riga Opera did not welcome the two with open arms. Leo Blech had once told my parents that the opera was a pit of vipers, where in secret conspiracies any weapon was fair game. All new arrivals, he said, were almost automatically regarded as dangerous rivals that people tried to get rid of. Envy and intrigues were the order of the day.

Arvīds was less affected by the ill will, but the hatred of the ladies poured down on Ida in streams. The fact that she was Jewish was already considered to be a serious flaw during the Soviet period, but when the Nazis invaded Latvia, her situation became life-threatening.

Ida told me her father had realized from the first moment what was in store for them. Immediately he turned to two Latvian doctors who were friends of his and went with them to the German military administration that during the first days was still managing all affairs in "Ostland." The two medical men testified that Ida was not Blumenfeld's biological daughter, but that he had adopted her from a Russian woman who died shortly after her birth. In reality, they had said, she was not called Ida, but had the Russian name of Iraīda. The doctors certified that they had been present at the birth, and so that the child would not learn its origin, no papers had been filled out. The military administration was not interested in Jewish affairs, and the matter was quickly settled. Mr. Blumenfeld was issued a certificate of adoption.

Thus Ida received a document that denied her Jewish origin, which had explicitly been entered in her Soviet passport. Literally in the first days of German occupation, when the power was still in the hands of the military, a few Riga citizens managed to "improve" their papers this way; shortly thereafter, when the German and local security agencies began their work, something like this was no longer possible. Ida's courageous, resourceful father and other members of her family were murdered.

Although Ida's papers were now supposedly in order, she still felt she was in danger. What was this? All this time she'd been Jewish, and now all of a sudden she wasn't anymore? If a person is surrounded by many envious people, such a question can be particularly risky. Ida stayed home, quiet as a mouse.

Many colleagues were scared of the prima donna Milda Brechmane-Štengele, who had a lot of influence at the Riga Opera. The artist, who was unquestionably outstanding, was a contradictory and sometimes malicious personality. We had already been told so by Leo Blech, whom she periodically hated – if only because this immigrant Jew sponsored not only her but also other female soloists. She was one of the persons of whom Ida was afraid.

Ida had one more "collective enemy": a couple of ballerinas who were in love with their conductor. The result was that Ida alias Iraīda, although she now had official papers, did not feel much safer than I did. That brought us closer to each other.

Ida was faced with a dilemma that demanded an imminent decision. She spoke to me about it very frankly several times. She was a little older than Arvīds and way past thirty; as is often the case with stage performers, she and her husband had kept postponing having a baby. Ida was aware that her status as adoptive daughter could be revoked at any time if some "benefactor" took a bit of trouble and did some research. As the wife of a Latvian, she wouldn't exactly have to face immediate death, but sterilization was unavoidable. In this unsafe, completely unpredictable situation, Iraīda decided to risk pregnancy.

A loyal friend of theirs who was able to support and protect them both to a certain extent although he had enough worries of his own was Mariss Vētra, the Opera's star tenor. Vētra's wife, a German Jew, had been jailed for a while in the prison of Einsatzkommando (Operational Command) 2. When Arvīds' and Iraīda's son was born in January 1943 – by that time I was no longer in Vidus iela – they gave him the name Mariss, in honor of Vētra.

Today, seventy years later, the world-famous conductor Mariss Jansons conducts the Bavarian Radio Symphony Orchestra and the Royal Concertgebouw Orchestra in Amsterdam.

Dima and I tried to keep up the appearance of a halfway normal life. This was hard and required enormous self-control, we did our best to struggle against our grief, for otherwise we would have completely lost our balance and clear-headedness. Yet we were always on the alert, and our sense of imminent danger was constantly growing. We began to discuss the possibility of leaving Riga and going to the provinces like some of our friends and acquaintances after they obtained forged IDs; in the countryside they were safer than in the city. One of them, a longtime acquaintance of ours, the dentist Guna Spera, had found a place on a farm as a laborer for her husband, Vladimir Vigdorchik, where they evidently did not have the slightest suspicion that their farmhand was Jewish. Guna herself and the children stayed in Riga; she had her dental practice on the corner of Brīvības and Elizabetes iela, right above the pharmacy. Wherever I happened to be hiding during the German occupation, if I had a toothache I would go to Guna. When you have a toothache, you're even willing to accept the risk of bumping into a patrol.

The Vigdorchiks had always seemed like a model family to me. Initially things had not been easy for them. They had married in the '30s, when antisemitic prejudices in Riga society were no longer as pronounced. And yet, as soon as personal relationships and marriage were involved, there were objections. Guna's family did not like the fact that she wanted to marry a Jew, and Vladimir's parents, too, were very upset that a Latvian girl was to be their daughter-in-law. But when they saw how harmonious the young couple was, they calmed down. Countless times I've noticed that prejudices vanish as soon as people get to know the actual persons more intimately. All of a sudden other laws come into effect. I was told that even members of the German military came to the defense of their Jewish workers in Riga's Little Ghetto whom they had gotten to know well, and did not hand them over to the SS to be killed.

More and more unmistakably, almost physically, I felt the noose tightening around Dima and me. It would have been naive to believe that nobody knew about our marriage and about the fact that I was hiding in the apartment. As time went on, the circle of those who knew inevitably became larger. Assuredly most of them were well disposed toward us or at least neutral; they would not have betrayed me of their own free will; but one could only speculate how they would act if they were interrogated.

We considered another possibility how we could save ourselves from the impending danger. We had heard that a number of people had managed to flee by fishing boat from the West Kurzeme coast across the Baltic Sea to Gotland. As an experienced yachtsman, Dima knew a lot of fishermen and sailors. In March of 1942 he began to resume these contacts, though to be on the safe side he kept the details from me. All I know is that there was hope something could be attempted in early spring. We started learning Swedish.

In midwinter, shortly after New Year's Day, I believe, our mutual friend Gabriels Civjans, whom everybody called Gava, unexpectedly appeared at our house. We had known only that he had been in the ghetto. Now we learned that his parents and sister had been shot, while he himself had been able to escape from the Little Ghetto. Like myself, Gava had been a student at the Esra-Gymnasium; in turn, his parents had been friends with Dima's parents. Gava was very attached to Dima, whom he admired like an older brother. The two of them were close friends.

After escaping from the ghetto, Gava went to Jūrmala to an aunt who was not Jewish. The wife of his late uncle was an extremely nice

Russian woman called Anna Filaretovna. Quartered in her large, beautiful villa were German officers to whom she introduced her nephew as a relative from the provinces, which aroused no suspicion. Gava was a slender, handsome, and cheerful young fellow who bore not the slightest resemblance to the caricatures of Jews promulgated by the Nazis. Besides, in spite of his nineteen years, he looked like a teenager who was not yet eligible for conscription, which is why he was able to move about relatively safely. Only a random passport control could have been dangerous for him.

Gava had lived through a great tragedy.

Ever since primary school he had idolized a classmate, Esther by name. Nobody challenged her title of being the prettiest girl in the school. I remember her clearly – her big amber eyes, her velvety skin, and the beauty mark on her left cheek. The last year of school, they became a couple, and in the ghetto they got married. But then Gava, being a young man who was fit for work, was separated from her and interned in the Little Ghetto. Esther, who was expecting his child, was sent on the death march and killed in Rumbula together with the other women, old people, and children. Gava survived, but no matter what happened in his eventful life, he could never forget Esther, and his lovely wife Lyalya and their two sons always understood and respected these indelible memories.

Gava, too, was one of the people Emīlija looked after. When he learned from her that we were alive, he immediately came running to our house. I have a vivid memory of how glad we were. That night the three of us sat in the Vidus iela apartment – and split our sides laughing. Gava told us about and acted out in pantomime his life with Aunt Anna in Jūrmala. Although the house was full of German officers, Gava, as the country relative, had a good life there. In order to appear even more credible, he pretended he knew no German (which was the everyday language in his family). One of the officers was dead set on teaching him German so that the boy would get along better in his new environment. Gava acted as if he was slow on the uptake and could simply not remember the German vocabulary, and when he did manage to memorize something, his teacher was as happy as a little child. Gava acted out these dialogues for us. He was hilariously funny.

Yet we also had to discuss serious things as well. It was clear that our friend could not stay in Jūrmala much longer. The Perov group at the prefecture that had helped to get me an ID had not been captured yet, and a replacement ID had to be obtained for Gava through them. For the document he needed a new first and last name, and thus we discussed this question too, which was great fun. I suggested that he keep his own initials, G.C., somehow I had the feeling that this hidden link to the past would bring him good luck. And thus we christened Gava Gunārs Cīrulis.[1] At the time, of course, no one could have imagined that this name would go down in Latvian literary history.

It occurred to Dima that his cousin Alexander Schönfeldt, a doctor, could help Gava, alias Gunārs. The Schönfeldt dynasty of doctors and psychiatrists was famous in Latvia: In Pārdaugava they had the psychiatric clinic and sanatorium Atgāzene, founded in the late 19th century by Alexander's father Max and his uncle Leopold. Connected to the sanatorium is a tragic occurrence that made headlines in the local and national press: In 1912, a patient, Baron von Rautenfeld, had gotten hold of a revolver and shot his attending physician, Max Schönfeldt. A romantic legend developed around this sad event and was even immortalized in a novel and in one of the first Latvian silent movies. According to this version Rautenfeld had fallen in love with a simple Latvian girl and wanted to marry her, whereupon his aristocratic relatives had him declared insane.

When we once happened to speak about this with our Schönfeldts, they waved the story aside: The baron had indeed married the lady's maid, they also had children, but Rautenfeld, they said, really was schizophrenic. Although he was not considered to be dangerous, his family did not want to keep him in the house and finally brought him to the Schönfeldt sanatorium. There Rautenfeld

---

1. Gunārs Cīrulis (1923-2002), Soviet Latvian writer and well-known witness of the Holocaust in Latvia. His stories *Das Meer bewahrt keine Spuren* (1976) and *Der Glückspilz* (1986), as well as a young-adult mystery, *Die mysteriöse Quittung* (1983), have appeared in German translation.

got the fixed idea that his relatives had conspired against him in order to get rid of him and pocket his inheritance. That was why they had bribed the doctor, he claimed. I don't know to what extent this suspicion was justified.

When I made friends with Dima, I also got to know the Schönfeldts. The sanatorium Atgāzene was managed by Alexander, aka Alik, whose sister, Elsa, also worked there. In the first Soviet year, the sanatorium was expropriated or "nationalized," but the former owners were allowed to continue their medical work and to live on the grounds. Later the Germans set up a military hospital there, and when the Soviet power returned, the sanatorium became a department of the hospital of the so-called Baltic Military District.

Alexander Schönfeldt told me a lot about the turbulent past of the widely known sanatorium. Here, they specialized in the treatment of alcoholics; during Latvian independence, even patients from abroad came there looking for a cure. I remember especially clearly the stories about the brilliant Russian actor Vasily Kachalov, who was a regular client in Atgāzene and often came there from Moscow. He was a charismatic man, absolutely irresistible – and completely untreatable, because he was unwilling to submit to any pressure and kept leaving the sanatorium. For instance, he was magically drawn to the station restaurant, which was open around the clock; it was here that the truck drivers came to fortify themselves every morning after delivering their goods to the central market. Kachalov was so fascinated by this company that you couldn't keep him away. He claimed he was not an alcoholic at all; he was just so fond of the atmosphere and the crowd at the pub. The characters there inspired his roles, he said.

Maria Schönfeldt, Alik's mother, was the younger sister of Yevgenia Osipovna Feinmane, Dima's mother. Thus both sisters had married Jewish doctors. During World War I Maria was said to have been in a relationship with the governor-general of Livonia, who had also issued considerable title deeds in her name. Even at an advanced age Mrs. Schönfeldt was a charming and attractive lady.

The young Schönfeldts had been baptized Russian Orthodox and were considered to be Russian, but now that no longer had much significance: Ill-wishers had spread the rumor that old Mrs. Schönfeldt was in reality also Jewish, which meant that her children were also full-blooded Jews and belonged in the ghetto. The elderly lady took the documents she had been issued by the erstwhile governor and went straight to the Reich Commissioner for the Ostland, Hinrich Lohse. Her decision to start at the very top proved to be correct. If she had turned to the prefecture or another Latvian local administrative office, she would hardly have gotten anywhere.

Mrs. Schönfeldt introduced herself to Lohse and told him about her connections to the court of the Czar in St. Petersburg. The dignified lady made such an impression on Lohse that he promptly handed her a written confirmation of her noble descent and thus of her family's immunity. This paper could be regarded as an effective guarantee of the family's safety.

When she came home, Mrs. Schönfeldt gave the document to her son and daughter – and hanged herself. She could not bear the disgrace of having tried to ensnare a miserable petty Nazi henchman and of spreading her past before him. She was old, she had done her duty toward her children, and left life of her own free will.

Alik was somewhat older than my husband, whom he loved very much, and I too was welcomed in his family. When I was still living in hiding in Vidus iela, he came to visit us a couple of times. After his mother's death it slowly began to dawn on him that in spite of the documents he had to get out of Riga, because there were people who wanted to destroy him. Alik had a good friend from former times, the German Balt Dr. Harry Marnitz.[2] From 1941 until the end of 1943 he was the head of the department of "health and social welfare" at the General Commission of the German civil administration of the General District of Latvia, and he got Alik a job. Since many physicians had been drafted into the army, there was a shortage of doctors everywhere, and Alik agreed to go to Indra in the province of Latgale, not far from the Russian border. He was the only doctor for a

---

2. In Latvian, Harijs Marnics (1894-1984); the physician and massage therapist, who came from the Governorate of Livonia of the Czarist empire, developed a holistic treatment method known as key zone massage.

vast territory – and did not even have a nurse or an assistant at his side. When Gunārs Cīrulis was "born," it occurred to us that he could work with Alik as an orderly. It all happened completely legally: The physician Dr. Schönfeldt sent a formal letter of request, Mr. Cīrulis went to the appropriate agency with his replacement ID, settled everything, and left for Indra. That must have been in March of 1942, for Dima still received a few witty letters from Gunārs from Latgalian exile. He wrote that Alik had quickly shown him what needed doing, and that he was doing fine.

He came to Riga one more time to pick up his few possessions at his aunt's house. He told us life in Indra had in the meantime become rather unpleasant. One of the armed so-called "self-defense" groups was active there, and if it ever occurred to them to check who it was that had come from Riga, and who this Gunārs Cīrulis was, then… At the time the Germans were recruiting young guys all over Latvia to send them to Germany to work for the labor service. Gunārs deliberately ran into them, and they took him as well. He did not want to stay in Latvia until his replacement ID had expired.

From Germany, too, Gunārs was able to send us a postcard: He was working as an orderly in northern Germany, because already upon entering the labor service he had stated he had "experience in the medical field." Later our contact broke off and I did not hear about Gunārs' further adventures up to the time of his flight to Switzerland until after the war, when he returned to Riga.

While still in Indra, Gunārs wrote to us that Alik's uncontrolled consumption of alcohol was causing him a lot of worry. Of course, you could understand Alik in his situation, yet his weakness cost him his life. Later I found out that he had often drunk in the company of the auxiliary police and had once disastrously opened his mouth too wide while under the influence. Just as drunk as he, they took him out in the yard and shot him.

Dr. Marnitz, who, incidentally, was a member of the Nazi Party and medical colonel in the Storm Troops (SA), made a huge fuss because of the shooting of Schönfeldt and of the Latvian doctor Lidija Kirchenšteina, who had also worked for him in the border region – he protested all the way to Berlin, but the Security Service of the SS had more influence, and Marnitz was summoned back to the Reich from Riga.³

---

3. *Lidija Kirchenšteina* is the sister of the Social Democrat Augusts Kirchenšteins, who became the president of Soviet Latvia in 1940.

THE CURTAIN FALLS IN VIDUS IELA

Time went by, and May 9th, 1942 arrived. All this time we had been prepared for the possibility that the auxiliary police might search the apartment – either by chance during one of their raids while the Hauptmann was away, or else because they had had a tip that I was hiding there. In case of an emergency Dima and I had worked out a special "scenario," using some of the building's advantages. Ours was a corner building with an entry on each of the two streets, and the apartment, too, had two entrances. The so-called parade door of the house was located in Vidus iela 9, while from the kitchen a door led by the back stairs to the courtyard and from there to Vīlandes iela. If push came to shove Dima would try to delay the intruders so that I could run away through the kitchen into the yard.

One day the fatal doorbell rang. Dima went to the door, I heard a loud and aggressive conversation in Latvian. While the back door was not visible from the apartment door, a couple of steps were all you needed to look into the corridor that led to the kitchen. Since all the doors were open, I didn't manage to reach the back door. I merely had time to slip into the so-called maid's room, in which nobody had lived since Manya left us in the fall of 1940. It was used to store old newspapers that were saved for various purposes, stacked-up chairs, and, in the corner, an old sewing machine.

Later, I often thought about what happened then.

When I entered the room, I instinctively turned the key that was on the inside, and just as automatically pulled it out and pressed myself against the wall next to the door. I heard the heavy boots of the policemen in the corridor, they went into the kitchen, inspected it and stated: "Nobody here either!" And then they rattled the door of the maid's room. I felt somebody peering through the keyhole. "Oh, nothing but old junk in here…" If I had left the key in the door or merely stood facing the keyhole, that would have been the end of me. I listened – the steps walked away again. I did not hesitate – after all, they could have changed their mind and broken into the maid's room anyway. I unlocked the door quietly and slipped into the kitchen. And yet another happy coincidence: The door did not squeak, and I was wearing outdoor shoes with soft rubber soles in which I could move without making a sound.

I went into the corridor. And saw that at the other end one of the policemen was standing with his back to me. Legs apart, arms akimbo – exactly like in the movies. On a clothes rack next to the kitchen door that led to the back stairs hung our everyday outdoor clothes. I grabbed my overcoat and scampered out of the apartment – the policeman hadn't stirred. No doubt his attention was on what was happening in our room. I could hear banging and crashing. Apparently his companion was emptying the cabinets on the floor.

I ventured outside the courtyard onto Vīlandes iela, far enough to see the corner of Vidus iela. There stood the car in which the policemen had arrived. I pressed myself against the wall of the house and decided to wait until they left. It took quite a while, maybe an hour, till I saw them come up to the car – carrying heavy suitcases, a couple of paintings under their arms.

And they led away Dima. That was the last time I saw him. Later I learned that we had been betrayed. To this day I haven't been able to find out who did it and under what circumstances. Dima was accused of having hidden his Jewish wife and was incarcerated in the Central Prison. By some curious chance Dima shared his cell with the lawyer Blankenstein, who had also recently been arrested – despite his status as the Swiss honorary consul. They were not immediately shot, however; that was done only in the case of captured Jews. In the case of all others, they tried to write a "proper" indictment. It mattered that they hadn't found me.

Emīlija learned that Dima adamantly denied I had even stayed at the apartment. He said the clothes had belonged to the previous occupants and he had pinched them – all the tenants who moved into formerly Jewish apartments did that, he added. That gave me reason to hope. The two of them might manage to escape safe and sound. Such cases had been heard of – if the accused was not a Jew.

When the police drove off with Dima, I realized I had to disappear as quickly as possible. But where should I go? Our rooms were sealed off, that was certain. There was no place for me to return to.

Suddenly, I thought of Mr. Wiechmann. He was someone I could trust. He immediately let me into his basement apartment in which he was quartered along with another army driver and the orderly of our Hauptmann. Luckily they were both on a trip with their superiors; Mr. Wiechmann said that as long as he was alone I was welcome to stay. He also offered that I could use the phone. The first person I called was Emīlija, who was deeply distressed by Blankenstein's arrest a few days previously, but did not succumb to despair and had already been able to establish contacts with the Central Prison. As she did everywhere else, there too she knew a fellow Catholic from Latgale, an older man who had been working as a prison officer since the Ulmanis period.

"It was no big deal," Emīlija explained. "I told him that one day, maybe quite soon, he'll have to come before God, and the work he is ordered to do is wicked. So if there is a chance to do something good, it's high time, and he must do it now." That was how he became our liaison.

Emīlija had the amazing gift of being able to awaken people's conscience and reminding them that they were God's creatures. She was better at this than many priests, especially when dealing with a member of her own religion.

Thanks to this prison officer whom Emīlija had induced to think about his immortal soul, we had a fairly good idea of how Dima and

Andrzej Blankenstein were doing in prison. Once I received a microscopically small slip of paper with greetings from Dima and the news that he was safe and sound and hadn't given up hope that nothing would be proved against him. I kept this tiny piece of paper for many years until, in 1950, during the house search I mentioned above, it was taken from me along with other notes from the same period.

After talking with Emīlija, I phoned Mama's Russian friend Katya Nemirovska, although I knew I could not stay with her long because her husband was Jewish. His hiding place was not in her apartment but somewhere else. After giving it some thought, Katya said I could stay with her for one or two days.

However, I spent the first days after Dima's arrest with Sergeant Major Otto Wiechmann. He calmed and encouraged me at a moment when I was in deep shock. I will be forever grateful to him for his loving sympathy and help.

In our apartment at Vidus iela 9, the drama continued even after the curtain fell for Dima and me. When the police searched the apartment, they naturally found the Babsts. The Russian Andrey and his twelve-year-old daughter were not in danger, but Vera's papers proved to be unsatisfactory. Andrey later told me he tried to convince the officials he would soon get additional documents from Liepāja. He hoped that by means of bribery he would get the necessary certification about his wife's ethnic origin. But before that could happen, about a week later, Vera was arrested. She died in prison soon thereafter. No one knows how it happened. He was simply told she had died.

Andrey and Natasha Babst survived, and immediately after the German retreat in October 1944 I met them again. They were no longer at the Vidus iela apartment, to which I too was unable to return, for the Central Committee of the Communist Party of Latvia had promptly confiscated the whole building for its members. A certain Comrade Soldatenko had moved into my parents' apartment and had found the Babsts an apartment in Rūpniecības iela as compensation. He would not acknowledge my claims; after all, he said, I hadn't lived there anymore. He even refused to hand over our furniture and books that the German officers had not gone off with. The new owner of the apartment did not give in until Mr. Babst and the caretaker, Oboļēvičs, threatened they would go to court with me and testify; he said I should pick up the things in two days' time. When Oboļēvičs and Babst brought me to the door with a truck two days later, it turned out that Soldatenko had moved and had taken the best pieces of furniture with him. So I collected what was left and, in October 1944, said goodbye to Vidus iela 9 forever.

I BECOME A FUGITIVE

When my parents had just left for the ghetto, I received an ampoule of cyanide from Father's physician, Dr. Goldberg. He had obtained this poison both for himself and for some of his patients who were in danger. The little ampoule had a wonderfully calming effect on me. I sewed it into the strap of my bra in such a way that when I bent my head I could reach it and crush it with my mouth, for instance in the event that my hands were tied behind my back. Every time I changed my underwear, my dose of poison was also transferred. Even during the Soviet period, I kept it in my first-aid kit for a long time, just in case. At some point in the 'sixties I finally got rid of the little glass vial.

But that was not enough. It could have happened that I fell into the torturers' hands without having a chance to swallow the cyanide. They wouldn't be able to force me to divulge anything only if I actually didn't know anything. That was why I decided, and discussed with Emīlija, that I would try not to remember the streets and houses she brought me to, or better still, not to even recognize them. That wasn't too hard for me – not only because I barely knew my way around all of Riga, but also because I had become a lot more nearsighted. Besides, Emīlija usually zigzagged back and forth like a hare in order to confuse any pursuers. Something that helped me a lot was the self-control I had practiced from early childhood, to which I now added autosuggestion. I successfully avoided becoming aware of certain types of information and forced myself not to remember them. That is why in later years I was unable to find again the houses in which I spent a short time, but had only a vague idea in what district they were located. Also, if possible, I was not supposed to know the last names of the people who saved my life: We used only our first names when talking to each other. That way I felt sure I could never divulge their names.

Who knows what would have happened to me if it hadn't been for Emīlija. She took me under her wing and brought me from one hiding place to the next, to strangers only she knew and considered to be trustworthy who risked their own lives and those of their children if they took me in even for a while. Emīlija had packed a knapsack with a change of clothing and the most important daily necessities. Later, in fall and winter, she got me warm clothes.

Initially the hiding places changed very often – I could stay for one night or a week at most. Several times I had to leave a hiding place because of the neighbors. They were not always bad people, not at all, but hopelessly curious, talkative, and eager to stick their nose in other people's business. And more than anything I was afraid that other people could come to harm on my account. One mustn't forget that anyone who helped the Jews was punished harshly and cruelly.

It was harder to go underground, among other reasons, because during the war ration cards had been introduced, and naturally people only got those if they were legal. Under these circumstances an additional person who needed to be fed represented a great burden for a family, a burden no one could expect them to take upon themselves. At least there was the black market, where goods were not so much sold for money but exchanged for other goods. As long as the gold jewelry Father had provided lasted, this problem did not cause me a headache, but unfortunately the two heavy belts were getting lighter and lighter. Around that time, I learned to earn my living with my own hands, as I will describe later.

Among the several dozen people with whom fate brought me together during those years, only a very few risked their lives because they were eager to get the gold rings I carried in my linen belt. But I feel nothing but sincere gratitude toward them as well, because they were in no way obligated to put themselves in danger in order to save my life, even if they did take payment for it. It is thanks to them as well that I am still alive. The majority of the people who gave me shelter did it completely selflessly and not for material gain. Each of them may have had his or her own motives: moral conviction, religious views, abhorrence for the occupying power, simple human compassion for a young woman who had become a widow and orphan practically simultaneously – and who herself according to orders from above must also be surrendered to the executioners. They did not feel like heroes by any means; rather, they felt it went without saying that they should listen to the voice of their conscience. And not only in my case. I know women whose families had suffered greatly during the Soviet year – and yet when ragged, half-starved Russian prisoners of war were driven past them, they spontaneously handed them their last piece of bread. These tortured people, for them, were no longer Russians or non-Russians, enemies or friends, representatives of some political power. None of that mattered in the face of the existential suffering of living human beings. And wherever the columns of Soviet prisoners of war came past, there were women who distributed milk or bread among them, depending on what was available to them in a time of war and scarcity. The guards chased them away and punished them, but the silent manifestation of humanity continued.

The first weeks of my flight were the hardest: As yet there was no stable chain along which I could be passed from hand to hand. Emīlija was forced to improvise, and all in utmost haste.

After leaving Aunt Katya, I spent several nights with a woman called Tamara Dworkin. At one time I had met this strikingly beautiful young woman, blond, with sparkling blue eyes and a face like pale pink porcelain, among my parents' circle of acquaintances: She was married to a wealthy man, much older than she, who owned a knitwear factory. Tamara originally came from Liepāja. Her parents had been deported to Siberia on June 14th, 1941, but since she had gone to Riga upon her marriage, nothing happened to her initially. She must have been roughly eight years older than me.

Her life history, inconceivable though it may seem, was to some extent characteristic for the period, which of course was inconceivable in and of itself.

In the spring of 1941, shortly before the mass deportations and the German attack of the Soviet Union, Tamara's husband unexpectedly died of a heart attack. When the Germans occupied Latvia, she landed in the ghetto. Then came the December day when along with other women, old people, and children she was driven in the death march to Rumbula. Together with a girlfriend and the friend's four-year-old son, Tamara managed to escape. While still in the grounds of the ghetto, they were able to hide in a basement. They were not the only ones. Evidently the executioners had noticed their disappearance; at any rate, two days later, a special unit of Latvian police led by two German Security Service officers showed up to comb the houses and basements of the ghetto. More than twenty people were discovered and rounded up, including Tamara. A high-ranking SS man caught sight of her: Karl Jäger, one of the leaders of the "action." It must have struck the man like lightning, for he immediately called Tamara aside away from the column and asked: "How did you get here?"

She did not tell me the rest of the conversation. But Tamara did not have to go on the death march. Soon, Jäger had her brought from a temporary accommodation to his apartment in the so-called Vorburg on Kronwald-Ring (present-day Ausekļa iela). That was where I had gone to school; now, top-ranking members of the SS and the Security Service had taken the district over. In one block of houses, there were big workshops in which Jewish men were made to perform forced labor. Tamara lived with Jäger as his mistress, but officially as his housekeeper. He provided her with the necessary papers, beginning with a replacement certificate made out in the Russian name of Tamara Pavlova. All the subsequent steps seemed to fall into place automatically: Tamara knew a lawyer called Dzenis, a sixty-year-old bachelor who – god knows by what means – allowed himself to be persuaded to enter a sham marriage with the young woman. Tamara Dworkin alias Pavlova, née Kopelovska, became Tamāra Dzene and was issued an official passport. Dzenis had a spacious five-room apartment in Parka iela, present-day Alfrēda Kalniņa iela, where Tamara registered her residence. Most of the time she had to live on Kronwald-Ring with her employer; it was only when he went on prolonged business trips that she stayed in her own room at Dzenis' place, who of course was not allowed to touch her.

Soon after her rescue, Tamara visited the Jansons, whom she knew from Liepāja and with whom she could speak openly. At first Iraīda only told Dima and me about her, and then brought us together. Sometimes Tamara even came to us in Vidus iela, although Jäger in his insane passion tried to keep her locked up in his apartment. Her visits were made easier by the fact that we were practically neighbors. Tamara was terribly afraid of Jäger and told us that the man had totally lost his mind, was hysterical, suffered from severe depressions, and had also begun to drink excessively. He had already been cautioned because of this. Tamara had heard that he had initially been different. She believed Jäger was by no means a monster by nature and that this was the reason for his insane behavior. Before the war he had allegedly studied law and even defended his dissertation, which is why he preferred to be addressed as "Herr Doktor" contrary to military etiquette.[1]

Tamara did not hide how much she was oppressed by the fact that she owed her life to such a configuration of circumstances. She would have felt better if she had simply been the bed slave of this man. But he loved her to the point of insanity, she said, as though he wanted to make amends to her for what he had done to others – and his obsession terrified and confused her. With her official papers Tamara could easily have fled, but she realized that Jäger would "track her down even in a mousehole," and during this hunt not only she but many others would also pay a heavy price.

In order to wring at least some sort of meaning from her

---

1. This is the origin of the misunderstanding that has also crept into some documents that Jäger was a physician; moreover, another Karl Jäger operated in the region: the commander of the security police and the Security Service (SD) of the General Commission for Lithuania headquartered in Kaunas. According to Tamara, the Jäger we knew was the personal aide-de-camp of the Higher SS and Police Leader Friedrich Jeckeln, who was responsible for murdering the Latvian Jews in the Riga Ghetto.

deplorable situation, Tamara tried to get hold of information that could save the lives of people at risk. There were no more mass actions, for most of the Latvian Jews had already been killed, and yet individual persons who had gone underground here and there were still being hunted. When he was drunk, the high-ranking SS officer sometimes divulged details about imminent raids, and then Tamara would pass on warnings to those who worked in the Vorburg workshops. She could do nothing more. The German, Czech, and other Jews who had been deported to the Riga Ghetto were not within the scope of Jäger's responsibility.

Jäger's superiors gradually got tired of his private excesses and decided first to transfer him and, if he did not improve, to send him to the front. Before he left Riga, he made sure that the woman he loved so passionately was provided for. Initially Tamara was to return unobtrusively to her fictitious husband. At a later time she would then have the prospect of a position as a secretary in a military office, somewhere in Velikiye Luki or Pskov, I believe.

When Dima was arrested and Emīlija found it difficult to come up with a hiding place for me, I phoned Tamara. At the time she happened to be living with Dzenis. Naturally I had to keep out of his sight, but by chance he happened to be on a business trip and we were able to take advantage of this circumstance. Thus I spent a few days in Parka iela while Tamara was getting ready to leave Riga.

Shortly after the end of the war I met her again. From Tallinn, her last residence, she had returned to Riga, where the KGB promptly arrested her. In the proceedings against Tamara (there was no real trial) I, too, had to testify. It was not an option to deny that she had lived with an SS big shot; that fact was well known. Yet I tried not to say anything superfluous. She was accused of having collaborated with the Gestapo and of having betrayed Jews who had gone underground. Allegedly she was not evacuated with the Germans only because they left her in Tallinn as a spy and informant. I don't know how the other witnesses were interrogated, but in my case they kept trying to get me to incriminate Tamara. Wasn't it she, they asked, who had betrayed my husband and me? But I acted as if I couldn't understand the question and simply told them what everyone knew anyway. Not for a second did I suspect Tamara.

From none of the witnesses was it possible to elicit even the slightest shred of evidence that could have been used for a real indictment, which is why – a rare case in the USSR – the charge was dropped. Nevertheless, it was administratively decided, without a court having passed sentence, to send Tamara Dworkin to a camp in the Urals for five years as an untrustworthy person.

It must have been around 1949 when I ran into Tamara by chance at a streetcar stop on tram line no. 6. She had only come for a few days to straighten out some papers and would be leaving the next morning to go to the far east of the Soviet Union. Tamara had been pardoned after one and a half years of work in the forest, and she had succeeded in locating her deported father in Krasnoyarsk. Her mother had died at the beginning of the deportation, she herself had remarried, and now the three of them – including her father – would try to start a new life in the most distant corner of the Soviet Union. She never wanted to return to Riga, she said; people here would never forget her past. Her new husband, she said, knew nothing about it, and she wanted it to stay that way.

I was very gratified that Tamara commended me for my testimony at the KGB hearing. She had been shown the interrogation records, and thanks to the founder of the Jewish Museum of Riga, the historian Margers Vestermanis, I too had an opportunity to look at them in the 'nineties. And I must admit that I was relieved when I read my statements. I don't need to be ashamed of them. When I read Tamara's extensive answers to the KGB's questions about her rescue and her existence among the SS men, I realized how radically the life story that had gone on record differed from the one she had confided to me in private in Vidus iela or at the Jansons' place in Eksporta iela. Thus there are several versions of the circumstances of Tamara's rescue: the one recorded in documents that she was forced to invent for the KGB interrogators; the different versions of the story she later told acquaintances; and the one engraved in my memory. Clearly I consider the confession Tamara made in order to vent her feelings to me, her companion in misfortune, to be reliable – and not the facts doctored within the realm of possibility intended for the ears of the KGB. Together with other cases I've experienced, this episode has confirmed my belief that it is shortsighted and naïve (perhaps even biased?) to rely uncritically on the fetish of records and documents, particularly if the latter were created under totalitarian conditions.

For many years I did not know whether Tamara's new life was a success. At the beginning of the new millennium, chance brought me into contact with a person who informed me about Tamara Dworkin's subsequent fate. The publicist and historian Anita Kugler was doing research for a book about a unique historical personality – the Jewish SS officer Scherwitz, who had been active in Riga, among other places.[2] In this connection she had also found references to the last part of Tamara Dworkin's life, the part I did not know about, and had even met her in person. It turned out that in 1963 Tamara had managed to obtain her rehabilitation (in the ruling it says, "her fate was a private tragedy [...] the judgment was an error on the part of the court") and had emigrated five years later – at first to Israel and from there, in 1972, to the Federal Republic of Germany. While she was still in the Soviet Union, her third marriage had been dissolved. Abroad, she had married for the fourth time and had again been divorced. She lived in Frankfurt, worked in a publishing house, and had later lived in a comfortable old people's home, where she died.[3]

---

2. For Fritz Scherwitz (1903-1962) cf. Anita Kugler: *Scherwitz. Der jüdische SS-Offizier*. Cologne: Kiepenhauer & Witsch, 2004.
3. In 1975, Tamara Dworkina gave evidence against Viktors Arājs; cf. Andrej Angrick, Peter Klein: *Die "Endlösung" in Riga. Ausbeutung und Vernichtung 1941-1944*. Darmstadt: Wissenschaftliche Buchgesellschaft, 2006, fn. 72.

THE BAPTISTS COME TO MY HELP

Until the beginning of 1943 I was constantly on the move, because I usually found shelter only for a short time. It is impossible for me to say when I stayed where and what the people who took me in were called. Now, too, only an occasional event or face surfaces in my memory of some of these kaleidoscopic periods of time – without a specific connection to a place or date. It's different with people and places I was able to get to know for a longer period and more intimately.

On dark winter evenings I sometimes went for walks and looked at the brightly lit windows, like movie screens showing scenes from a fantastically peaceful life. The time before Christmas, especially, has remained in my memory – people decorating Christmas trees and wrapping presents.

There were two parallel worlds – mine and that of "normal" people, the dark street and, in the bright window, the Christmas tree as a symbol of the holiday in the light of candles and of shining decorations. Two worlds at the same time and in the same place, but the boundary between them was insurmountable.

In the summer of 1942, Emīlija took me to the home of a young religious Baptist couple who had a little baby. I lived with them for quite a long time – two months. That is why I know the last name and address of this family: They were called Treiģis and lived at Lāčplēša iela 37. Many inhabitants of Riga are familiar with this building, among other things because later, for decades, the Jaunatnes teātris (Young People's Theater) was located there. Before the Soviet occupation, however, the house belonged to the Baptist community. After the re-establishment of the Latvian Republic it was returned to the community when expropriated real estate was restored to its previous owners. When I found refuge there, the building served not only as a house of prayer but as a residential building as well.

The Treiģis family's quiet apartment faced the courtyard. They lived a secluded life, and we got along very well. In general, among the Baptists I encountered there were no Nazi followers, on the contrary: In some way, they were in contact with their co-religionists in the U.S., where there were strong and wealthy congregations. I don't know how they managed it, yet not only during the first Soviet year but also under the Nazi occupation, the Riga Baptists, as they told me at the time, used to receive material support, including books and newspapers, from the American congregations,

The Treiģises' neighbors, of course, realized another person had moved in with them. As usual I was passed off as a relative who had graduated from secondary school in the country and had now come to Riga to look for work. Nobody paid special attention to me. But then, a loud and jaunty fellow called Ansis, somewhat older than me, moved into the apartment next door, of all places. One night, after a few drinks to give himself Dutch courage, Ansis came to visit. He brought all kinds of country delicacies and asked Mrs. Treiģe to set the table. He felt like spending the evening with us, he said. Mr. Treiģis couldn't very well throw him out, for we knew he was in the auxiliary police.

So we sat down at table together. Baptists do not drink alcohol, but Ansis had brought a bottle with him, drank, ate, and got more and more talkative. And started to brag about his exploits: how, waiting for the Germans to invade Latvia, he had joined an armed troop of Latvian volunteers, the so-called *pašaizsardzība* (self-defense), who intercepted people on the highways going north and east, refugees who together with the Red Army were on their way in the direction of Estonia. He said they'd bumped them all off, but he had especially enjoyed shooting communists and Jews. We sat there as if petrified listening to his swaggering talk. The neighbor told us in detail how they had captured a group of Komsomol members and forced them to dig a pit for themselves before shooting them. When the first Germans appeared, they had already been able to produce a whole list of "exploits," thus proving that the Latvians were no mean allies. I didn't even care how much of what he told us was truth and how much was bragging. Merely the fact that he believed the murder of unarmed people was something to boast about and to be proud of felt so abhorrent to me that I felt sick to my stomach. He was the reason I had to leave this hiding place. I had just begun to entertain the faint hope that I could come to rest here for a little while. The constant roaming from house to house meant that each time I had to adjust to different circumstances and new people who, though compassionate, were unknown to me. And the feeling that I was responsible for the fact that they were taking such a huge risk on my account never left me.

The Treiģises were sorry that because of the nasty neighbor I had to part from them earlier than originally planned. They found me a place to stay with other Baptists – in an old age home that the community ran at their own expense. It was located in a two-story wooden villa with a garden; I managed not to memorize the address, and the name of the home's director.[1]

This house had a great advantage. Shortly before my arrival, the home's domestic help had gotten married and given notice. Quite officially, they were looking for another maid, and it was I who played that part. I could have lived there undisturbed if the old people hadn't proved to be so unbelievably curious. With no ill intent or mistrust, simply out of boredom, they questioned me every chance they got. Where are you from, dear? Where do your parents live and what do they do? Do you have any brothers and sisters? The director and I

---

1. After the original Latvian edition of this book was published, I received a letter from a reader with photos of the old age home Saulrieti (Sunset), located in Baseina iela 2a, and of its onetime occupants. I thus also discovered the name of its director; it was Alma Bertliņa.

had made up a fictional biography for me, but soon enough I realized how many pitfalls that implied: Suddenly, for instance, it turned out that one old lady had lived almost next door to "my parents' house," and she joyfully began not only to tell me all about it, but also to ask me all sorts of questions.

So I began to work as a cleaning woman, although I had never mopped a floor or scrubbed a toilet in my life. You could hardly have imagined anyone more spoiled than me. But gradually I began to cope with all the chores, which made me very proud. I kept hearing Mama's voice: "The difference between intelligent people and unintelligent ones is that intelligent people don't find it difficult to do even unaccustomed work or work they haven't been trained to do. They watch, reflect, figure things out, try them, and then know what needs to be done. Unintelligent people only know how to do what they're trained to do or what they've been used to since childhood."

There was plenty of work. The director of the home was extremely fussy, she demanded that the many rooms should always be immaculate. In the kitchen, bathroom, laundry, and toilet the brass faucets had to be scrubbed with cleanser until they shone like pure gold. That's when I grumbled to myself. But otherwise life in the home was good. There was enough to eat, and I also instinctively felt safer from pursuers here than in an apartment house.

The home's director had a separate little apartment in which I was given a tiny room. I learned not only to clean house: She also taught me to mend silk stockings and to fix ladders with a special little hook. During the war and even years after the war, this was a skill in high demand that proved extraordinarily useful to me. Synthetic silk stockings were expensive and hard to get even in the black market, which is why you had to lavish care and attention on them. Once I had fixed a stocking, it looked like new.

The director was a single woman in her late forties whose faith had a strong touch of militant lack of compromise and a certain missionary aggressiveness. Various restrictions were imposed on me that I silently accepted in view of my situation. I was not allowed to read any worldly literature or to have newspapers and magazines in my room. The residents of the home rarely listened to the radio, and if they did, only heard music broadcasts. Only the director listened to the news; she had a shortwave receiver in her room. She did not conceal from me the fact that she also followed the forbidden foreign news broadcast in English. This was a bond between us.

On the nightstand in my room were two bibles – one in Latvian and one in English. Naturally I had already read the Bible as an outstanding cultural monument of the human race, but now I again turned to its texts with enjoyment and studied them quite thoroughly.

The people I met at the home were decent and honorable. They spoke a great deal about their American brothers and sisters, who had great influence in their country and fought for the moral purity of their nation. Unfortunately, the director tried with all her might to convert me to her faith. Right from the start I had explained that I respected all denominations without belonging to one myself. I tried not to affront the director by too obvious an attitude of rejection, but she only wanted one thing from me: that I should be christened as a Baptist.

Such a step would have ensured that I had protection and a refuge. It would have harmed no one. And yet: I could not have justified my action to myself.

After two months I realized things could not go on as they were. Once I categorically said no, the director's benevolent attitude would change, for she had her principles. It was better that I should leave of my own accord. Emīlija had not visited me at the old age home, there were others who needed her help more urgently at this time. But now I sent her sister a message that I had to leave this place.

Emīlija came, she agreed with me, and after expressing my gratitude for everything, I left the home soon thereafter. Perhaps that was the right thing to do for another reason as well: The old people's attempts to discover every last detail of my biography might have had unexpected and sad consequences.

PERFER ET OBDURA – BE PATIENT AND TOUGH

Near the New Church of St. Gertrude lived a family with whom Emīlija had previously made an agreement that they would take me in on a short-term basis if there was a sudden emergency. They were religiously neutral people who simply had compassion for a persecuted young woman. One factor here was the fact that I came to them at a dramatic moment: The family's only child, a young man my age, had been conscripted into the auxiliary police battalion, which was under German command. The parents were very alarmed, for they had no illusions that their son was going into battle for an independent Latvia. In the meantime, those who kept their eyes and mind open had realized that Hitler found a free Latvia as undesirable as did Stalin. My new hosts, however, also saw no possibility of keeping their son from being drafted. They reasoned that if they lived in the country, it would be easier to hide, to say the boy had left quite a while ago and hadn't been seen since. In the big Riga apartment house, however, the neighbors had seen him coming and going all this time. If he disappeared after receiving the conscription order, the parents would be severely punished. In their opinion, I had appeared at exactly the right moment. Who would suspect that in an apartment where the only son was on the point of enlisting in the German army there were persons persecuted by the regime?

It was not only the son of the family who had to join the army, but one of his friends as well. That was why he had come to Riga from the country, and now the two of them were waiting for the departure date. They spent the days that remained drinking without interruption as they said goodbye to their lives – they were firmly convinced they would not come back. I shall never forget the last evening as we all sat around the table drinking. We drank and wept, each of us weeping for ourselves and at the same time out of compassion for the others. I grieved for my own fate, and also felt terribly sorry for the two young men who had been virtually condemned to death. I felt for the parents and understood their grief, and they in turn felt pity for me. So we kept crying until finally we were all totally drunk.

Still, I could not stop being vigilant, for the two conscripts, who kept repeating that they were drinking at their own funeral, were wallowing in self-pity. They were still so young, they said, they had never even properly gotten to know a woman. After the parents went to bed, they pestered me half to death. I didn't hold it against them, even though it wasn't easy to ward them off. But they were so drunk they finally simply fell asleep.

I shall always remember this hiding place, for it is here that I received the news that my husband had most probably been shot. All this time we had been able to maintain some degree of contact, even though only sporadically, thanks to Emīlija's acquaintance, the prison warden. That was why I clung to the hope that Dima would somehow save himself. After all, like the lawyer Blankenstein, he was not classified as Jewish and thus had not been incarcerated in the Jewish cell block. He was accused of only one thing: that he had kept his Jewish wife hidden, which he steadfastly denied, however. He claimed I had gone to the ghetto. That's what it said in the house book, and the caretaker, Oboļēvičs, also confirmed it. These assertions were not believed, for a number of people had seen a wanted poster with my photo at the police station, as Emīlija reported. We did know, however, that in the prison Dima and Blankenstein were treated in a relatively civilized fashion– they were allegedly neither beaten nor tortured. That was why Emīlija and I did not give up hope.

But then dysentery erupted in the Central Prison and, of all places, in the wing where the two men were housed. The sick were neither separated from the healthy nor given medical treatment. There was an announcement that the facility had to be disinfected so that the epidemic would be kept from spreading; the prisoners – both those who were sick and those who were possibly infected – were rounded up and taken away. No one saw them again. Everyone realized what had happened to them. The epidemic was terminated by killing actual as well as potential patients.

And yet for years – even after I married for a second time, got divorced, then remarried and became a mother – every once in a while the irrational idea suddenly appeared in my imagination that Dima was still alive. Perhaps he had been transferred to a different prison or to a concentration camp and remained somewhere in the West after the war instead of returning to his native country, which was occupied by the Soviets. Although reason told me this was impossible; after all it was well known what had happened in the prison, even though, as is typical of totalitarian regimes, there was no evidence to this effect. There were moments when suddenly I seemed to see my husband coming down the street toward me like a mirage. I recognized him even from a distance, and until the very last moment, when I saw a total stranger before me, I felt I would go with him without hesitation and without looking back.

When Emīlija gently told me the news, the two of us were alone in the room. Something strange happened to me. Suddenly everything went dark. I literally became blind. I sat there frozen and could no longer see. I heard Emīlija speaking words of comfort to me. But the darkness did not give way.

Emīlija had to go somewhere in a hurry, she told me to wait and said she'd be back soon. She had not even noticed what had happened to me. So I remained sitting there – numb, cold, and blind. Calmly I settled all my accounts with life. After all, I was still of sound mind and realized quite well that no one could hide or rescue a completely helpless creature – it was hard enough to help somebody who was in good health. That meant that my life was over too. I decided to get out of the apartment somehow and to bite down on my cyanide ampoule in the gateway or the yard.

I don't know how long I remained that way – was it an hour, half an hour, maybe even longer? I had lost all sense of time. When I had thought my thought to the end and decided what I must do, my sight was restored as abruptly as I had lost it. And with the light, great strength and peace flooded into me. I knew I would survive, and since then I haven't doubted it for a single moment. I shall live – that was my duty toward the dead whose lives I shall continue, and this will be our triumph over "them," as I secretly called the monstrous adversary. Physically and mentally something was going on within me, a kind of transformation. After a moment of being blind, I had received new sight, as it were.

At the same time, I felt as if all my limbs had been amputated. This feeling of amputation overwhelmed me every time that, one after another, I lost through death all the people with whom I had grown together so closely that we shared the same circulation. I had the almost physical sensation of being anesthetized. There was no pain, there were neither tears nor despair – inside me everything had become numb, a zone of glaciation. I remained that way for a long, long time, I even began to think it would be for life. Only gradually – in another life by then – I began to thaw.

Later I was sometimes asked whether I suffered from guilt feelings because my husband had lost his life in order to save mine. In fact, I have never felt anything that even resembles self-reproach. I know that people in similar situations have lived the rest of their lives with a heavy burden, tormented by a sense of guilt. I have no such sense of guilt. It was not I who was guilty, but rather the bloodstained system of totalitarian power – and the people on whom this system has been able to lean. I know with certainty that I would have acted without hesitation exactly like Dima if our roles had been reversed.

I believe that all my dead – the people I loved and who loved me – wherever they may be now, are happy that I'm still alive. I don't know if there is a life after death. If there is, then I am convinced they are looking down on me with benevolence. I feel not guilt, but responsibility toward them. I try to live my life honorably, because I am living in their stead also. I would feel guilty only if I had squandered my life.

At the end of 1942 I was taken in by the family of a janitor in Marijas iela on the other side of Matīsa iela. This refuge was located by Emīlija's brother-in-law Juzefs, who was also a janitor. During the first Soviet, the subsequent National Socialist, and finally the second Soviet occupation, the janitors in the cities became people of consequence. Both regimes tried to make them into snitches and informers, which some of them certainly did become; but in my experience there were quite a few who warned or even saved the lives of the residents of their buildings. Moreover, the janitors were relatively well informed, for the local authorities often summoned them to give them instructions. Among other things, the janitors brought the ration cards and rental invoices to the individual apartments, and so they knew or at least suspected what was going on where. Quite a lot depended on them.

My new hosts were unusual inasmuch as the janitor's wife, too, could have been persecuted like me. She was a Gypsy by birth, and Gypsies, too, were murdered by the Nazis. Her maiden name was Marcinkēviča, she was married to a Latvian and had his last name – Broders, if I remember correctly. Until recently they had lived in another part of town, which is why no one here knew about her origin. I never met her husband, evidently he earned his living doing farm work in the country. They had two children. Mrs. Broders proved to be an energetic, terrific woman. As long as I ate at her table, I had enough to eat, because she speculated with food on the black market. She got the food from the country, presumably from her husband, and she could have easily fed the whole building.

She had a brother who was also married to a Latvian; he had taken her last name. Unlike his sister, who looked like a Gypsy, he did not resemble his Gypsy ancestors in the least. Mr. Melderis was not only above all suspicion as to his ethnic origin: He had even found a job accompanying groups of Jewish men who were still employed in the workshops of the Wehrmacht. These survivors, who were interned in the Little Ghetto, were considered to be privileged because the members of the Wehrmacht frequently stood up for them and would not surrender them to the German SS or to its Latvian henchmen who regularly "cleansed" the columns of Jewish men capable of work; they maintained that these workers were indispensable to the Wehrmacht. If one of the army units was transferred, the Jewish workers lost their protection – and later their lives. While the soldiers were getting ready to go to the front and the workshops in the barracks were being liquidated, some of the Jews managed to escape.

Not long before, I had been able to find out that my father was still alive and together with other men was working in one of these workshops. In the morning they were brought to the barracks from the Little Ghetto, to be returned there at night. It was this column that the brother of my hostess accompanied. He seemed to be a decent person, cautious but not cowardly, and had made it possible for some of the Jews to meet friends or relatives who lived in freedom. When I was told a meeting with my father had been arranged for me, I hardly dared believe it for fear of painful disappointment. Mr. Melderis had been able to change the route slightly; it led past his sister's house. He and his sister had agreed that he would bring Father into the backyard of the house for ten to fifteen minutes. That's how I unexpectedly met Father one more time.

He looked better than I had expected. He had lost a lot of weight, though admittedly not only because of the frugal provisions, but also as a result of the daily hard physical labor, which is why he appeared healthy and strong. His clothing, too, looked clean, though very plain. I observed in him the same defiance, the same determination that had taken root in me as well. His stance would not admit that in memory of Mama we should embrace in tears or that he should start comforting me. "We only have ten minutes," he said, "and that's why we have to discuss how we can both survive and what specifically needs to be done right now." He spoke laconically and matter-of-factly, no doubt he had prepared for our meeting and weighed every word.

Father told me that they – a small group of Jewish men – were planning to escape; outside, there were people who would provide them with papers and weapons. They had been able to organize all this thanks to the limited freedom of movement they had been able to have in the workshops of the Wehrmacht. His characteristic optimism filled him with confidence that their flight would succeed; he had, however, also considered what must be done if he were killed and only I survived. He said he had had time to deposit money abroad in two places, and he impressed upon me how I could get access to it after the war, to whom I should turn – after all, I would not have the necessary documents. By the time he had told me all this, the time allotted to us was over. Without crying, we embraced in silence for a few moments. Then he left, and I looked after him. I never saw him again.

Soon thereafter, Emīlija brought me the news that the group that had planned the escape and the people who had obtained the papers had been discovered, brought to the Central Prison, and shot there. They had prepared very carefully and found the necessary resources, but never managed to flee – they had been betrayed. Now I really had no one left in the world.

A MILDER CLIMATE IN PĀRDAUGAVA

At the time when I was living with Mrs. Broders, people were talking of nothing but the battle of Stalingrad, which went on for a long time. Of course, the German news reports and the British radio news to which people listened secretly did not correspond in the least. Although officially all radios had been either confiscated or registered, there was still, hidden away somewhere in every household, a *vefiņš,* as the little short-wave receivers of the State Electrotechnical Factory (VEF) were lovingly called. I too usually had access to such a radio.

The winter was dreadfully cold that year – not only in Russia, where it proved to be a powerful additional weapon against the Germans, but in Latvia as well. My life with the janitor's wife was good – there was no lack of firewood, and the apartment was always so hot that I walked around in a cotton robe and barefoot in slippers (the latter, of course, also in order to save my stockings).

One night, when I was sitting at the table with Mrs. Broders and her two children, there was a knock at the door. A police check, which as usual consisted of Latvian policemen. Luckily they were not searching for people but for stocks of food. Mrs. Broders, who was actively engaged in black marketeering, was sufficiently shrewd and circumspect not to store the merchandise in her apartment. After the deportations and the outbreak of the war shortly thereafter, many Riga apartments stood vacant, and she had converted one of them in her building into a small storehouse. The apartment was not heated, so that the temperature was perfect for this purpose. She kept a few pork knuckles and other trifles that could not be obtained for ration cards in her own pantry, but that wasn't enough for her to be accused of black marketeering.

Mrs. Broders knew what to do: She first seated the policemen at the supper table. They paid no attention to me, but the mistress of the house explained without being asked: "That's our neighbor's daughter. Go home, dear, I'm sure they're waiting for you." In the hallway, I grabbed an overcoat that was hanging on a hook and crept out in the yard to wait for the uninvited guests to leave again. But they had probably come precisely because Mrs. Broders served such copious meals. Later she told me she had immediately put a couple of bottles of *dzimtene* ("homeland," the generic name for homemade liquor) and some snacks on the table – plus the pork hocks that had been found during the search, wrapped in paper for them to take with them. In the warm room and with good food before them, the men were no longer in a hurry at all. They weren't ready to leave until a few hours later.

Meanwhile I waited, alternating between an adjacent stairwell and the yard, in the frost that had come to us all the way from Stalingrad. I was wearing a short little skirt and the overcoat, which according to prevailing fashion reached only to my knees, leaving the calves bare; only my feet in felt slippers were reasonably warm.

That evening I ruined my legs for life. The frostbites penetrated deep into the tissue. Both legs, particularly the right one, were soon covered with suppurating ulcers that wouldn't heal. These later tightened into hard, knotty scars that broke open during cold weather even years later. To this day I still struggle with various leg ailments. If I could have immediately seen a physician at the time, the consequences would probably not have been as severe. The only remedy I used was Mrs. Broders' good country foods – butter and sour cream. Vitamin deficiency also slowed down my recovery. Thanks to the slippers, at least my feet were not affected. I comforted myself with the thought that things could have been a lot worse: one more hour in the icy cold, and I would have become a helpless invalid.

Soon thereafter, a milder, more favorable climate, if you will, set in in my life.

First, Emīlija found me accommodations with Anna Ivanovna, a member of the Russian intelligentsia. The old lady lived in Āgenskalns in the ground-floor apartment of a wooden house whose furniture consisted mainly of bookshelves.[1] She reminded me of a gray-haired high school student, for she lived completely in the world of the ideals and ideas of her youth, which were also familiar to me from the Russian novels of the prerevolutionary period. Anna Ivanovna was totally impractical and unfit for real life, which is why she led a very frugal existence. Here I was in a familiar milieu. We talked about philosophy, ethics, and literature, and sometimes completely forgot what was going on outside our four walls.

While I lived with her, my frostbites healed. In the beginning it even seemed my troubles were over. My legs didn't look pretty, but that didn't worry me at the time.

In every place where I found shelter, there were always reasons why I was rarely able to stay more than one or two months. To the neighbors I was usually passed off as a relative who had come to Riga to take care of something. As long as I was still suffering from the suppurating frostbites on my legs, the fact that I needed to consult Riga doctors could serve as an especially credible reason. Yet such a "visit" must not be extended too long. Thus I was also forced to leave Anna Ivanovna, with whom I had felt very secure. She died soon thereafter.

As chance would have it, I spent almost all the remaining time up to the Germans' departure from Riga in the district of Pārdaugava, which I had previously hardly known at all. From Anna Ivanovna, I came straight – from hand to hand, so to speak – to the Levitin family, Russian Old Believers who lived in Torņakalns, and thus once more

---

1. *Āgenskalns:* Riga neighborhood on the left bank of the Daugava River, directly across from the Old Town, the historic center of the former Hanseatic city.

into new, totally unfamiliar circumstances. The Levitins lived in a little crooked old two-story wooden house with vegetable beds, rabbit hutches, and stacks of firewood in the yard. The Old Believers had been living in Latvia for generations since the time of Catherine the Great, for the Orthodox Church, which did not tolerate religious deviation, persecuted them fiercely. They found refuge in Livonia, among other places, where orthodoxy was not predominant; thanks to the German Balts, more tolerant social conditions prevailed here.

The Levitin family was unusual because the mistress of the house, who was Jewish by birth, had converted before her marriage and had taken the name Maria. In both families, Maria Borisovna's decision had a profound effect, a trauma from which neither the Jewish nor the Old Believer family was ever entirely healed. Even several years later, when the Levitins already had two children, the marriage was not accepted by either side. They lived in very modest circumstances but were very happy together. I am very moved when I remember their love and mutual commitment. Mr. Levitin, a tall, good-looking man, a roofer by trade, was deeply religious without being fanatical. He followed all the prescriptions of the Old Believers and observed their rituals; at night, he would pick up books that were blackened with age and read texts I could decipher only with difficulty. When I came to them, they had been together for over twelve years; Maria was very young when they had married. The children were born just in time, before the German invasion, for according to the racial laws introduced by the Nazis Maria Borisovna had to be sterilized in order to be able to remain with her husband.

While I was with the Levitin family, I learned how to sew. It is my most vivid everyday memory from the time I spent with them. Maria herself didn't sew, nor did she have a sewing machine, which is why I took on this task.

The first thing I sewed was nothing as simple as an apron or nightgown, but a winter overcoat for little Benita, whom everyone called Lyalya. It was a luxury an ordinary roofer could not afford during the war. We ripped and altered whatever we could find in the house. Women developed the skill of combining old pieces of fabric in such a way as to create fancy new outfits.

Maria gave me a raspberry-colored plush curtain, and gray cotton wool intended for stuffing the chinks in the windows. For the lining, she sacrificed a worn silk blouse. Time is something I had plenty of, and so I studied in detail an already existing coat and set to work. At first I made the batting, spreading and stitching the gray cotton wool to the pieces of blouse, and the rest followed later piece by piece. The culmination was a gray and white rabbit skin, which I used for the collar and the muff. The little coat turned out really pretty, and three- or four-year-old Lyalya looked like a little doll in it. I was proud of my achievement – with my new skill I was able to give back something to the people who shared their bread with me.

In the Levitins' three little rooms on the top floor of the wooden house we were cramped, but lived together harmoniously, respectfully, and, thanks to the children and Maria's character, even cheerfully. The worst thing about our day-to-day life was the butchering of the rabbits – I couldn't take part in that, not if you paid me. Which seems almost ludicrous, considering the historical context.

The residents of the lower floor were not nosy, and we had nothing to fear from them. It seems to me that it didn't even occur to Maria that she and her family could get into difficulties on my account; for her it was something natural and self-evident to help people in trouble.

Later the Levitins were struck by misfortune. The husband fell from an icy roof while working, became disabled, and began to drown his sorrows in alcohol. His son, too, trying to take his father's place at work, suffered a severe head injury and became an invalid. Both died shortly after the war, followed by Maria a few years later. Only Benita remained alive – little Lyalya, whom I met a few times when she was already a young woman and had a family of her own.

The only person who visited me at the Levitins' house now and then was Emīlija. She had news to share about acquaintances, some of whom were also in hiding – the dentist, Dr. Vigdorchik, Doctor Goldberg, Riva Šefers' family, and others. When it was time to move to a different place, Emīlija said she had found a new hiding place for me. Strictly speaking, two places – both in the immediate vicinity of the Levitins' house. The two homes belonged to two prominent families who were willing to take me in.

At first I found shelter with Mrs. Melnikov in Zaļenieku iela, then a mere dirt road that led to Ēbeļmuiža. The road was bordered by private homes in large gardens. My parents had known the Melnikovs; while I couldn't remember them, I knew that the opera director Peter Melnikov, Pyotr Ivanovich, had died not long ago, in late 1941. He came from a dynasty of musicians; his father, the famous bass-baritone Ivan Melnikov, had been a friend of Modest Mussorgsky and the other musicians of the "Mighty Handful." Pyotr Ivanovich, who had been connected with the opera stage from early childhood, was in Moscow and at the Mariinsky Theatre in St. Petersburg, aka Petrograd, until the early '20s, when he emigrated and devoted the last twenty years of his life to being a director at the Latvian National Opera.

When I came to the Melnikovs' house in the late winter of 1943, only the widow, Maria Aleksandrovna, her daughter, and a woman by the name of Stepanida Dmitriyevna Makars lived there. Although Stepanida did all the work in the house and garden, she could actually not be called a domestic servant. She was a member of the family.

Mrs. Melnikov came from the educated and wealthy Moscow family of the Kryukovs and during her first marriage had been the wife of a powerful banker with whom she had three daughters. With heart and soul, she lived for the theater and for music. During the chaotic period of the revolution, she got divorced and married Pyotr Melnikov.

Maria Aleksandrovna had an older sister called Pyereta, whose actual name – Peripetuia –, which she hated, came from the Russian Orthodox calendar of saints. Her husband was Vasily Lushsky, a well-known actor at the Moscow Art Theatre, a colleague and friend of Stanislavski and Nemirovich-Danchenko, who was later awarded the title "People's Artist of the USSR," with all the privileges and guarantees associated therewith. The powers that be even overlooked his wife's upper-class origin, which is why Maria Aleksandrovna's sister was the only one in the family still to live unmolested in

Moscow after the revolution and was even allowed to keep her villa in the very center of town, right on the Arbat, which their father had given his daughter at the turn of the century when she married the actor. The two-story Italianate villa with its little garden and fountain looked like a relic from a lost world.

When Maria Aleksandrovna precipitously left Soviet Russia together with her second husband, she was not permitted to take the children from her first marriage with her. She hoped that a little later, when she was a Latvian citizen, she would be able to get them out, but did not manage to do so, and for almost two decades she was unable to see her daughters, only learning about their growing up in Moscow from occasional letters.

Alya, the only daughter the Melnikovs had in common, who was born when Maria Aleksandrovna was in her mid-forties, had Down syndrome. When I came to them, the sweet and friendly girl was around twenty, but had developed to the level of an eight-year-old. Her realm, which she never left, was the garden.

Like Mrs. Melnikov, Stepanida Dmitriyevna, who came from St. Petersburg, was also a widow. Towards the end of World War I, she had been working as a sales clerk in a shoe store and had fallen in love with a handsome customer, whom she married. Mr. Makars, who was Latvian, returned to his native land with his wife in the early '20s in the course of Latvian repatriation; here, his parents had a flourishing farm. Stepanida's husband died early, and the son he had from his first marriage, whom she had raised, succumbed to consumption while still young. Thus she was left on her own. Her brother-in-law inherited the farm, and she took a job as housekeeper with the Melnikovs. Stepanida spoke fluent Latvian, which could not be said of Maria Aleksandrovna.

The two women and the handicapped daughter lived together as a family. Stepanida kept house, for Masanna, as we called Mrs. Melnikov, had no clue about house and garden work. Stepanida comforted and took touching care of me as well. Masanna, who had been a great beauty in her youth, as I could see from her photographs, was well into her sixties. After her husband's death, she rarely left the house because her daughter needed her care. Now and then an occasional friend or student of her late husband from his years at the opera came to visit her.

I slept in a small room behind the pantry and kitchen. Mr. Melnikov had purchased the little wooden house, which was surrounded by a large, unkempt garden, shortly before the first Soviet occupation. It had three rooms, a spacious kitchen, and the above-mentioned small room. Pyotr Ivanovich had cherished great plans to remodel and renovate the house, but had no longer been able to implement them. On the other hand, the modest house had not been "nationalized," or rather, expropriated. I loved the park-like garden with its meadow, the tall horse-chestnut trees, and thick hazel bushes that kept prying eyes from noticing much of the occupants' daily routine. Thus after a long time I was again able to enjoy the spring and summer sun, lie in the green grass, and look up into the sky.

My second refuge was not far away. All I had to do was run down Zaļenieku street a short distance and cross Jelgavas šoseja – the present-day Vienības gatve – and I was in Atgāzenes iela 8 at the Schiemanns'.[2] In these two houses, alternating between them as necessary, I spent around a year and a half up to the end of July 1944.

---

2. *Jelgavas šoseja:* Latvian for Jelgava Highway, the main arterial road going south in Pārdaugava (the section of Riga on the left bank of the Daugava).

PAUL SCHIEMANN

Again it was Emīlija to whom I owed my refuge with Paul and Lotte Schiemann. When she accompanied me to the Schiemanns' house for the first time, I had no idea that this encounter would have consequences for the rest of my later life.

The German Balt Paul Schiemann was a prominent figure on the political stage, a protagonist of European history. I was aware, of course, that in the 1920s and '30s he had played an important part both in developing the young parliamentarian republic of Latvia, and in the League of Nations. He was a deputy of all four elected parliaments (Saeima) of Latvia and editor-in-chief of the *Rigasche Rundschau*, an influential German Baltic newspaper my family had also regularly read. As an opponent on principle of the National Socialist regime in Germany and of its sympathizers in Latvia, he was an authority and a widely read publicist. Admittedly in those days I had only a vague idea of the scope of his activities. At the time when I was welcomed into the Schiemann home, *Herr Doktor*, as he was generally called, was 67 years old. Illness and old age – he suffered from diabetes and TB – had severely restricted his political activity. But it was precisely this circumstance that protected him from too intense a scrutiny on the part of the occupation authorities.

His wife Charlotte, called *Frau Lotte*, came from Bavaria and had played leading parts at various German theaters in both light comedy and drama. Shortly before World War I, on tour in Riga, she had met Paul Schiemann, whom she married in early 1914. Although there was a good German theater in Riga, her acting career was thus practically over, for as the wife of Schiemann, the well-known and socially active editor-in-chief of the *Rigasche Rundschau*, she no longer had time to go on the stage.

Frau Lotte was an extremely fun-loving, vivacious, and charming woman. Unsentimental and matter-of-fact, while at the same time understanding and compassionate, she had a great sense of humor. Her presence brought a bohemian lightness into the house. At the time she too must already have been over fifty, but everybody thought she was younger.

In the Schiemanns' marriage there was a time when Frau Lotte separated from her husband and married a baron, whom she, however, left after two years to marry Schiemann for the second time. While I was there, she had a family friend and admirer, the thirty-year-old Eugen, evidently the brother of one of her woman friends, to whom she assigned all kinds of tasks. He used to accompany Frau Lotte to large parties and to the opera. Herr Doktor, who was worn out by his illnesses, was glad that his wife was not forced to give up all amusements on his account. His thoughts were occupied with other problems, and he accepted the minor details of day-to-day life with Olympic calm.

Paul and Lotte Schiemann dearly loved each other. Frau Lotte admired her husband, touchingly took care of him and, on days when he felt more lively, organized cheerful little parties in which I, too, participated on occasion. It almost felt like home.

A wonderful relationship developed between Frau Lotte and me. Always ready for a laugh, she was frivolous but not banal. For me, there was something deeply comforting about her sense of humor. She poked fun at everyone, from Hitler to the Führer's representatives in Riga to the crème de la crème of Latvian society, which she knew well, since she was frequently invited to their social gatherings and went to them on occasion. When she returned, she amused us with the latest gossip from circles loyal to Hitler: which Latvian lady had which Wehrmacht officer as her lover, what sort of jewelry had been given to this or that operatic star, etc. The German officers, who had plenty of looted goods, were highly sought-after lovers among women in various social circles.

Frau Lotte also reported that many a Latvian family was searching for German ancestors so they could feel just a bit superior to their compatriots. Although a large part of the local elite had been carried off by the Soviet repressions, many had been able to save themselves, and a number of them were now collaborating with the occupiers, almost unbeknownst to the rest of the inhabitants of Latvia. Thanks to Frau Lotte, I, living invisible deep underground, was able to catch a glimpse of what was behind the scenes. Nevertheless, I regarded these marginalia as material for satire rather than as historical information.

Schiemann himself was disgusted by such gossip. He said that brainless calculation and greed for power, hypocrisy, and dangerous self-deception, not to mention the atrophy of humanity, did not even deserve an ironic smile. You could tell what bitterness and disillusionment about the society he had formerly known so well were expressed in his rare, his very rare verbal eruptions.

Otherwise, life in the Schiemanns' house went on as though the occupying power outside its walls didn't exist. We simply ignored it. As for me, I was treated as a totally normal, welcome guest.

At the time when fate brought me together with Paul Schiemann, he was a sick man, as I mentioned above. He knew he didn't have long to live anymore. Yet he tackled one more project: writing down his experiences, which he wanted to pass on to future generations.

He was already so weak that he could sit at his desk for an hour a day at most; he lacked the physical strength to write a large book. When he hid me in his house, fate unexpectedly sent him a secretary who was ideally suited for his undertaking. Happy that I was able to make myself useful – this time not by cleaning, sewing or mending clothes, but as a typist – I hurled myself into the unexpectedly exciting task, which promised to satisfy my boundless curiosity.

We worked in a room on the top floor used as Schiemann's study and bedroom both. Mostly he lay on the bed while I got settled at the desk. I wrote down Schiemann's words by hand, only to type them later. Herr Doktor spoke slowly, in a weak voice, to save his strength. Often he had already thought through the passages or even written them down, so that I could type them directly.

He began with his biography: his childhood in Jelgava, the years as a high school and university student in Germany, his early career as a journalist in the Baltic provinces of Russia, in Tartu and Tallinn, until, in 1907, he began working at the *Rigasche Rundschau*, with which he was to be associated all his life. His experiences in World War I seemed like an adventure novel to me: officer in the Imperial Russian Army, severely wounded in the arm, which almost had to be amputated, an Odyssey involving various places, rulers, and armies, between the Russian Revolution and the gradual forging of the identity of the Baltic nations. During the final phase of the war, he found himself in Berlin, where he encountered the champion of Latvian independence who had gotten to safety there. They immediately discovered they shared a common language and began to work together, since the situation was favorable for founding a Latvian state. Naturally, the consequence of Schiemann's collaboration with the Latvians was severe criticism on the part of the German Baltic minority in Latvia to which, of course, he belonged. Among its barons and patricians, he was considered to be a black sheep because he actively supported the Latvian independence movement and later the young state.

In his conversations with the young woman I was then, only moderately enlightened when it came to politics, he always emphasized like an axiom: The native population of Latvia are the Latvians, and everyone who lives in this country must respect that. But historically Latvia is also the native land of several other ethnic groups that have been rooted there for generations – and that, too, must not be ignored.

Since I hadn't read Schiemann's writings, I was hearing his clearly reasoned core idea for the first time. I was able to accept it without objections, and basically I still share his idea today: All those who reside in Latvia must learn to get along with each other, respecting each other and together supporting the Latvian state, their homeland, with sincere loyalty – while at the same time recognizing the right of all minorities to education in their own mother tongue and to the cultivation of their own cultural traditions. Admittedly, at that time, when I had to struggle with completely different existential dangers, I was not capable of going more deeply into the concepts discussed by Schiemann, concepts that have remained relevant to this day – for instance, the idea of an "a-national state," from which follows the separation of multinational activities from state and political concerns.

Full of enthusiasm, Schiemann participated in drafting a constitution for the Republic of Latvia, which later enjoyed global recognition.

During the '20s and early '30s, he was one of the most prominent Saeima deputies and intermittently also a member of the Riga City Council; moreover, he held important European offices: until 1939, as vice president of the Congress of European Nationalities, founded in Geneva in 1929, and in 1939 as founder of the "German Association for National Pacification in Europe" in Vienna. Schiemann was regarded not only as a pioneer of the European minority movement, but also as its official spokesman.

In our work there were periodic interruptions, since I repeatedly had to go stay at Mrs. Melnikov's. Occasionally the Schiemanns would have people visiting – Frau Lotte's relatives from Bavaria and, if I am not mistaken, relatives of Theodor Schiemann, Herr Doktor's uncle. This Schiemann was a well-known conservative historian who had settled in Germany in the late 19th century and had gradually become "Germanized," as his nephew quipped – the German Balts were in the habit of strongly emphasizing the difference between them and the "Reich Germans" in general, and already as a child I had noticed that they even had a touch of arrogance, a certain snobbishness in this regard.

As soon as house guests were expected, I had to clear out and go across Jelgavas šoseja to stay at the Melnikovs'. When visitors were announced for a couple of hours, I would remain upstairs, while Herr Doktor sat with them in the drawing room downstairs or asked them to come out on the porch if the weather was nice.

Without Schiemann I would probably hardly have thought as intensively about the founding period of the sovereign Republic of Latvia. I got a sense of the people of that time, their ideas and ideals, the relationships between them. After all, each of them had his own view of what the young state should look like. And was that state not a utopia anyway?

Schiemann sensed that he would not manage to finish telling his life story. But except for occasional slightly ironic allusions he avoided referring to his premonition in our conversations.

It wasn't as if I only wrote down what Schiemann said; often our work turned into a dialogue between two unequal interlocutors. Schiemann liked me to express my thoughts or ask a question to find out more. He encouraged me to do so, and this gave me the feeling that I was thinking and acting rationally. The most important insight I gained was that even in the most tragic moments of life one must fight to keep one's sovereignty and intellectual freedom instead of letting oneself be controlled by circumstances. At the time, Schiemann had his back to the wall, yet he lived and conducted himself as his self-respect demanded.

As he dictated his memoir, he only occasionally referred to his broken, wrecked lifelong dream: to shape Latvia into an exemplary democracy that would serve other states as a model of the integration of different minorities – Germans, Russians, Jews, Poles, and Lithuanians. He said this had by no means been a utopian vision; in Latvia, he said, all the conditions for it had been present.

The foundation of his political ideal was shaken in the early '30s. When Hitler came to power in Germany, his influence grew in the circles of the German Balts (whom, incidentally, the Nazis called "Baltic Germans" in analogy to "Sudeten Germans"), although the majority of Germans in Latvia, especially the older generation, were quite skeptical and even hostile toward Hitler. Schiemann, however, had to give up his position as party chairman of the German Balts in the Saeima, and as early as 1933, he resigned from his job as editor-in-chief of the *Rigasche Rundschau* because he had been required to adjust the newspaper's ideology to that of the Nazis, something he found unacceptable.

The Ulmanis coup d'état of May 15th, 1934 was a catastrophe for Schiemann. I questioned him particularly insistently about this period (when I had still been in secondary school). I realized that his dream of Latvia as a model democratic state had collapsed at that time. Schiemann rejected nationalism as a guiding state ideology and driving force of policy not only as an archaic and backward model that dated back to the 19th century; he also recognized it as a fundamental danger for the Latvian state and the Latvian people. He did not conceal from me the flaws of the parliamentary Republic of Latvia – the wrangling of the parties, the corruption of the public servants, the machinations of the nouveaux riches – and was nevertheless convinced (exactly like my father) that these were all growing pains. The democratic, parliamentarian structures of Western Europe, he said, had also only taken shape and stabilized over centuries; one couldn't expect that in our country everything would come to maturity within a few years. I was also reminded of Father when Schiemann said he had been happy to see that the Latvians were gradually shedding their complexes and overcoming the irrational fears that they would lose their identity, something that was typical of the collective psychology of a people that had been oppressed for centuries. In my opinion it is these complexes that lead to wrong reactions in every more or less critical or only seemingly threatening situation, because people's logical judgment is impaired and they follow impulses triggered by past injustice.

I did not really have the opportunity to question him about his time in Vienna and the year 1938, when Hitler annexed Austria and Schiemann returned to Riga. Although political adversaries in Latvia did not have to fear for their lives, he could not accept the authoritarian Ulmanis regime with its grotesque leader cult and narrow cultural horizons. He no longer took part in the official social life, and besides, his illnesses were beginning to get the better of him.

After the signing of the Hitler-Stalin pact, Paul Schiemann categorically refused to follow Hitler's call to return "home to the Reich": As long as Hitler was in power, he said, he would not set foot on German soil. Admittedly he also did not assess the Soviet threat correctly – and when the first Soviet tanks rolled across the eastern border of Latvia, it was too late to leave, say, for Switzerland. The Schiemanns were caught in a trap and had no choice but to retreat into their four walls like a snail into its shell.

The contents of our conversations were no longer included in the memoir, which breaks off with the founding of the Republic of Latvia; we managed to complete only the section between 1903 and 1919. Only one text, written in manuscript by Schiemann, which he had no longer been able to dictate to me, was added to the book edition of his memoir – a brilliant essay in which he pithily and accurately analyzes the year 1940/41. That was how I found out a great deal of new information about political events in the first Soviet year, which I would also like to include in these memories.

Schiemann told me that at the start of the Soviet invasion he cherished naïve hopes – though this was only for a short time, and he was not the only one to do so. Initially, he said, people wanted to believe the Soviet promises that democratic elections would actually take place and the Saeima could be reinstituted in accordance with the constitution. Together with his former colleagues he had started to put together lists of candidates for the election, and onetime Saeima deputies had been particularly enthusiastic. Yet the general respect enjoyed by Schiemann was so great that at dangerous moments well-informed people had warned him – both during the Soviet and, later, during the Nazi occupation. It's true that one section of the leftist Social Democrats had managed to change their allegiance, dyeing themselves red as soon as the Red Army invaded Latvia and thus gaining the trust of the powers that be; nevertheless, former colleagues from his time in parliament discreetly informed Schiemann that there would be no elections based on party lists. He immediately grasped the situation, and when his supporters urged him to run as a candidate in the parliamentary election, Schiemann declined. And sure enough: In one fell swoop, the non-Communist lists of candidates were transformed into lists of persons who were due to be arrested or immediately shot.

A similarly ominous situation came up barely a year later. Shortly before June 14th, Schiemann was warned in strictest confidence by persons well-disposed toward him to stay away from home for a while and to go into hiding somewhere unobtrusively. Although Schiemann was already so ill that he hardly ever left his room, he followed the advice. The NKVD actually did come to take him away, and if he hadn't been warned, Schiemann would have ended his life in Siberia – if not already on the way there.

A few days later, Hitler's Germany attacked its ally, the Soviet Union. If ever there was a persona non grata in Latvia for the Nazis at the time, it was Schiemann. Exhausted by his illnesses, he could not have gone underground for any length of time, since he needed constant medical care. Frau Lotte believed that it was precisely this infirmity that to a certain extent saved her husband – to whom would he have posed a threat? Schiemann confided to me that a cousin of his wife's had a high position in the Gebietskommissariat in Riga and was not at all eager for his "dirty family secret" to come to light. Herr Doktor joked that this was why the relative held his hand above his house like an umbrella. That was how Schiemann came to remain relatively unscathed. Strictly speaking, however, he was under a kind of house arrest. He knew that his mail and possibly some of his phone calls were being monitored. He only rarely left the house to go and see doctors, while his primary physician normally came to see him at home. Schiemann's closest friends and a few acquaintances came to visit only rarely. All these circumstances were quite favorable for hiding a persecuted person in the private house with a little garden that was concealed behind a thick hedge.

Although Paul Schiemann always emphasized that he was "only a democrat and a liberal," he also maintained good relations with the former Social-Democrat Saeima deputies – not only during the entire Ulmanis period but also during both occupations, to the end of his life. Obviously these relations were not impaired by the fact that their positions were irreconcilable. The former deputies came in order to convince Schiemann to support the initiatives of the opposition or because they wanted to hear his views on various issues. Naturally I did not meet them, because I was lying low upstairs, quiet as a mouse, but usually I was the first to hear what Schiemann thought of what had just been discussed, as he often came up to my room agitated or even indignant. I have especially vivid memories of two incidents.

A few Latvian acquaintances of Schiemann's whom I did not know had come to see him. After the guests left, I heard him climbing the stairs heavily, muttering angrily and complaining. The guests, he said, had enthusiastically told him about the "Latvian Legion," a "legion of volunteers" of the Waffen-SS established in February 1943 on Hitler's orders. Now, they told him, we could finally go to war against Stalin and restore a free Latvia. "These people are either idiots or deluded!" Schiemann grumbled. You couldn't expect the young guys to grasp the situation. They were assured that it was their patriotic duty and that they would be fighting for their fatherland, and they believed it. But if grown-up people with political experience said stuff like that, it was absurd, irresponsible, even an egoistic crime against the youth of their people. These men were either blind or didn't want to face the truth. "You can't fight fire with fire!"[1] Hitler, said Schiemann, did not need a free Latvia, he needed cannon fodder. What is more, it was clear that Germany would ultimately be defeated, so that in this game, rashly, they'd be betting everything on the losing card. And it would be the young men who would pay. The only way to stay out of this game would be by keeping a cool head and preserving one's honor – Latvia had no horse in this race.

Unfortunately Schiemann was to prove right.

A second time, I saw him worried and upset after a small delegation appeared at his house that consisted, among others, of several deputies of parties that had formerly been represented in the Saeima. If I'm not mistaken, they included Fēlikss Cielēns, Pauls Kalniņš, and the latter's wife Klāra. I haven't read the declaration of the Latvian Central Council, but am familiar only with Schiemann's version of it. A few years later, the Soviet security agencies interrogated me twice regarding this declaration, but they probably realized at some point that I really didn't know anything specific.

After showing the guests out, Schiemann returned to his study

---

1. Literally, "You can't drive out the devil with Beelzebub!" (German proverb: *Man kann den Teufel nicht mit Beelzebub austreiben!*).

dejected. This was yet another utopia, a completely illusionary project and pure wishful thinking that the moment Hitler was weakened it would be possible to regain Latvia's autonomy, an overture, so to speak, to the restoration of its independence. "If we, men who are respected in Latvia, sign such a declaration, which is built on sand, we are deceiving the people and encouraging them to act irrationally and adventurously – and will have unjustifiable victims on our conscience. This is not 1918 – the British navy cannot and will not show up in the Bay of Riga. And we are left with no choice but bravely to accept that Latvia's present situation is tragic. The only thing I can compare it to is a stalemate in chess. An impasse as far as the restoration of independence is concerned."

Paul Schiemann was convinced that Latvia could be saved only by a coup in Germany itself – if Hitler's opponents succeeded in getting rid of him and assuming control of the German Reich. Then peace could immediately be concluded with the Western states as long as the Red Army was still within its legal borders and had not yet invaded Latvia. As an ally the Soviet Union would then be forced to accept this status quo and to sign the peace treaty. Only then would there be hope for Latvia and the two other Baltic states to regain their independence. On the other hand, if nothing changed in Germany, the war would have to be continued until the longed-for Allied victory – yet in that case Stalin would advance far to the west, and nothing and nobody would then be able to force him to retreat from the liberated and at the same time conquered territories again.

Schiemann repeatedly spoke about this sole hope. And also about how hard it was for the average Latvian to admit bluntly that there was no other salvation for Latvia. Neither the volunteer legion of the Waffen-SS nor the Latvian Division of the Red Army could save Latvia. The wise saying of a general and First World War veteran comes to mind: "Both have the right enemies – and both the wrong friends."

Schiemann had a very clear point of view. The fact that he condemned the Soviet regime in principle did not prevent him from recognizing the heroism of the Russian people without reservation, and from deeply deploring the immense, often unnecessary losses of human lives incurred by the Red Army, which had been weakened by Stalin's crimes. He held the righteous struggle of the people per se in high esteem: They were defending their homeland, although officially in the name of Stalin – just as they had fought in the name of the czar in 1812.

I couldn't help noticing that even talking about these things exhausted the sick politician so much that I sometimes had the feeling he would presently draw his last breath.

Around the beginning of the summer of 1944, when the Red Army was already standing near the eastern border of Latvia, Paul Schiemann visibly collapsed. His strength left him. The deadlock in which Latvia found itself, its unenviable fate, weighed on his mind terribly. He repeated many times that the only salvation now, at the last moment, would be an uprising in Germany or at least the assassination of Hitler. At the time I was still too ignorant to be able to assess the political situation in Germany. When I later analyzed the statements of Schiemann I still recalled and his behavior, I had the growing conviction that perhaps he was maintaining indirect connections and had information about the preparation for the later attempt on Hitler's life in the "Wolf's Lair" [Wolfsschanze]. He exuded a strange restlessness, tense expectation, and his thoughts kept returning to his hypothesis about the only possible way out. I shall never learn whether this suspicion was grounded in reality or is merely a product of my imagination.

At that time, in May/June 1944, Schiemann had to decide what he himself should do. The Germans were already beginning to retreat from Riga, and Frau Lotte, a thoroughly practical, realistic woman, was of the opinion that they should gradually start packing their bags. All Germans would be in deep water once the Soviets came back, regardless of whether they were guilty or not. I admired Schiemann's sense of justice and his ability to understand even an unloved adversary when I heard him say: "You won't even be able to blame the Russians, particularly if you consider what the Germans have done to them…"

Still, Schiemann had declared that he would not set foot on German soil as long as Hitler was in power. He was incapable of going against his principles, of deleting the meaning of his whole existence. Thus he was incapable of fleeing to Hitler's Germany. He did urge his wife to go to her relatives in Bavaria. But Frau Lotte too had her principles. She refused to leave her severely ill husband, and remained in Riga.

In this difficult situation, Schiemann was nonetheless worried about me as well. "Little lady," he said (that was what he jokingly called me), "you have at least one alternative. Compared to certain death, the Red Army is the lesser evil. At least you'll have saved your life." Schiemann had also considered how he could help me later, once the war was over. He felt that after Hitler's imminent defeat and the inevitable cleansing of Germany I should go to Berlin or the West in general, because in Latvia I had lost everything. Here I would be tortured by the memories. Besides, one could only speculate what Soviet rule would look like after the victory. For a short time, Frau Lotte fantasized whether I ought not to try and get forged papers and leave Latvia together with the other refugees. But that would have been too dangerous. We had no illusions: At the slightest suspicion, there would be plenty of people among the refugees who, with malicious joy, would immediately deliver me up to destruction. Just in case, Schiemann did give me the address of a friend, the actor Paul Wegener. If I later came to the West, I was to look him up without fail and give him Schiemann's regards. Wegener would help me under any circumstances. At the time I was glad that the famous stage and screen star had kept his decency even during the Nazi era. But I already suspected that I would not be able to fall back upon this offer of help.

Paul Schiemann did not live to learn of the failed attempt on Hitler's life on July 20th, 1944 at the Führer's headquarters. He died on Midsummer Night, 1944. Although he was very weak, we were not expecting him to die at that time, as his condition had not noticeably deteriorated.

When I thought about those days later, I had the feeling that Schiemann had simply "switched off" his will to live in order to be able to die. There are people who are able to do that. This is how he dealt with the unsolvable dilemma he was facing.

Paul Schiemann's death was a significant turning point for me as well. During the almost one and a half years I spent with him and the Melnikovs I had recovered to some extent and begun to feel almost like a normal person, if that was at all possible.

The night Schiemann died was the last I spent under his roof. The next morning, Frau Lotte gave me the address of her relatives in Bavaria and made me promise to be sure and look her up if I managed to get to Germany.

The Schiemanns' house filled with people, preparations were made for the funeral, and Frau Lotte did not want to stay in Riga one day longer than necessary. She was already packing her suitcases to leave Latvia forever, and I went to the Melnikovs' house. The German authorities would not authorize a large funeral service; the interment, in which I naturally could not participate, was under observation, and those present were allegedly photographed.

I never saw Frau Lotte again, nor did I hear from her for years. For just as many years, I did not know the fate of the typescript of Schiemann's memoirs. In the mid-'eighties – the perestroika had already begun – the phone rang one day and my childhood friend, the historian Pēteris Krupņikovs, rather mysteriously announced his visit – plus a surprise. He handed me Paul Schiemann's book *Zwischen zwei Zeitaltern* (Between Two Eras), published in 1979 in the series of the Carl-Schirren-Gesellschaft, which publishes, among other things, German Baltic literature.

In the introduction of the book it says that the author's widow, Mrs. Charlotte Schiemann, gave the typescript to the publishing house and told them that the memoir was written shortly before Paul Schiemann's death and thus remained unfinished. Included in the book was a separate manuscript about much later events in Latvia in 1940/41. The introduction also states that Schiemann dictated his memoir to a young Jewish woman whom he and his wife kept hidden in their house. It was obvious to me that Frau Lotte had not mentioned my name in order not to cause me unnecessary problems in case I was still alive and had remained in the Soviet Union. In the 'seventies there was already fairly accurate information in the West about the way the Soviet security agencies dealt with the few Latvian Jews who had survived the Holocaust.

I remember Paul Schiemann with respect and gratitude – an extraordinary man who had a profound influence on my life – not only as someone who saved me and as an example of humanity, but also as the model of a steadfast, sovereign personality.

In February 2000, at my instigation, Paul and Charlotte Schiemann were awarded the title "Righteous Among the Nations" by the memorial Yad Vashem in Jerusalem. The award has also been received by other persons in Europe who saved Jewish lives during the fateful years of the Shoah. Their names are engraved in the Wall of Honor in the Garden of the Righteous Among the Nations in Yad Vashem. A few years prior to this, the proposal that Emīlija Gajevska's name be immortalized there was implemented, and it is wonderful for me to know that the remembrance of these three so different personalities is united in this place as a testimony to the highest human values. For, as it says in the Talmud, "Whoever saves one life, saves the world entire."

THE SOLUTION DRAWS NEAR

Twice during my years in hiding, people who themselves belonged more or less to the "inferior" ethnic groups despised by the "master race" posed a threat to me. Before I came to Mrs. Melnikov and the Schiemanns, I had found a short-term refuge with a woman who lived alone, a pensioner in Ogre who had a house with a large garden. She was a genuine Latvian Social Democrat and in the 1920s had worked in the Saeima as a secretary or something similar. I liked Ogre, a quiet small town southeast of Riga located at the confluence of the Ogre and Daugava rivers; the place seemed relatively safe, the old lady was uncomplicated and very approachable, you could talk to her about politics and find out interesting things about Latvia's parliamentary period.

Since she could no longer take care of her garden on her own, she hired a laborer, a Ukrainian prisoner of war who hated the Soviet power with all his heart. Even more, however, he loathed the Jews and the Poles to an extent that he could talk from morning till night about how right Hitler was to wipe out all the Jews one after the other and to bump off the Poles as well. In my entire life I've never met, face to face, another antisemite as pathological as him. It's true that he had no idea I was Jewish, but we women lived in constant fear that he would find out one day. That's why I had no choice but to disappear again after barely a month.

A slightly less dangerous, but still unpleasant situation occurred at Mrs. Melnikov's house. In the summer of 1943 she too found someone to help with garden work – an eighteen-year-old Russian girl from a kolkhoz near Velikiye Luki, one of the civilians deported by the Germans from the occupied territories to do forced labor. In Riga, too, there were camp-like collection points where you could engage prisoners of war to work for you. At the time this was even an advantage for the forced laborers, since they usually got decent food and urgently needed clothing – and often even a small salary in cash.

When we saw Manya the first time, we all felt very sorry for her. She was as thin as a rail, nothing but skin and bones, and wore an old shawl instead of a coat. The girl was bathed, dressed, and given plenty of food, so that she soon recovered and turned into a good-looking young woman. Then we noticed that Manya was gaining weight suspiciously fast. When we questioned her, she confessed that a German soldier had raped her and that she was expecting a baby.

According to regulations, the forced laborers had to return to the camp at night, but Manya begged Mrs. Melnikov to get permission for her to spend the nights with us as well. The matter was arranged, and Manya merely needed to report regularly as proof that she had not run off. Once she regained her strength, the Soviet citizen in her began to come to the fore. If in the Ukrainian man I had, as it were, encountered a model antisemite, then in Manya we – the inhabitants of both houses, including that of the Schiemanns – had come face to face with a fanatical Komsomol member. Prior to this, none of us had ever made closer acquaintance with anyone of this type.

As she looked around her, Manya saw everything exactly as she had been taught to do during her political education classes. The guidelines she had learned made it possible for her immediately to classify people without any doubt whatsoever. Mrs. Melnikov, the formerly wealthy fancy bourgeois lady and reactionary emigrant, had taken her in in order to exploit her mercilessly. I was a capitalist brat, which is why I immediately became the target of her mistrust and proletarian hatred. When kindhearted Frau Lotte hired Manya for pay, good food, and clothing to help her in the house and garden for a few weeks, Manya's class hatred promptly turned against her as well, and became even stronger towards me. Namely, Manya noticed that in the Schiemann house – that is, the house of the German enemy – I was treated like their own daughter, since I sat at a desk all day long writing, while she had to do menial work. Frau Lotte had hoped that Manya's Soviet way of thinking would change as soon as she got to know a different kind of life, but the opposite happened. In everything Manya observed in the house of the Melnikovs and the Schiemanns and in our interpersonal relationships, she saw only a confirmation and graphic illustration of the communist dogmas. She interpreted every act of kindness and every selfless gift as hypocrisy or deceit. The only person she accepted was Stepanida, who, of course, was also being "exploited." She regarded the help she was offered as a matter of course, without gratitude, since in her opinion she was only getting back what the hated exploiters had "sucked from the blood and sweat of her class brothers." Gradually we all began to keep at a distance from Manya, especially me. Our only hope now was that she would not report me to the German authorities or the Latvian police, because these were fascists.

As the time of the birth came closer, Manya remained safely at the Melnikov house, something that had been officially authorized thanks to a lot of effort and bribes. In the fall of 1944, when the Red Army and the Soviet power had recaptured Riga, Manya and the baby needed a very special kind of assistance. Mrs. Melnikov wrote to Manya's parents at the kolkhoz that their daughter had given birth to a baby fathered by a Russian prisoner of war whom the Germans had later murdered. Thus Manya, her reputation as a Komsomol member unblemished, was able to return to her native village, where, according to what she told us, moral standards were extremely strict. Then, for the first time, she really thanked us.

In the summer of 1944 the situation in Riga became far more tense. In Mrs. Melnikov's neighborhood lived a shoemaker called Ignatjevs. We knew he had close links to the partisans – both to the reds in Latgale and the Latvian nationalists in Kurzeme. When he had had one drink too many, he openly told us about them. I asked him to take me to the partisans.

Ignatjevs looked at me oddly and said he wouldn't take a Jew. Transporting Jews was too dangerous – if he was caught, the consequences were far more serious than in the case of non-Jews. The partisans, too – both one lot and the other – were not too eager to accept Jews. And so my plan went nowhere.

After Paul Schiemann's death I spent one more month at the Melnikovs'. I couldn't stay any longer, as I had initially hoped. The Red Army was already on Latvian territory, and Riga was starting to look like a front-line city. On the outskirts of Riga, the Germans were positioning anti-aircraft batteries, and Mrs. Melnikov's garden was chosen for one of them. The residents had to vacate the house.

Mrs. Melnikov, Alya, and Stepanida took the basic necessities with them and found a home with nearby acquaintances where, however, there was no room for me. These people were Russians by birth from Vidzeme, who had been evacuated to Russia during World War I and hadn't been able to return. Before the October Revolution they had fled not westward, like most of the white émigrés, but eastward, to Harbin in Chinese Manchuria. At first they did quite well there; a large Russian Orthodox community had settled in the city. But in 1932 Harbin was occupied by the Japanese, and the Melnikovs' future neighbors traveled across the entire continent back to Riga.

They were nice people. Their daughter Nina was older than me, an intelligent, vivacious blonde, though suffering from ill health. She was married to a young Latvian whose name was Osvalds Tabaks, and lived with him in Pleskavas iela, the former Marijas iela. I knew the two of them well because they often visited Nina's parents in Torṇakalns. Osvalds worked in the VEF factory as a technician; the production of the works was considered to be of military importance, so that for the time being he was not drafted into the so-called volunteer legion. Osvalds and Nina had once mentioned that I could hide at their place for a while if I had nowhere else to go.

That moment seemed to have arrived. However, I could no longer get in touch with anyone, for as the front moved closer everything was turned upside down, the infrastructure collapsed, and the phone went dead. Besides, I wouldn't have known whom to call, for Osvalds and Nina had no phone, and ever since Blankenstein had been arrested, Emīlija no longer had a fixed abode and spent the night now here, now there. We had agreed, however, that in case of emergency I would go to her sister, Marija, and the latter's husband, Juzefs. I knew the house in Riga Old Town where they worked as caretakers. At first I wanted to try and stay with them, and as a "reserve" I had the Tabakses in mind. And so I set out, not knowing whether I would even find anyone at home.

I shouldered my backpack, which contained all my possessions, and set off. Public transportation had broken down, so that I had to cross the Daugava on foot in order to reach the Old Town. From afar I could already tell that German soldiers stood at the bridgehead, checking the papers of the pedestrians. These were not SS men but ordinary Wehrmacht soldiers. I saw that they stopped people, waved a few to the side and searched their luggage, while others were allowed through.

I relied on my instinct. I seem to remember I didn't even slow down, but walked toward them resolutely. When I had come closer I found myself face to face with a few young fellows, smiled at them, reached for my backpack, and asked: "Shall I open it?" They smiled at me too, and one of them waved me through to the bridge. They let me through without stopping me, and I crossed the Daugava to "Mary and Joseph," as I called the Karčevskis family. This was one of the unbelievable and inexplicable strokes of luck that saved my life.

In the big apartment house near St. Peter's Church, with its inner courtyard and rear building, I found the two caretakers at home in their apartment; immediately, Emīlija appeared as well, and we considered what we should do now. The Karčevskis family consisted of six persons, and I could spend maybe one night in the small caretaker's apartment in the rear building, but not stay there for a longer period.

At the time, in August 1944, many Riga residents were already leaving the city, mostly in the direction of Kurzeme. Juzefs said a few apartments were also vacant in the buildings of which he was in charge – and until the owners returned he had been entrusted with the keys. Everybody knew they could rely on him one hundred percent. Juzefs put me up in a basement apartment in which all the furniture had been left behind – including even a radio, much to my delight. The windows, which were at the level of the sidewalk, remained blacked out, and once a day Marija brought me something to eat – bread, milk, cheese, sometimes soup or even a meat dish. It was enough to live on. Practically all day long I listened to the BBC, turned down low – I feverishly shared the experiences of the Allies, of the navy, the troops landing in Normandy; in my imagination I was in the ranks of the Resistance approaching Paris. In turn, the Soviet broadcasts reported that the front was moving closer in the east. And that meant that the "lesser of the two evils," as Schiemann had referred to the Red Army, was drawing near as well.

Day in, day out, my only company were the rats, with whom I got along splendidly. I neither found them disgusting nor feared them, although I had read that starving rats will attack even people. I gave them some of the food Marija brought me, sometimes even a bit of cheese. While I myself was eating, the little creatures were courteous – they would come out of their cracks, look at me with shining little eyes, and wait for me to invite them to table.

One day Marija did not show up. I wasn't too worried – I still had a piece of bread, and I could drink water from the faucet. But when she did not come on the second and third morning as well, I was alarmed. I thought about what I should do and decided to bide my time and not to leave my hiding place for the time being.

Late in the evening of the third day, Juzefs brought me something to eat – and an issue of *Tēvija* dated August 25th. From this antisemitic rag, I found out that in a house not far away, in Peldu iela 15, the janitor's wife, Alma Pole, had hidden seven Jews, including one woman. The men had managed to get hold of a couple of weapons. But now somebody had given away the hiding place. The hunt for the unfortunates, whom the paper described as "Jewish criminals," ended in a bloodbath. There was a scuffle, and one of the policemen was killed. The people who were captured in the encircled house were shot dead on the spot, but Juzefs said one of them had probably managed to escape across the rooftops. The pursuers thought the fugitive had not been able to break out of the encirclement and hidden in one of the adjacent buildings, which is why they had started searching the apartments in the neighborhood. Juzefs' building, too, had been painstakingly searched, but the police left the locked-up apartments undisturbed; Juzefs had explained to them that the residents had fled the Russians to Kurzeme and nobody could get in without breaking down the door. Still, guards were posted around the block of houses, and Juzefs could not venture out to come and see me until they had left. The incident had ended well for us, but we no longer felt really safe and decided that I must leave the house. Years later, I learned to my great surprise that there had been Jews concealed in another empty apartment – namely, my classmate Riva Šefere, whom I mentioned earlier, and her brother. At the time I knew nothing about this – so strict was the secrecy observed by our saviors.

At the end of August, I moved to my last place of refuge: to Marijas iela, officially still called Pleskavas iela, to Osvalds and Nina. At that point the SS began to mobilize even the workers who had been exempted from conscription as indispensable for the legion of volunteers, but Osvalds had no intention of complying with the conscription order. As the chaos began to spread, he hid in the basement of his house, but he did go upstairs to the apartment fairly often as well. The neighbors weren't interested in him, they were all preoccupied with their own affairs, for it was clear that the end of German rule was imminent. When I asked Nina if she could take me in, she merely laughed: "What's the difference – if I hide one, I can hide two as well."

Nina herself during that period was suffering from severe asthma and a lung disease, and seldom left the house. She was considered chronically ill and had been declared an invalid and unable to work, but earned money on the side with typing jobs at home. During those weeks I spent with them in September and October 1944, we had a very hard time. Only Nina had ration cards; it was hardly possible to get anything on the side. Once someone brought us a big piece of meat with a bone teeming with maggots. We boiled it in vinegar water, the maggots rose to the top, we poured off the water, and then added fresh water and boiled it till it was soft. The soup turned out perfect. We neither got poisoned nor did we die. However, we did lose a lot of weight – when I left my hiding place, I weighed a hundred and four pounds.

Soon there came a time when in Riga scarcely a single night passed without an air raid alarm, when everybody had to go into the basement. Osvalds, who lived there during the day, came up to the apartment in the evenings by the servants' staircase, and I stayed upstairs as well. Nina, on the other hand, did the opposite: As soon as the sirens wailed, she went down to the air-raid shelter. This was also done so that the neighbors would believe she lived alone. We were not particularly scared of the air raids. I was still in that insensible trance, but Nina and Osvalds too were fairly untroubled, and even reckless.

Like many of my previous hiding places, I was no longer able to identify this house in Marijas iela later on. I guess it was somewhere near Stabu and Bruņenieku iela. Quartered right across the street from us was a German military headquarters. I remember the late October evening when the rest of the occupants of the house sat in the basement as usual. Osvalds and I, on the other hand, were looking out the window watching the evacuation of the headquarters. The Soviet artillery was already strafing the city center. What was happening on the street looked like a stage show, and we had great seats, like being in a box at the theater. I couldn't tell whether the Germans tried to burn any papers or to blow up the building, they simply came running outside, jumped into their vehicles, leapt on their motorbikes and raced away. All they took with them were a few boxes. Papers and scraps of paper fluttered out the open windows, swirled about in the air, and slowly settled on the pavement, covering it like strange snowflakes.

As soon as this horde was gone, the inhabitants of the adjacent houses appeared on the "stage" and, ignoring the shells that were still falling and exploding fairly frequently, began to loot the stores. Along its entire length, Marijas iela was bordered by larger and smaller businesses in which there was still merchandise. Osvalds and I observed that the men tended to be interested in so-called industrial goods, which under the Germans were sold according to a special point system, while the women pounced on the grocery stores. Particularly comical were the men who emptied out, as if intoxicated, a lingerie shop on the opposite side of the street. Many came with bicycles or handcarts and grabbed bras and women's undies by the bundle.

Then the shooting intensified, the street emptied, and Osvalds and I realized there was no longer anyone to whom we could be betrayed. The last act was over; I had already watched the last but one the day before from my sixth-floor window, when from the early hours of the morning people carrying bundles and suitcases streamed toward the harbor like ants on foot or in vehicles – all those who did not want to or could not remain under the Soviets. When the headquarters were gone, the shops had been looted, and there was no longer any sign of the Germans, Osvalds and I also went down to the basement for the last night. It was a strange night – without German or Russian occupying forces, at least in our neighborhood.

When, filled with strange, unaccustomed feelings, I came creeping out of the basement after almost three and a half years of being in hiding as a fugitive, the world that greeted me after the artillery thunder of the past days was unusually silent. It was about five in the morning, this lovely, serene and sunny morning of October 13th – or did it only seem that way? No one would try and arrest or kill me without further ado anymore; and yet I could almost feel in the air the uncertainty about what would happen next.

The basement door led to a courtyard shared with several adjacent buildings. And on steps like those I had just climbed sat a man. Something about the way he was sitting looked familiar. When I came closer to him, I recognized Harry Niss – Emīlija had at one point brought me the news that he had married my childhood friend Vivi Misroch, whom I mentioned earlier, in the early phase of the ghetto's existence. He had been hiding in the basement of a nearby building for the last twenty-four hours.

I only knew Vivi's husband by sight. Yet when we met in that backyard, we hugged each other like brother and sister. The story of

Vivi and Harry is one of the few, the very few, that had a happy ending. On that October 13th we only knew that Vivi, her mother, and younger sister had escaped the "action" because they worked as seamstresses in the workshops of the Wehrmacht barracks, though later they were deported to the Stutthof concentration camp. All three of them survived. Her mother Lilly – my mother's bosom friend in Riga – and Vivi's sister Eva walked westward together with French prisoners of war after the camp was liberated; Vivi, however, returned to Riga in order to look for her husband, and there she did indeed find him again. It was like a fairy tale. We managed to find a place to stay in the same building, which made me very happy. But that lasted only a short time. Harry, quite a bit older than we, was firmly resolved, from the first day after the war, to escape from the Soviet Union. As soon as the Polish-Soviet treaty on the repatriation of Polish citizens was concluded, Harry (and not only he) succeeded in obtaining a forged Polish birth certificate, leaving the USSR together with his wife, and emigrating from Poland to Palestine. But that's another story. It's true that at the time I felt I was losing a sister, but of course I was glad for the two of them.

After meeting Harry, I went out on Marijas iela. It was completely deserted as far as the eye could see. And then I saw the first Soviet soldier – looking for mines. Small in stature, with Asiatic features, quite undistinguished-looking. And yet for me he was a hero: a soldier of the great alliance against Hitler, even if he himself was perhaps not really aware of it. On any other occasion I would probably have regarded him with unconcealed dislike, but now I was filled with great relief and emotion at the sight of him, and an almost petrified tension within me was released.

Unfortunately I also realized that at that moment I was not destined to feel the heartfelt, pure joy that would have spontaneously filled me if I had encountered the other allies. The fact that we had survived, we who had been denied the natural right to life – was doubtless more important than anything else. Nevertheless, after my experiences with the Soviets, I hardly had any illusions as to what the future held for me. I didn't know how to act toward my liberators. I had always believed that ingratitude was a feeling unworthy of me.

The soldier who risked his life searching Marijas iela for mines saved my life as well. I didn't care who he was – at that moment I was filled only with deep gratitude. And at the same time I began to have other, more complicated feelings. I recalled Paul Schiemann's words: "You can't pick and choose your liberators."

Only a few days later, it was no longer Red Army soldiers who were predominant in the streets but members of the Soviet power structure. Now began the historical period that the Czechs later astutely summed up as follows: "They came as liberators and remained as occupiers."

I felt quite chaotic. During the Nazi occupation things had been simpler – I had known who my enemies were, who it was that wanted to destroy me, and had used every ounce of energy to resist and foil their plan. Now it became more and more difficult to tell friends from enemies.

May 9th, 1945 produced a similar contradictory emotion in me.[1] I too was happy, of course, that people would no longer be killed and that no more bombs would fall in a Europe that was half in ruins. That an inhumane regime had been defeated. But the other, no less inhumane regime continued to exist. As long as Europe was still at war (and even a while later) quite a few of us cherished the naïve hope that some things in this state would change for the better. There were rumors that after the victory over National Socialism and the enormous sacrifices it had cost, a freer wind would blow, that the autocratic rule of the Communist Party would end and the omnipotence of the secret service – the NKVD – would diminish, and the like. Russian friends told me, for instance, that in Belarus rumors were circulating that the kolkhoz system was to be abolished in order to make it possible to reconstruct agriculture more quickly. The process of the peace negotiations and conferences, the wording of the peace treaties, and the course of action of the government bodies in

---

1. The capitulation of the German Reich was signed in Berlin-Karlshorst on May 8th at 11:00 p.m. local time, when it was already 1 a.m. in the Soviet Union. That is why in Russia to this day VE Day is celebrated on May 9th.

the Soviet Union itself quickly shattered these illusions and hopes. The trap had snapped shut.

My personal struggle was not over yet. I knew I would have to continue to defend myself day after day. This would be a different kind of struggle, but it, too, would require all my strength. And I was completely on my own.

The waves had engulfed my lost Atlantis. I stood on an alien, forbidding shore, and hidden in impenetrable, dense swaths of fog an unknown continent lay before me.

AFTERWORD

This memoir was written over a period of more than ten years. Often, for months, I did not have the energy even to approach the bookshelf that held the first drafts and notes. It was hard to control the memories as they came to life again. If I had given in to their vehemence without imposing limits on it, my life would have gone haywire.

The plan to settle my heart's debt to the lost world and its people by means of this book would not have been possible without the support of many friends and companions. I should like to thank them from my heart.

For years, Gunta Straumane interviewed me and wrote down my accounts of the past in Riga and in Berlin. The copy she made of the tapes was the basis of the book that I could never have written without her unselfish help, her understanding, and empathy.

Marta Dziļuma, the niece of my late husband Valdis Grēviņš, was an invaluable help in the final Latvian editing of the memoir. My thanks to Marģers Vestermanis, who devoted his time to me, bringing a number of blurred memories into sharper focus by reconciling them with historically documented facts and dates. Through the years, Lilija Dzene persistently encouraged me to overcome my inner resistance and to tell my story. She gave me the feeling that my book might be relevant to Latvian readers. I am indebted to her for valuable suggestions that became part of the final version of the manuscript. Last but not least I would like to thank my former student, the theater director Alvis Hermanis, who facilitated the publication of the book's original edition by making available for it the funds he received when he was awarded the Konrad Wolf Prize in 2010.

The German edition of the book would not have materialized if it hadn't been for the dedication of my translator, Matthias Knoll, my Berlin friends Henning Rischbieter and Veronika Arendt-Rojahn, and the competent and sensitive support of my editor, Katharina Raabe. I should like to thank them as well.

AMSTERDAM PUBLISHERS
HOLOCAUST LIBRARY

The series **Holocaust Survivor Memoirs World War II** consists of the following autobiographies of survivors:

Outcry. Holocaust Memoirs, by Manny Steinberg

Hank Brodt Holocaust Memoirs. A Candle and a Promise, by Deborah Donnelly

The Dead Years. Holocaust Memoirs, by Joseph Schupack

Rescued from the Ashes. The Diary of Leokadia Schmidt, Survivor of the Warsaw Ghetto, by Leokadia Schmidt

My Lvov. Holocaust Memoir of a twelve-year-old Girl, by Janina Hescheles

Remembering Ravensbrück. From Holocaust to Healing, by Natalie Hess

Wolf. A Story of Hate, by Zeev Scheinwald with Ella Scheinwald

Save my Children. An Astonishing Tale of Survival and its Unlikely Hero, by Leon Kleiner with Edwin Stepp

Holocaust Memoirs of a Bergen-Belsen Survivor & Classmate of Anne Frank, by Nanette Blitz Konig

Defiant German - Defiant Jew. A Holocaust Memoir from inside the Third Reich, by Walter Leopold with Les Leopold

In a Land of Forest and Darkness. The Holocaust Story of two Jewish Partisans, by Sara Lustigman Omelinski

Holocaust Memories. Annihilation and Survival in Slovakia, by Paul Davidovits

From Auschwitz with Love. The Inspiring Memoir of Two Sisters' Survival, Devotion and Triumph Told by Manci Grunberger Beran & Ruth Grunberger Mermelstein, by Daniel Seymour

Remetz. Resistance Fighter and Survivor of the Warsaw Ghetto, by Jan Yohay Remetz

My March Through Hell. A Young Girl's Terrifying Journey to Survival, by Halina Kleiner with Edwin Stepp

Roman's Journey, by Roman Halter

Beyond Borders. Escaping the Holocaust and Fighting the Nazis. 1938-1948, by Rudi Haymann

The Engineers. A memoir of survival through World War II in Poland and Hungary, by Henry Reiss

Spark of Hope. An Autobiography, by Luba Wrobel Goldberg

Footnote to History. From Hungary to America. The Memoir of a Holocaust Survivor, by Andrew Laszlo

Farewell Atlantis. Recollections, by Valentīna Freimane

The Courtyard. A memoir, by Ben Parket and Alexa Morris

Run, Mendel Run, by Milton H. Schwartz

The series **Holocaust Survivor True Stories**
consists of the following biographies:

Among the Reeds. The true story of how a family survived the Holocaust, by Tammy Bottner

A Holocaust Memoir of Love & Resilience. Mama's Survival from Lithuania to America, by Ettie Zilber

Living among the Dead. My Grandmother's Holocaust Survival Story of Love and Strength, by Adena Bernstein Astrowsky

Heart Songs. A Holocaust Memoir, by Barbara Gilford

Shoes of the Shoah. The Tomorrow of Yesterday, by Dorothy Pierce

Hidden in Berlin. A Holocaust Memoir, by Evelyn Joseph Grossman

Separated Together. The Incredible True WWII Story of Soulmates Stranded an Ocean Apart, by Kenneth P. Price, Ph.D.

The Man Across the River. The incredible story of one man's will to survive the Holocaust, by Zvi Wiesenfeld

If Anyone Calls, Tell Them I Died. A Memoir, by Emanuel (Manu) Rosen

The House on Thrömerstrasse. A Story of Rebirth and Renewal in the Wake of the Holocaust, by Ron Vincent

Dancing with my Father. His hidden past. Her quest for truth. How Nazi Vienna shaped a family's identity, by Jo Sorochinsky

The Story Keeper. Weaving the Threads of Time and Memory - A Memoir, by Fred Feldman

Krisia's Silence. The Girl who was not on Schindler's List, by Ronny Hein

Defying Death on the Danube. A Holocaust Survival Story, by Debbie J. Callahan with Henry Stern

A Doorway to Heroism. A decorated German-Jewish Soldier who became an American Hero, by W. Jack Romberg

The Shoemaker's Son. The Life of a Holocaust Resister, by Laura Beth Bakst

The Redhead of Auschwitz. A True Story, by Nechama Birnbaum

Land of Many Bridges. My Father's Story, by Bela Ruth Samuel Tenenholtz

Creating Beauty from the Abyss. The Amazing Story of Sam Herciger, Auschwitz Survivor and Artist, by Lesley Ann Richardson

On Sunny Days We Sang. A Holocaust Story of Survival and Resilience, by Jeannette Grunhaus de Gelman

Painful Joy. A Holocaust Family Memoir, by Max J. Friedman

I Give You My Heart. A True Story of Courage and Survival, by Wendy Holden

In the Time of Madmen, by Mark A. Prelas

Monsters and Miracles. Horror, Heroes and the Holocaust, by Ira Wesley Kitmacher

Flower of Vlora. Growing up Jewish in Communist Albania, by Anna Kohen

Aftermath: Coming of Age on Three Continents. A Memoir, by Annette Libeskind Berkovits

Not a real Enemy. The True Story of a Hungarian Jewish Man's Fight for Freedom, by Robert Wolf

Zaidy's War. Four Armies, Three Continents, Two Brothers. One Man's Impossible Story of Endurance, by Martin Bodek

The Glassmaker's Son. Looking for the World my Father left behind in Nazi Germany, by Peter Kupfer

The Apprentice of Buchenwald. The True Story of the Teenage Boy Who Sabotaged Hitler's War Machine, by Oren Schneider

Good for a Single Journey, by Helen Joyce

Burying the Ghosts. She escaped Nazi Germany only to have her life torn apart by the woman she saved from the camps: her mother, by Sonia Case

American Wolf. From Nazi Refugee to American Spy. A True Story, by Audrey Birnbaum

Bipolar Refugee. A Saga of Survival and Resilience, by Peter Wiesner

In the Wake of Madness. My Family's Escape from the Nazis, by Bettie Lennett Denny

Before the Beginning and After the End, by Hymie Anisman

I Will Give Them an Everlasting Name. Jacksonville's Stories of the Holocaust, by Samuel Cox

Hiding in Holland. A Resistance Memoir, by Shulamit Reinharz

The Ghosts on the Wall. A Grandson's Memoir of the Holocaust, by Kenneth D. Wald

Thirteen in Auschwitz. My grandmother's fight to stay human, by Lauren Meyerowitz Port

The series **Jewish Children in the Holocaust** consists of the following autobiographies of Jewish children hidden during WWII in the Netherlands:

Searching for Home. The Impact of WWII on a Hidden Child,
by Joseph Gosler

Sounds from Silence. Reflections of a Child Holocaust Survivor, Psychiatrist and Teacher, by Robert Krell

Sabine's Odyssey. A Hidden Child and her Dutch Rescuers,
by Agnes Schipper

The Journey of a Hidden Child, by Harry Pila and Robin Black

The series **New Jewish Fiction** consists of the following novels, written by Jewish authors. All novels are set in the time during or after the Holocaust.

The Corset Maker. A Novel, by Annette Libeskind Berkovits

Escaping the Whale. The Holocaust is over. But is it ever over for the next generation? by Ruth Rotkowitz

When the Music Stopped. Willy Rosen's Holocaust, by Casey Hayes

Hands of Gold. One Man's Quest to Find the Silver Lining in Misfortune, by Roni Robbins

The Girl Who Counted Numbers. A Novel, by Roslyn Bernstein

There was a garden in Nuremberg. A Novel, by Navina Michal Clemerson

The Butterfly and the Axe, by Omer Bartov

To Live Another Day. A Novel, by Elizabeth Rosenberg

The Right to Happiness. After all they went through. Stories, by Helen Schary Motro

Five Amber Beads, by Richard Aronowitz

To Love Another Day. A Novel, by Elizabeth Rosenberg

Cursing the Darkness. A Novel about Loss and Recovery, by Joanna Rosenthall

The series **Holocaust Heritage** consists of the following memoirs by 2G:

The Cello Still Sings. A Generational Story of the Holocaust and of the Transformative Power of Music, by Janet Horvath

The Fire and the Bonfire. A Journey into Memory, by Ardyn Halter

The Silk Factory: Finding Threads of My Family's True Holocaust Story, by Michael Hickins

Winter Light. The Memoir of a Child of Holocaust Survivors, by Grace Feuerverger

Out from the Shadows. Growing up with Holocaust Survivor Parents, by Willie Handler

Hidden in Plain Sight. A Family Memoir and the Untold Story of the Holocaust in Serbia, by Julie Brill

The Unspeakable. Breaking my family's silence surrounding the Holocaust, by Nicola Hanefeld

Eighteen for Life. Surviving the Holocaust, by Helen Schamroth

Austrian Again. Reclaiming a Lost Legacy, by Anne Hand

The series **Holocaust Books for Young Adults** consists of the following novels, based on true stories:

The Boy behind the Door. How Salomon Kool Escaped the Nazis. Inspired by a True Story, by David Tabatsky

Running for Shelter. A True Story, by Suzette Sheft

The Precious Few. An Inspirational Saga of Courage based on True Stories, by David Twain with Art Twain

Dark Shadows Hover, by Jordan Steven Sher

The Sun will Shine Again, by Cynthia Goldstein Monsour

The series **WWII Historical Fiction** consists of the following novels, some of which are based on true stories:

Mendelevski's Box. A Heartwarming and Heartbreaking Jewish Survivor's Story, by Roger Swindells

A Quiet Genocide. The Untold Holocaust of Disabled Children in WWII Germany, by Glenn Bryant

The Knife-Edge Path, by Patrick T. Leahy

Brave Face. The Inspiring WWII Memoir of a Dutch/German Child, by I. Caroline Crocker and Meta A. Evenbly

When We Had Wings. The Gripping Story of an Orphan in Janusz Korczak's Orphanage. A Historical Novel, by Tami Shem-Tov

Jacob's Courage. Romance and Survival amidst the Horrors of War, by Charles S. Weinblatt

A Semblance of Justice. Based on true Holocaust experiences, by Wolf Holles

Under the Pink Triangle. Where forbidden love meets unspeakable evil, by Katie Moore

Amsterdam Publishers Newsletter

Subscribe to our Newsletter by selecting the menu at the top (right) of amsterdampublishers.com or scan the QR-code below.

www.ingramcontent.com/pod-product-compliance
Lightning Source LLC
LaVergne TN
LVHW091717070526
838199LV00050B/2432